Sabrina Merkel

AF239086

Building Evacuation with Mobile Devices

Building Evacuation with Mobile Devices

by
Sabrina Merkel

Dissertation, Karlsruher Institut für Technologie (KIT)
Fakultät für Wirtschaftswissenschaften
Tag der mündlichen Prüfung: 28. Februar 2014
Referent: Prof. Dr. H. Schmeck
Korreferent: Prof. Dr. A. Oberweis

Impressum

 Scientific Publishing

Karlsruher Institut für Technologie (KIT)
KIT Scientific Publishing
Straße am Forum 2
D-76131 Karlsruhe

KIT Scientific Publishing is a registered trademark of Karlsruhe
Institute of Technology. Reprint using the book cover is not allowed.

www.ksp.kit.edu

Print on Demand 2014

ISBN 978-3-7315-0207-4
DOI: 10.5445/KSP/1000040428

Building Evacuation with Mobile Devices

Zur Erlangung des akademischen Grades eines
Doktors der Ingenieurwissenschaften

(Dr.-Ing.)

von der Fakultät für Wirtschaftswissenschaften
des Karlsruher Instituts für Technologie (KIT)

genehmigte

DISSERTATION

von

Dipl.-Inform.Wirt Sabrina Merkel

Tag der mündlichen Prüfung: 28. Februar 2014
Referent: Prof. Dr. H. Schmeck
Korreferent: Prof. Dr. A. Oberweis

2014 Karlsruhe

CONTENTS

ACKNOWLEDGEMENTS

I would like to express my deepest appreciation to all those who supported me in completing this thesis. Foremost, I would like to express my sincere gratitude to my advisor Prof. Dr. Hartmut Schmeck for providing me with the possibility of working and pursuing my research at his chair. Thank you for encouraging me to ask questions and for teaching me that it is not a sign of ignorance but the first step to improvement and new knowledge.

Apart from my advisor, I would like to thank the rest of my thesis committee: Prof. Dr. Andreas Oberweis, Prof. Dr. Hansjörg Fromm, and Prof. Dr. Detlef Seese, for accepting the request to serve as reviewers in the examination committee and for taking the time to give insightful comments, to pose hard questions, and to provide helpful advise.

My sincere thanks also goes to my colleagues and friends of the research group *Efficient Algorithms* for the wonderful working atmosphere, their constant encouragement during the last years, and many enjoyable lunch and coffee breaks. In particular, I would

i

like to thank Christian Gitte, Birger Becker, and Fabian Rigoll for many inspirational conversations and their profound support in advancing my research and writing this thesis. Likewise, I am especially grateful to Ingo Mauser, Sebastian Kochanneck, Dr. Florian Allerding, and Dr. Pradyumn Shukla for their honest and encouraging feedback and many helpful suggestions. I am deeply grateful that I got the chance to share some ideas and time with all of you.

Moreover, I am grateful to Christoph Brunner and Matthäus Malkowski for reviewing parts of this thesis, for listening and discussing many underlying ideas, and for providing good advice and moral support.

Last but not least, I would like to express special thanks to my family, my parents Margarete and Alwin Merkel, my sister Doreen Merkel, and to Matthäus Malkowski for their permanent support and for always being there for me. You have helped me to stay calm and positive in stressful times and gave me the courage to pursue this path until the end. Thank you for always believing in me.

Karlsruhe, April 2014 *Sabrina Merkel*

ABSTRACT

A rapidly growing world population and an increasing density of settlements demand ever-larger and more complex buildings from today's engineers. These requirements can often be met due to a continuous development of new building fabrics and construction processes. In comparison to this technological progress, the development of novel equipment for emergency evacuation of buildings has been quite stagnant in recent years. Current evacuation support facilities are mainly limited to stationary exit signage and emergency maps displaying recommended escape routes. Such emergency maps can be easily overlooked and are often perceived as confusing and unclear, especially when someone is in panic. However, the main problem with contemporary building evacuation support equipment is its inability to adapt recommended escape routes to the ever changing environment during the evacuation process. Neither fire outbreaks, smoke formation, blocked passages due to debris of collapsed masonry can be considered, nor can the current distribution of people inside the building be taken into account when planning potential escape routes. Nevertheless, these factors strongly affect potential congestion emergence and, hence, the evacuation time.

The increasing propagation of mobile devices designed for wireless communication, such as smart phones, tablet PCs, or general devices for personal digital assistance, opens up an opportunity to improve the support of evacuees during an emergency evacuation of a building. In emergency cases, the mobile device can alert its user via ringing or vibrating and display an individual escape route on its screen. By pointing out respective directions, the device can navigate its user to a safe exit. The advantage compared to traditional escape route signage lies in the possibility to update the recommended escape route according to new information about the current evacuation situation. Such information can be gathered by the device via wireless communication between devices and the environment. In this thesis, the *Organic Building Evacuation Support System*, or OBESS, is introduced. OBESS is a concept for an adaptive building evacuation system based on the paradigm of controlled self-organization from the research area of *Organic Computing*. To achieve this characteristic system behavior, an exemplary implementation of the Observer/Controller Architecture is presented. The Observer/Controller Architecture is a generic system architecture developed in the context of *Organic Computing*, designed specifically for the purpose of realizing controlled self-organization. The support system consists in part of mobile devices, which have the ability to establish an ad hoc network via local communication with each other. This way, local communication provides a mean for the dissemination of information about the current evacuation situation in the network. This information can then be used to find the optimal escape route for the user of each device. In OBESS, all computations are meant to be performed in a decentralized way, directly on the mobile devices in order to avoid having a single point of failure in the system. This approach increases the robustness of the evacuation system, which is a crucial characteristic, especially for emergency applications.

There are two algorithmic challenges that have to be mastered in order to realize such a decentralized evacuation support system based on mobile devices. Firstly, the devices have to compute escape routes based on uncertain and incomplete information regarding the evacuation situation. Amongst other reasons, this is partly due to the fact that communication over an ad hoc network is generally delayed and that the network can get disconnected from time to time since participating devices move through the building. So far, the task of decentralized escape route planning based on uncertain information has received little attention from researchers. Since it is a key prerequisite for a robust evacuation support system based on mobile devices, a large part of this thesis is dedicated to developing solutions for this problem. The second crucial requirement for the realization of the building evacuation support system proposed is the ability to determine the locations of mobile devices in the building. Since signals of the most commonly used localization technique, the Global Positioning System (GPS), are usually not available indoors, this task alone can be a challenge. For static sensor networks, which have similar characteristics to mobile ad hoc networks, many localization techniques which are independent from GPS-signals have been proposed over time. Since an important difference between sensor and ad hoc networks is the mobility of the devices in the network, this thesis investigates the effect this mobility has on various distance estimation techniques, which ultimately form the basis for localization algorithms in OBESS. It is shown that mobility of devices has a significant impact on the accuracy of computed locations and, therefore, has to be dealt with explicitly. For this, several solutions are suggested and evaluated in this thesis. In addition, this thesis presents an optimization approach to improve the localization infrastructure for mobile devices in specific buildings and discusses the potential of the Observer/Controller Architecture for improving the accuracy of indoor localization.

CHAPTER 1

INTRODUCTION

A continuously increasing global population and settlement density combined with huge progress in the building and construction industry led to the emergence of ever-larger and more complex buildings. Recently, the world's tallest construction, the *Burj al Khalifa* in Dubai, was brought to completion in October 2009. This imposing structure consists of 900 apartments, which are distributed over about 190 floors. Although probably being the most prominent example of today's engineering skills, there are many more to name. The *Ghery Buildings* in Düsseldorf, Germany, clearly illustrate the ability and willingness to construct buildings which diverge from simple geometric forms. Another illustrative example of complex architectural design is the *Habitat 67*, a model community and housing complex in Montreal, Canada, where houses are assembled in an irregular structure. In contrast to such developments, most buildings' precautions for emergency evacuation are comparatively underdeveloped. Hence, they fail to

1

profit from technological progress, which has found its way into most other areas of everyday life. The fact that an infrastructure whose main purpose it is to save human life does not keep up with technological achievements is surprising, at best, if not worrying. Therefore, it is an urgent matter to investigate how new scientific insights and findings, for example in the area of computer science, can be exploited in order to improve emergency management in modern buildings.

1.1 Motivation and Problem Statement

Today's approach to prevent disasters and support a well-ordered evacuation of buildings is to install safety devices, such as sprinkler systems, fire or smoke alarms, fire extinguishers, exit signs, and emergency maps. In general, such emergency maps display the current floor, recommendations for escape routes, and the locations of first-aid kits or fire extinguishers. Apart from that, there are usually stationary signs installed throughout the building, which are meant to direct people to nearby exits or safe areas. Figure 1.1 displays some examples of such signage. A major drawback of such kind of emergency facilities is the fact that they are usually developed when the building is constructed and are permanent without provision for frequent changes. The route guidance which is provided by exit signs and emergency maps is designed based on expectations regarding the evacuation process, which are obtained from statistical data and expert knowledge. However, the resulting escape routes can be suboptimal in case the situation in the building differs from the expected scenario, for example in terms of the number of evacuees or their distribution across the rooms, et cetera. Furthermore, the escape routes are not necessarily optimal for people with special needs due to disabilities or other handicaps.

Fahy and Proulx [62] published reports from survivors of the attacks of September 11th, 2001, which indicate that the main obstacles during their escape were congestions in bottleneck-areas and closed or blocked passages due to smoke formation or damaged building fabrics. Conventional evacuation signs are unable to adapt to the specific evacuation situation in the building, to changes in the environment during an emergency situation, or to personal needs of specific evacuees. Another serious problem is that navigation signs are stationary and sometimes easily overlooked in panic situations (cf. Morishita and Shiraishi [165]). Smoke formation and lack of illumination can further aggravate this situation. Even people who are familiar with the building's layout can have difficulties to find their way to the exit under such circumstances (cf. Fahy and Proulx [62]). Furthermore, conventional emergency maps are often hard to apprehend, especially when in panic. Since they are fixed to the wall, they cannot be rotated, which is common practice for some people in order to orient themselves on a map.

For all these reasons, today's evacuation support equipment in buildings should be reconsidered and replaced with more innovative solutions, which can overcome the identified deficiencies. A modern evacuation system should have digital illuminated screens, which show navigation instructions towards safe areas or exits of the building. Ideally, some of these screens are portable devices, which can be carried by evacuees. This way, frequent searches for new signs during the evacuation process can be avoided. Evacuation devices should provide the possibility to assess the current evacuation situation, detect changes in the environment, and adapt the navigation instructions accordingly. Furthermore, it is desirable to integrate personal information about the devices' users in the process of finding suitable escape routes.

Figure 1.1: Standard navigation signs for building evacuation.

1.2 Objectives and Approach

The widespread distribution of mobile devices, such as smart phones or tablet PCs, provides a chance to achieve a changeover in evacuation support for buildings. These devices are portable and equipped with digital illuminated screens, which can display a building's layout and navigation instructions to guide their users. Mobile devices typically possess means for wireless communication via short-range communication modules, which could provide information about the current situation in the building. Moreover, the devices are able to form a so-called *Mobile Ad Hoc Network (MANET)*, or ad hoc network for short, i.e., a network which consists of dynamically built-up connections between devices which are located within sufficiently close proximity. Each device in such a network forwards messages that it receives to all other devices in its communication range. This allows for dissemination of information in the network, which increases the knowledge each device can obtain about the environment. In addition, mobile devices possess computing capacities, which are needed in order to determine navigation instructions and to dynamically adapt them according to newly available information. There is no need for a central computing unit in the building, which makes the evacuation support system scalable and robust against a single point of failure. The fact that each evacuee can have his own mobile evacuation device provides the potential to personalize evacuation route planning. Individual preferences and needs, such as for disabled or elderly people, can be taken into account.

However, the scalability and robustness a system gains from decentralized computation and information acquisition via local communication have their price. The lack of global knowledge poses a special challenge for evacuation route planning. Firstly, the available information basis can be incomplete in case the ad hoc network is disconnected, or if there are no devices located in a certain area of the building which can report about its state. Secondly, messages received from nearby devices can be obsolete or outdated because of the delays which arise during the forwarding process. Furthermore, information exchanged between the devices could, from the outset, be incorrect either as a result of error-prone computations or when human users report false information to their devices, be it accidentally or even on purpose. Although these are considerable shortcomings, the above described advantages justify a thorough investigation of the potential that mobile devices hold for the improvement of evacuation support in future buildings. Since the task of evacuation route planning on mobile devices differs from standard path-finding problems which require global and certain knowledge, the first objective of this thesis is:

1. Proposing and evaluating methods to determine optimal evacuation routes on mobile devices which regard user preferences, take into account uncertain information gathered via local communication, and are adaptable to detected changes in the environment.

5

In order to be able to navigate their users, the devices have to be able to determine their current locations in the building. Since there is usually no GPS-signal available indoors, the localization alone becomes an ambitious task. To tackle this problem, the devices' ability to organize into ad hoc networks and exchange messages with other devices in this network comes in handy. While localization of mobile devices in an ad hoc network has not yet received much attention, there are a vast number of localization techniques proposed for a *Static Sensor Network (SSN)* in the literature. SSNs have similar characteristics to MANETs but differ in the fact that the devices are stationary. Mobility of the devices, however, can fundamentally affect the applicability of localization algorithms designed for SSNs to MANETs, which leads to the second objective of this thesis:

2. Investigating the applicability of localization algorithms designed for SSNs to MANETs and developing reasonable adjustments.

Due to the mobility of the devices, their surroundings change constantly. This is why the evacuation route planning, as well as the localization process, have to be able to adapt to new and unforeseen situations. Such a requirement calls for self-organization amongst the involved devices. Self-organization enables a system to autonomously operate in unpredictable and interchanging environments. If predicting all potential system states at design time poses a problem, it is advisable to embrace self-organization as a design principle. At the same time, self-organization always bears the risk of undesired system behavior emerging from local interactions between the system's components due to the lack of global coordination and supervision. This can be disastrous, especially when it happens in a life-threatening situation, such as a building evacuation. As a consequence, it is desirable to allow for a certain amount of control in an otherwise autonomous evacuation support system. *Organic Computing* (cf. Müller-Schloer and Schmeck [169], Müller-Schloer et al. [170], Schmeck [213], VDE/ITG/GI [235]) deals with the design of self-organized technical systems in order to make them flexible in their reaction to changes in the environment or the system's objectives. At the same time the system remains trustworthy and robust with respect to failures and disturbances. The *Observer/Controller Architecture (O/C Architecture)* (cf. Branke et al. [23], Müller-Schloer [168], Richter [193], Richter et al. [195]) is a generic design framework developed to build such organic systems in a way that they exhibit the previously described life-like characteristics. Pursuing the goal of a controllable and self-organizing *Organic Building Evacuation Support System (OBESS)*, the third objective of this thesis is:

3. Developing a concept for a controllable, self-organizing evacuation support system by applying the generic O/C Architecture to the mobile evacuation devices in the system.

The aforementioned objectives lead directly to the major contributions this thesis provides for the research areas of evacuation route planning, localization in MANETs, and Organic Computing.

1.3 Major Contributions

The first major contribution relates to the research area of evacuation management. A concept for an evacuation support system in buildings is presented, which consists of a MANET, an SSN, and a Central Control Unit (CCU). The presented system emphasizes decentralized computations and local communications between its

7

components, which makes it scalable and robust against a single point of failure. In addition, two algorithms for decentralized evacuation route planning on mobile devices are presented, which are designed to integrate uncertain information about other evacuees' locations in the building. This information is gathered via local communication and subsequent dissemination over ad hoc network connections to other mobile devices in the building. It is shown that the evacuation process can be accelerated compared to a situation without communication between the devices, even though the information can be incomplete, outdated, and error-prone due to the characteristics of the scenario. Both algorithms are designed in a way that they can adapt to changes in their environment and one method regards user preferences in the optimization of escape routes. Since the strongly expanded use of mobile devices is a rather recent phenomenon, the idea to use mobile devices to support the evacuation of a building has not yet been subject to extensive investigations. The proposed methods for distributed and adaptive escape route planning on mobile devices advance the research in this area.

The second set of contributions relates to the task of localization, more precisely, to determine the locations of mobile devices in an ad hoc network without the use of GPS-receivers. While this challenge has received much attention for static devices in SSNs, mobility is rarely addressed. The usual proposition to account for mobility is to constantly repeat the respective algorithm in order to find the devices' new locations when they moved. However, an extensive study about the impact of mobility on localization algorithms presented in this thesis shows that simple repetition leads to an unpredictably high inaccuracy in the resulting locations. Experiments reveal details about the effects various mobility models have on the quality of localization results and identify main influencing factors of these models, such as speed or direction of movement. A modification of a distance estimation algorithm is suggested, which is shown to reduce the error produced by mobility of the devices. Additionally, two indicators are proposed which can characterize the mobility of devices in a network based on locally available information. As a consequence, localization results could be corrected in order to account for the distortion brought by the specific mobility pattern. Moreover, a distributed, nature-inspired procedure to synchronize devices in a MANET is successfully tested and, based on it, a method is developed for distance estimation, which is shown to improve the mobility induced localization error. Furthermore, a novel distance estimation approach is introduced and experiments are presented to demonstrate that by applying this algorithm the accuracy of localization can be improved for various network topologies and especially for MANETs. The quality of the results produced by localization algorithms mostly depends on the placement of specific devices in the network which possess knowledge of their own positions. This thesis contributes an *Evolutionary Algorithm (EA)*, which can be used to optimize the locations of such devices. Valuable insights about an optimal device placement for localization during a building evacuation process are obtained by an experimental study. These findings contribute to both, the research field of evacuation planning and localization for MANETs.

Moreover, a contribution is made, which relates to evacuation management, localization, and Organic Computing as well. Organic Computing is concerned with the design of self-organizing technical systems in order to make them adaptable and trustworthy at the same time. A generic O/C Architecture was developed for such systems, which provides for online and offline learning mechanisms, i.e., learning at runtime and in a simulation, in order to achieve

9

these goals. In this thesis, a conceptual system architecture is proposed, which applies the generic O/C Architecture from Organic Computing to the mobile devices in the building evacuation support system. It is shown how the generic architecture can be implemented for evacuation route planning and localization. It is further introduced how offline learning can be used to evaluate the quality of an evacuation instruction with respect to the current evacuation situation in the building before it is suggested to the user. Apart from that, the O/C Architecture offers a chance to improve localization. The study of localization algorithms presented in this thesis reveals that various localization techniques can deliver high quality results under different environmental circumstances. When determining to use a specific localization algorithm at design time, there can be circumstances under which another localization algorithm could deliver better results. Here, a concept is proposed which uses online and offline learning mechanisms provided by the generic O/C Architecture in order to switch between various localization algorithms at run time. Learning mechanisms are applied to improve this decision process over time. This is a novel approach to the task of localization, which opens up a new perspective for research in this area.

1.4 Structure

This thesis is structured as follows. Chapter 2 describes the research context of this thesis. A short introduction of MANETs is given and the main research topics regarding these networks are discussed. Subsequently, the research area of Organic Computing and the related O/C Architecture is described. In addition, an overview of the concepts of swarm intelligence and nature-inspired computing is given and their role in organic systems is discussed.

The chapter proceeds with a description of current research in the area of evacuation management, including evacuation modeling and optimization approaches, as well as an overview of state-of-the-art concepts for evacuation management systems with mobile devices. Subsequently, the task of localization is introduced and various approaches to the problem are described with focus on localization of devices in MANETs and SSNs. Chapter 2 concludes with an overview of state-of-the-art localization systems.

A concept for OBESS is presented in Chapter 3 and the main elements of this system, as well as their functionalities, are described. An examplary application of the generic O/C Architecture to mobile evacuation devices follows and the potentials this architecture provides for the improvement of evacuation planning and localization are discussed.

In Chapter 4, two distributed evacuation planning algorithms are developed, which can be employed by mobile devices to navigate users to an exit while taking into account information about other evacuees derived from local communication. Simulative experiments show that this information can be used to improve the overall evacuation time compared to route planning without communication, even though the devices have only uncertain information about their environment.

Chapter 5 investigates various methods to locate mobile devices in ad hoc networks without the use of GPS-receives. A standard localization algorithm, which has been proposed for static networks, is stressed under various mobility models and important influencing factors of the mobility pattern on the localization accuracy are identified. Additionally, various methods to improve the localization results for MANETs are presented and discussed. The approaches are investigated thoroughly, compared, and evaluated in simulative experiments. Concluding this chapter, an EA

11

is proposed, which optimizes the placement of specific devices in order to improve localization accuracy. This approach is tested in a simulative evacuation scenario and provides valuable insights into the characteristics of an optimal placement and into the factors which influence such an optimal solution.

Chapter 6 summarizes the research presented in this thesis and subjects it to a critical evaluation which leads to the prospects for future research in order to advance the vision of OBESS.

CHAPTER 2

RESEARCH CONTEXT AND STATE-OF-THE-ART

In this chapter, the research context of the work presented in this thesis is outlined and fundamental principles are explained. Firstly, a short introduction to MANETs is given. The chapter proceeds with a description of the concept of Organic Computing and its generic O/C Architecture, which forms the basis for the software architecture of the mobile devices in OBESS. Subsequently, the state-of-the-art in evacuation management research is described in detail. The chapter concludes with an introduction to the task of localization and state-of-the-art localization methods are described.

2.1 Mobile Ad Hoc Networks

MANETs are networks which consist of a number of mobile devices with the ability to communicate with other nearby devices using

13

a short-range wireless communication module, like infrared, Bluetooth [20], or ZigBee [257] technology. Also, the devices forward messages that they receive to all other devices in their neighborhood. Hence, the devices are able to spontaneously form networks which make long-distance communication possible (cf. Ghosekar et al. [75]). In contrast to SSNs, the devices in a MANET are mobile and not necessarily equipped with sensors. Ad hoc networks have been subject to research since the late 1960s (cf. Abramson [1]) and have been widely studied in the literature since. There is a working group founded by the Internet Engineering Task Force (IETF) [107] to investigate MANET related issues. Apart from being mobile, the devices in MANETs are usually assumed to have limited resources in terms of memory, processing capabilities, and power supply.

In the work of Nan and Li [172], an overview of the main research areas for SSNs is given. According to these authors, the main research areas are resource management, optimization of the devices' lifetimes and their localization in the network, routing of information in the network, and optimizing the coverage of the network. It should be noted that the scientific questions in the area of SSNs can mostly be transferred directly to MANETs due to the similarity of SSNs and MANETs. Throughout this thesis, the localization task is the main focus, however lifetime optimization and optimal coverage is also touched upon.

When talking about routing in ad hoc networks, there is a variety of protocols proposed, which can mostly be categorized into *distance vector routing* or *link state routing* protocols (cf. Ballew [14], Tanenbaum [228]). While in distance vector routing each device communicates all distance information it possesses to its neighbors, in link state routing only distance information about the links to direct neighbors is communicated to the whole network. Many implementations of these protocol types are suggested and each protocol has its advantages and disadvantages, such as varying packet sizes or the number of messages needed to establish and maintain routing information. For the research presented in this thesis, however, there is no need for direct communication between specific devices because broadcasts are used to distribute information over the whole network. Thus, routing is paid little attention to. The communication model assumed for the network throughout this thesis is similar to the *Gossip Protocol* (cf. Haas et al. [81]). The Gossip Protocol is an alternative routing method to *Flooding*, which is the most basic way to disseminate messages in networks where each device simply forwards all information available to all neighbors. The idea of the Gossip Protocol, also called *Epidemic Routing*, is that each device only forwards the most recent information it receives and, thus, the communication overhead is reduced.

Another great advantage of decentralized ad hoc networks is that the information exchange can still function even if certain devices are broken. In contrast to networks which depend on a central unit for message routing, which is often the case in wireless local area networks, communication in ad hoc networks remains intact in case of individual failures of devices. This lack of a single point of failure makes the network's communication robust, even in regions where there is no existing communication infrastructure or where the available infrastructure is damaged. This characteristic makes the operation of such networks attractive in many application scenarios, such as geographic monitoring, target tracking, or evacuation management.

2.2 Organic Computing

Another research area touched upon in this thesis is *Organic Computing*. The Organic Computing initiative started with a position paper from the German Informatics Society (GI)[1] and the Information Technology Society (ITG)[2] in 2002 and was established as priority program 1183 by the German Research Foundation (DFG)[3] in 2004 [214]. The fundamental observation that led to the Organic Computing initiative was that future computing systems become smaller in size and at the same time increase in performance and quantity. Due to this development, computing systems become ubiquitous. Sometimes, they form possibly unlimited dynamic networks via local communication, hence, building complex, variable, and unpredictable structures. Such computing systems will likely be part of everyday life enhancing the functionality of our houses (cf. Allerding et al. [6], Bing et al. [19]), offices (cf. Davidsson and Boman [49]), cars (cf. Corona and De Schutter [45], Srovnal et al. [222]), manufacturing industry (cf. Liana et al. [135]), health-care facilities (cf. de Ruyter and Pelgrim [51], Soar et al. [220]), et cetera. Because of the dynamics of the environment such systems are deployed in, they are required to be flexible and adaptive to unforeseen situations. Since all potential states of the environment or the system itself cannot be accounted for at the time of design, some degree of self-organization is necessary to cope with the dynamics, complexity, and unpredictability of such computing systems. While there are different definitions for self-organizing systems, "...in the most general way the essence of self-organization is that system structure appears without explicit pressure or in-

---

[1]Gesellschaft für Informatik e.V.
[2]Informationstechnische Gesellschaft
[3]Deutsche Forschungsgemeinschaft

volvement from outside the system" Schmeck [212]. When external involvement is excluded, the desired behavior has to be established exclusively by interactions between the system's components. A system which adapts itself to a changing environment possesses almost life-like properties, such as self-protection or self-healing. This is the reason for the choice of name.

When a system acts completely self-organized, the question arises whether it is possible to trust such a system and how it can be guaranteed that no unexpected and possibly harmful system behavior arises. Organic Computing addresses the tradeoff between the desire to have an adaptive, flexible, and self-organized system which is also trustworthy and robust. While an organic system (in the sense of following Organic Computing principles) is encouraged to solve tasks in a self-organized way using feedback loops and learning, the possibility for a user to intervene in the case of an undesired emergent behavior is given to ensure correct system behavior. Another requirement of future computing systems identified and addressed by Organic Computing is the need to design computing systems according to human needs. This postulation refers to the need for user-friendly interfaces. Because of the complexity such systems exhibit, it is hard for a user to tell the system exactly what it has to do. A much more convenient and realistic way for users to communicate with such a system is by formulating objectives or goals instead of precise instructions.

So far, Organic Computing is used for the design of various system types, for example the control of traffic (cf. Fekete et al. [65]), self-organization of traffic lights (cf. Prothmann et al. [185]), design of a robot control architecture (cf. Brockmann et al. [25]), artificial vision (cf. Walther and Würtz [241]), energy management in smart homes (cf. Allerding et al. [6]), and many more (cf. Müller-Schloer et al. [170]). The application to a building evacuation scenario, however, is novel.

2.2.1 Organic Observer/Controller Architecture

One outcome of the Organic Computing initiative is a generic O/C Architecture. It allows for controlled self-organization in distributed technical systems (cf. Branke et al. [23], Müller-Schloer [168], Richter et al. [195]). The architecture provides means for observing, analyzing, and characterizing the current state of a *System under Observation and Control (SuOC)*, as well as the ability to predict its future behavior. This information is subsequently interpreted by the controller in order to direct the system into a desired system state and prevent unwanted emergent behavior (cf. Mnif et al. [163], Ribock et al. [192], Richter and Mnif [194]). While this all happens without external control, the possibility for a human user to control the system still is provided. User input can be made in terms of objectives and goals. Apart from the O/C Architecture, similar concepts are presented in other scientific disciplines like mechanical engineering (cf. Hestermeyer et al. [93]) or autonomic computing (cf. Kephart and Chess [121]). However, these architectures do not cover all aspects of an organic system. The main, but not only, difference is that the generic O/C Architecture emphasizes the role of an external entity to specify system-objectives. In the next section, the generic O/C Architecture is described, as it serves as a basis for OBESS. For a detailed introduction and distinction between the generic O/C Architecture and similar concepts, it is referred to the respective literature by Müller-Schloer [168], Richter et al. [195], and Branke et al. [23].

The generic O/C Architecture consists of four elements, which interact with each other: The SuOC, the observer, the controller, and a higher level entity specifying the system-objectives, which are usually provided by a human user but, in theory, could also be provided by another computing system. Further on, this higher level entity is referred to as "user". Figure 2.1 shows the basic elements of the architecture and their relationships. These components and their interactions are explained in detail in the following.

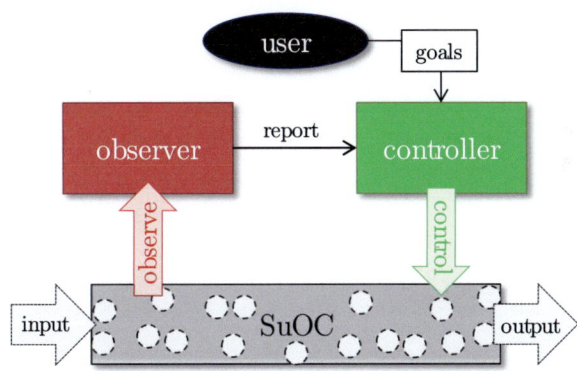

Figure 2.1: The main elements in the generic O/C Architecture and their interactions.

System under Observation and Control

The SuOC can be a set of interacting entities, as illustrated in Figure 2.1, or a single device. The behavior of this system is subject to the influence of the controller and is desired to satisfy the objectives given by the user. Still, it does not depend on the existence of neither the observer, nor the controller, nor the user. The system gets input from its environment, i.e., parameters which can influence the behavior of the SuOC but are uncontrollable by the system. Furthermore, there is output from the SuOC,

19

i.e., changes to those parameters in the environment that are visible to external entities outside the SuOC. In addition to input and output, the SuOC has internal parameters, i.e., parameters changeable by the system in order to influence its own behavior. These parameters are only accessible from the outside if specified explicitly as configuration parameters of the SuOC. An example of such a system could be those components of a car which are meant to collaboratively ensure a certain driving speed. The desired driving speed would be the objective given by the user. Input parameters could be outside temperature, the incline of the road, et cetera, and the output parameter is the driving speed. Internal parameters can, for example, be a certain motor configuration, which is regulated by the software of the car, but cannot be set explicitly by the user.

Observer

The system is observed, analyzed, and its current state is characterized by the observer. Furthermore, the observer is responsible for predicting the most likely future state of the system. Figure 2.2 shows the components of the observer and their interdependencies in the generic O/C Architecture. The observation model is selected by the controller and it determines how the other components in the observer work depending on the current objectives. It can, for example, decide which parameters of the SuOC should be monitored or what their sampling rate is. The monitor collects the specified parameter values from the SuOC according to the defined sampling rate and stores these values in log files. The preprocessor takes this data and prepares it for the data analyzer and the predictor module, for example by filtering or aggregation. The preparations needed are also specified by the observation model. In the data analyzer, meaningful attributes that are able to characterize the current system state, e.g., stochastic values are calculated from the pre-processed data. The observation model determines which values are computed. The predictor has some prediction methods at its disposal and selects a suitable one according to the observation model. With the selected prediction model and data from the pre-processor it forecasts the future system state. This is an important step because it increases the chance for the controller to prevent undesired system behavior before it actually arises. The output from pre-processor, data analyzer, and predictor is collected in the aggregator-module and forwarded to the controller.

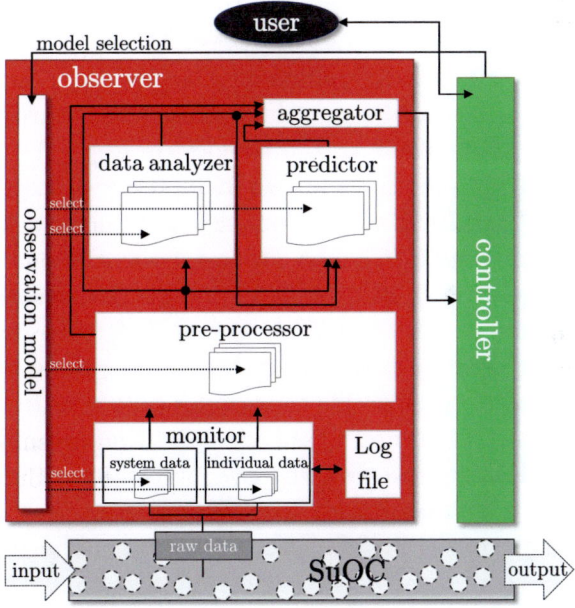

Figure 2.2: The observer of the generic O/C Architecture and its components.

Controller

The main purpose of the controller in the O/C Architecture is to select control actions, i.e., actions that influence the environment of the SuOC, the communication between its elements, or the behavior of the elements directly. Figure 2.3 shows the components of the controller and their relations. The selection of an appropriate action for a certain situation is done in the action selector. The mapping from system state to appropriate action is subject to a learning process (cf. Fredivianus et al. [70], Richter [193], Richter and Mnif [194] for detailed descriptions). This process can be distinguished into *online* and *offline* learning. Both learning mechanisms take place in different parts of the controller. During online learning, actions are executed which influence the SuOC. The quality of these actions is deduced from the system's response. For this, the controller keeps track of the previously applied actions and the subsequent system states in two history-stacks, namely action history and situation history. From this information, the impact of an action is evaluated with respect to the given objectives and a so-called fitness value is assigned to the situation-action pair. The result of the evaluation is reported to the adaptation module, which alters the fitness for the corresponding mapping in the action selector, giving this mapping a higher or lower chance, respectively, to be selected again for execution. Simultaneously to this online learning process, the O/C Architecture provides the possibility for offline learning. The offline learning is realized in a simulative model of the SuOC. The adaptation module creates new mapping rules, for example by applying mutation and reproduction mechanisms of EAs (cf. Weicker [246] for details), which can be evaluated in the simulative environment using standard fitness evaluation and selection mechanisms from EAs. Thus, only rules that perform well in the simulation are committed to the action selector and available for online learning. Although simulations are never exact reproductions of the real environment and, therefore, cannot guarantee the impact an action has, the offline learning still provides certain quality assurance.

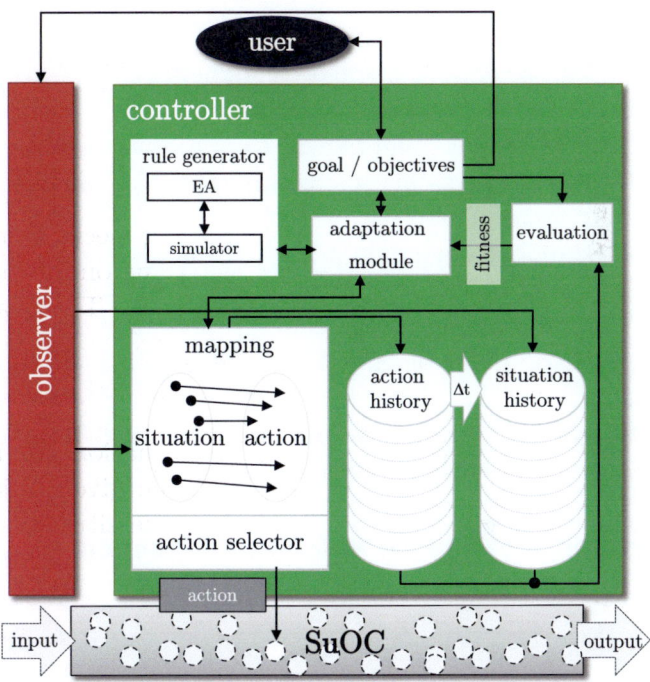

Figure 2.3: The controller of the generic O/C Architecture and its components.

2.2.2 Structure of Organic Systems

The generic O/C Architecture in the previously presented form consists of a central observer and controller which regulate a distributed system, but there are other structures as well. For example, a completely distributed O/C Architecture, where every element of a distributed system is an SuOC and has its own observer and controller. Also, a multi-level O/C Architecture is conceivable, where the distributed O/C Architecture has an additional central top-level observer and controller layer. Figure 2.4 shows these system structures. For the organic evacuation support system, each mobile evacuation device is designed according to the O/C Architecture. In addition, the system could benefit from a centralized O/C unit, such that the overall system architecture resembles the hierarchical system architecture illustrated in Figure 2.4(c). It is important to note that the mobile devices in a hierarchical system are perfectly functioning, even if the superordinate O/C Architecture breaks down. This is important in the context of emergency situations, in which a single point of failure is to be avoided. However, an additional central unit allows for users to communicate with the distributed system via a unique interface, which significantly facilitates the control of such a distributed system.

2.2.3 Swarm Intelligence and Nature Inspired Computing

Although the notion *organic* in Organic Computing does not imply the use of nature-inspired algorithms, these methods often fit well into the concept of Organic Computing. Nature-inspired methods transfer observed behavior in natural social systems, e.g., swarms of insects, into principles for the design of artificial technical systems. Creatures, especially when living in swarms, tend to self-organize in order to solve complex tasks. Prominent examples of swarms in nature who serve as algorithmic models are ant colonies (cf. Dorigo [56], Dorigo et al. [57]), bee swarms (cf. Karaboga and

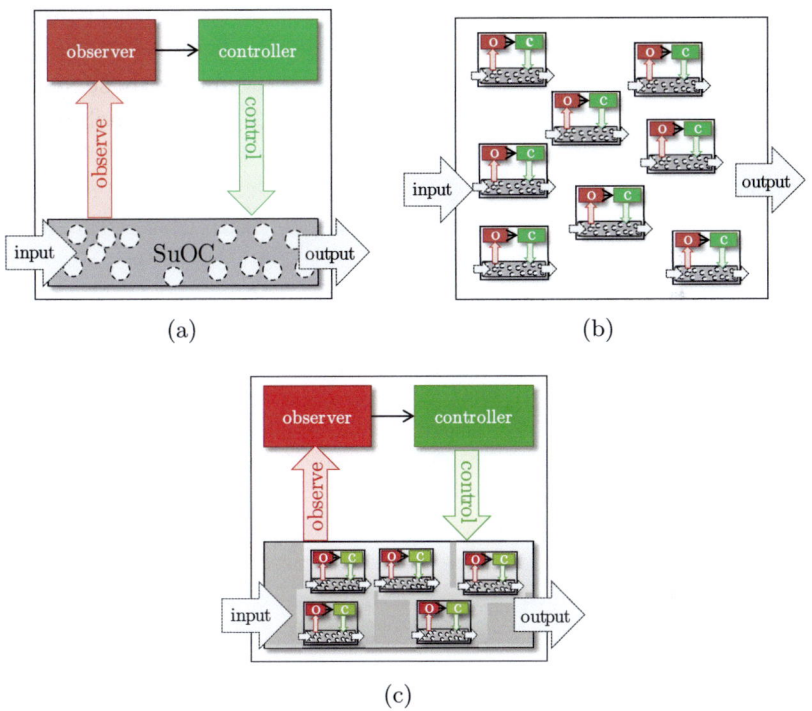

(a)   (b)

(c)

Figure 2.4: Different structures of O/C Architectures. The architecture of a centralized system (a), a decentralized system (b), and a hierarchical system (c).

Akay [116]), or fish schools (Neshat et al. [175]). The main characteristic of swarm intelligence is that a global behavior of the entire system arises as an emergent effect from simple local interactions between its components. This emergent global behavior, however, is unknown to the single entities (cf. Eberhart et al. [58]). Emergence denotes the phenomenon where local interactions lead to new global properties or structures which only arise from the interactions between its parts and would not appear with only few or a single individual. In the words of Aristotle: "The whole is more than the sum of its parts!". For OBESS, many nature-inspired algorithms have been investigated and proposed since they are very suitable for such distributed, decentralized systems. Also, due to the local communication between the devices, concepts from swarm intelligence can be transferred to mobile evacuation devices.

2.3 Evacuation Management

When it comes to evacuation management, there are generally two distinct topics which are addressed by researchers. One research subject is evacuation modeling, which has the objective to describe an evacuation process. The other research area concerns the optimization of an evacuation process by systematic intervention. In the following, these two aspects of evacuation research are described in detail.

2.3.1 Modeling

Figure 2.5 displays an overview of the research in evacuation modeling. According to Hamacher and Tjandra [82] and Schadschneider et al. [210], evacuation models can be distinguished into *microscopic* and *macroscopic* models. The objective of microscopic models is to describe an evacuation process as realistically as possible. Hence, the focus lies on modeling the heterogeneous character of individuals and their interactions. Microscopic models often form the basis for evacuation simulations. Their main purpose is the assessment of evacuation processes in order to either identify potential weak points or to evaluate improvement measures. Macroscopic models, on the other hand, provide the basis for optimization of route choices for evacuees. These models capture the evacuation situation from a global perspective and describe aggregated evacuation flows rather than interactions between individual evacuees or their characteristics.

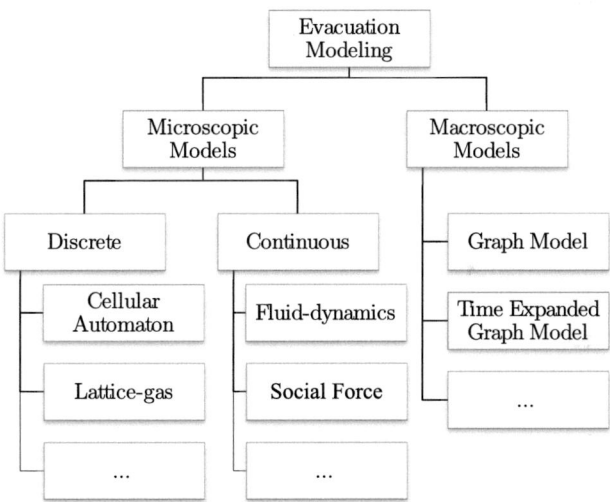

Figure 2.5: Overview of current research in the area of evacuation modeling.

Microscopic Models

Recorded data or systematic studies about the behavior of people in emergency situations are rare (cf. Brown [26], Yang et al. [252]). Therefore, microscopic evacuation modeling is not straightforward and receives much attention from the research community. Microscopic models describe the behavior of a number of, possibly different, evacuees and their interactions during an emergency situation. In such models, each evacuee is treated as a single agent with special characteristics, e.g., speed, risk aversion, size, et cetera. Microscopic models often serve as a basis for investigating the behavior of people with different characteristics during evacuation in a certain environment.

There are various microscopic models, which can be characterized into discrete and continuous models. Examples of discrete models are models which are based on cellular automaton theory (cf. Burstedde et al. [32], Gipps and Marksjö [76], Minoru Fukui [160], Schadschneider [209]) or lattice-gas models (cf. Guo and Huang [79], Song et al. [221]). The evacuation environment is divided into a grid or hexagonal patches and time is modeled in discrete steps, in which the evacuees move from one patch to another according to the rules defined by the model. Continuous models comprise models, such as the social force model (cf. Helbing and Molnar [89], Helbing et al. [90]), in which the movements are determined by forces that act on the evacuees, or dynamic fluid models or gas-kinetic models (cf. Helbing [88], Henderson [91, 92]), where movements follow the physical principle which describes the dispersion of fluids or gas. Additionally, there are so-called agent models (cf. Epstein et al. [59], Xiong et al. [251]), which allow for a distinct modeling of evacuees, such that two different evacuees can behave differently in the same situation (cf. Dawei et al. [50], Lo et al. [141]). Moreover, there are models of evacuee behavior based on game theory (cf.

Dawei et al. [50], Lo et al. [141]) or models inspired by nature, such as the model based on particle swarm optimization from Izquierdo et al. [109]. For an overview refer to Schadschneider et al. [210] and Zheng et al. [256]. Microscopic models usually form the basis for the simulation of an emergency situation, which can then be used to evaluate the evacuation process and improvement strategies. Many evacuation simulations have been developed over time. For an overview it is referred to the website of the evacuation modelling community [164].

Macroscopic Models

A macroscopic evacuation model is a graph representation $G = (N, E)$ of the evacuation environment (cf. Chalmet et al. [36]). The nodes $n \in N$ represent regions of the modeled environment in which people can be located (e.g., rooms, squares in a city, et cetera) and have certain capacities in terms of available space. An edge $e \in E$ between two nodes in the graph represents a path between the two regions described by these nodes. The edges are weighted with traveling costs, such as the distance between the connected nodes or similar properties which are decisive for route choices. The main purpose of macroscopic models is to find optimal paths for evacuees towards the building's exits. An example of a building layout and its corresponding macroscopic evacuation graph model is shown in Figure 2.6.

Some optimization approaches use a time-expansion of such a macroscopic graph as a basis. A time-expansion of a graph introduces multiple copies of each original node from the evacuation graph model. Each expanded node represents the state of the original node at a specific time step. Edges in the time-expanded graph connect nodes which can be reached in one time step, which implies that the travel time for each edge in the time-expanded

29

graph has the value 1. Capacities are adopted from the original graph. Figure 2.7 displays the time-expansion for the macroscopic evacuation graph model shown in Figure 2.6. For better readability, node capacities, initial allocations, and the travel time for edges are removed from the graph.

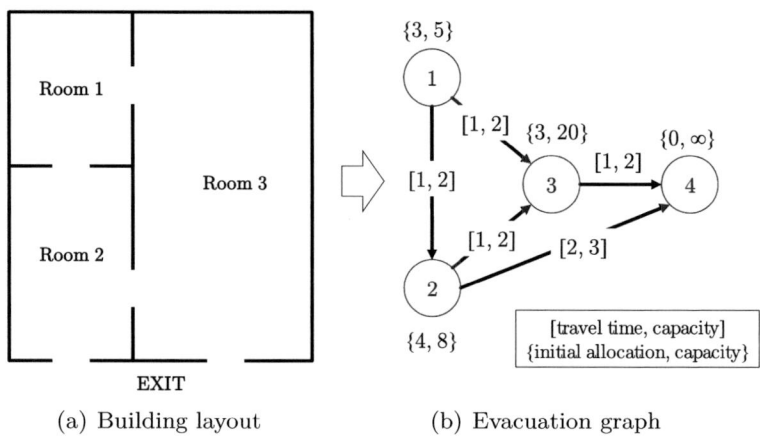

(a) Building layout　　　　(b) Evacuation graph

Figure 2.6: Example of a building layout (a), a corresponding macroscopic evacuation graph model (b).

2.3.2 Optimization

Evacuation optimization refers to approaches which are meant to improve the evacuation process. Usually, evacuation optimization has the objective to accelerate evacuation, but there are other objectives which can be considered, for example reducing the number of injuries. In general, optimization can happen in two ways, either indirectly by influencing the evacuation environment or directly by improving the route choice of evacuees. Figure 2.8

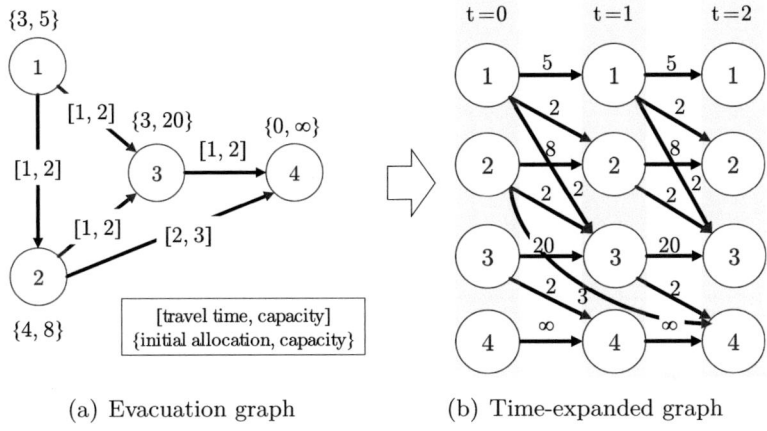

(a) Evacuation graph   (b) Time-expanded graph

Figure 2.7: Time-expansion of a macroscopic evacuation graph model.

displays an overview of the research in evacuation optimization presented hereafter.

The optimization of environmental factors ranges from finding an optimal room structure (cf. Kellenberger and Müller [120], Swenne and Bäck [225]) to defining the optimal number of doors, the optimal placement of doors, or their optimal width (cf. Alizadeh [5], Muhdi et al. [167], Varas et al. [234]). Furthermore, the deliberate placement of barriers, such as pillars, is subject to investigation in order to improve the evacuation flow (cf. Frank and Dorso [69], Johansson and Helbing [113]). Indirect optimization is generally evaluated via evacuation simulations based on microscopic models. Apart from environmental factors, the optimization of route choices is a well-studied topic. Route optimization is usually performed on the basis of a macroscopic graph representation of the environment.

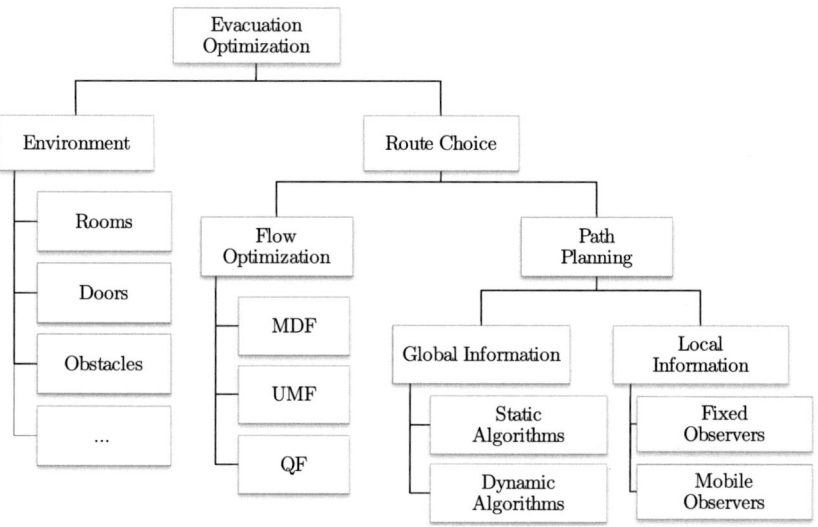

Figure 2.8: Overview of current research in the area of evacuation optimization.

Such a graph model can be used to perform either flow optimization or path planning. Flow optimization calculates optimal evacuation routes for sets of evacuees located at the same node in the graph. Such sets of evacuees are denoted as flows and the corresponding optimization problem reflects a network flow optimization problem. If the optimization objective is to maximize the number of evacuated individuals in a certain time period, the corresponding network flow problem is called *Maximum Dynamic Flow (MDF)* problem (cf. Ford and Fulkerson [68]). Maximizing the number of evacuated individuals in each time step is denoted as *Universal Maximum Flow (UMF)* problem (cf. Gale [71], Jarvis and Ratliff [111]). An optimal solution for a UMF problem corresponds to an optimal solution for an MDF problem, not only for the time period considered, but also for any smaller time horizon (cf. Jarvis and Ratliff [111]). Minimizing the time needed for a certain number of evacuees to reach the exit is referred to as the *Quickest Flow (QF)* problem (cf. Burkard et al. [31]). Since capacities of edges in the evacuation graph change during the evacuation process, these constraints are not properly reflected by a static network model as depicted in Figure 2.6. Therefore, flow optimization is generally based on a time-expansion of the evacuation graph model (cf. Section 2.3.1). It should be noted, though, that time-expanded graphs have several drawbacks. The most obvious one is that they can get very large with increasing number of time steps. Even more problematic is that the total time of evacuation has to be estimated beforehand in order to know how many expansions are needed. In the work of Lu et al. [143], a heuristic approach to solve the QF problem is presented, which does not require a time-expansion of the evacuation graph model. Instead, capacity reservations are modeled as a time series for each node in the graph. A routing protocol is adapted to schedule evacuees on paths towards the exit.

The scheduling is performed sequentially starting with evacuees closest to the building's exit. The occupied capacities are stored in the time series and considered when the next flow is scheduled until all evacuees left the building. The sequential scheduling reduces the necessary computations while still providing evacuation planning of similar quality as the solutions based on time-expanded graphs (cf. Sangho et al. [204]).

In contrast to flow optimization, path planning searches for an optimal route choice for a single evacuee instead of optimizing the flow in a network. Since only one evacuee is regarded in path planning, capacities can be neglected in the evacuation graph model and the optimization can be performed on a graph without time-expansion. Similar to flow optimization, path planning can have various objectives. If travel distance on the route is to be minimized, the problem is called a *shortest path problem*. If the optimization objective is to minimize travel time, the problem is called the *quickest path problem*. Path planning can be generalized into a *minimum cost path problem*, where costs represent any desired optimization objective. In case multiple objectives are considered at the same time, edge costs can be a weighted sum of multiple cost-components each representing one objective.

When global information about the costs of all edges in the graph is available, path planning can be solved deterministically using the algorithm described by Dijkstra [53] or the *A* *algorithm* of Hart et al. [84]. Dijkstra algorithm computes the lowest cost path between all nodes in a graph and a target node, whereas the A* algorithm concentrates the search on finding the best path starting at a specific node in the graph, which reduces the computational costs. The problem can also be solved by heuristic approaches. One of the most prominent heuristic method is the *Ant Colony Optimization (ACO)* from Dorigo et al. [57], a nature-inspired method based on the behavior of ants. Another heuristic approach to solve this problem is to use an EA, which are derived from the concept of natural evolution (cf. Weicker [246] for details). For path planning in an evacuation scenario, two approaches to find the lowest cost path according to multiple objectives are introduced and examined by Cheng [39] and Zong et al. [258]. The edge costs contain risk and travel time and ACO is used to find the optimal path through the building. A similar scenario is subject to investigation in Garrett et al. [72] and Saadatseresht et al. [202], where an EA is applied to solve the path finding problem for multiple evacuation objectives. It should be noted that the quickest path problem is also known and addressed in the evacuation modeling domain. Here, it is solved to model pedestrians which take quicker paths in order to avoid crowded areas which results in a more realistic walking behavior (cf. for example Kretz [126]).

In case of variable edge costs over time, a naive approach would be to compute the new shortest path from scratch whenever costs have changed. The D^* *algorithm* by Jarvis and Ratliff [111] avoids recomputation from scratch and reuses information from previous computations, which reduces the necessary computations significantly compared to total replanning from the beginning. The D^* algorithm is an incremental and heuristic search approach that performs local consistency checks before edge costs are newly computed. The process starts at the edge with detected change in costs and continues from there until there are only unaffected nodes left or the starting node of the search is reached. This limits necessary computations to nodes which are affected by the changed edge costs. This algorithm was further developed to result in D^* *Lite* by König and Likhachev [125]. D^* Lite is a less complex version of the D^* algorithm in terms of its structure. In addition, the number of computations which are required to find the new best path are shown to be equal or less compared to the D* algorithm.

There are scenarios where path planning is performed in a distributed system. In such cases, each system component has only a limited view on the graph, for example local information about some edge costs. The complete optimal path is then built incrementally on a next-hop basis by assembling locally optimal subparts. An application of distributed path planning based on local information to avoid traffic jams is presented by Prothmann et al. [186]. Here, traffic lights are equipped with means to observe the traffic flow at intersections. This information is exchanged with other nearby traffic lights and, similar to the distance vector or the link state routing protocol (cf. Tanenbaum [228]), the accumulated information is used to send waiting cars to the allegedly next best intersection with respect to the cars' destinations. A similar approach is presented by Filippoupolitis et al. [66] for evacuation navigation. Here, sensors observe danger indicators, such as smoke or heat, forward this message to stationary decision nodes, which exchange and collect information and decide based on these local observations to which neighboring decision node passing evacuees are sent. These methods rely on a fixed infrastructure which constantly observes a locally limited, but fixed part of the building. From these observations, information about arising congestions or risk values can be derived easily.

When mobile devices have to be used for observation, however, the observable area changes over time and the estimation of waiting times, as well as the prediction of emerging congestions, is not straightforward anymore. In the work of Wagoum et al. [237], a method is presented, which is similar to distributed path planning with mobile observers. It introduces a microscopic evacuation model that integrates local path planning with the aim of modeling a more realistic pedestrian walking behavior. A pedestrian which is slowed down by congestion on its current path is modeled to observe other pedestrians which are located in the same room and aim for a different exit. The pedestrian changes his route in case the evacuees which he observes progress faster and he starts following them. The presented method to model pedestrian behavior during an evacuation has similarities to route choice optimization approaches. However, this work belongs to the domain of evacuation modeling, since the goal is to achieve a more realistic walking behavior of evacuees, not to find the optimal paths. Hence, the chosen escape routes in this model can differ strongly from paths which result from route choice optimization approaches. The problem of distributed path planning on the basis of information collected by mobile observers is, among others, object of this thesis.

2.3.3 Evacuation Systems Using Mobile Devices

There are several projects investigating the usage of mobile devices in outdoor evacuation scenarios. For example, the project "REPKA: Regional Evacuation: Planning, Control, and Adaptation" of the German Federal Ministry for Education and Research (BMBF)[4] [2]. In REPKA, mobile devices are used to build a network and guide users to safe areas. Similar projects about the coordination of rescue forces or evacuees with the help of mobile devices are described in publications from Jang et al. [110], Lien et al. [138], Schau et al. [211], and Rodriguez et al. [199]. However, little has been done, so far, to investigate the potential of mobile devices for supporting building evacuation. An obvious reason for this is the challenge to localize devices indoors without being able to rely on GPS, which

---

[4]Bundesministerium für Bildung und Forschung

is the preferred localization technique for outdoor deployment of mobile devices in emergency management.

Nevertheless, first ideas about the application of mobile devices to support people during an emergency situation in a building are presented by Szwedko et al. [227] and Filippoupolitis et al. [66]. In the work from Szwedko et al. [227], reducing waiting times that occur due to overcrowding is addressed. The authors propose an evacuation system, where users carry mobile devices and scan QR-Codes or RFID chips in order to send their current location to a central server. This server runs a so-called *Scavy algorithm*, which computes the next destination for the mobile device's user, thereby, trying to achieve a load balancing in the building. Although this system is shown to prevent overcrowding at specific destinations in the building, it has several drawbacks. Firstly, it takes time to read a QR-Code or scan an RFID chip, which is hindering to people leaving the building as quickly as possible in case of an emergency. Additionally, it requires physical proximity between the user's device and the QR-Code or scanner, which is hardly possible for several users at the same time and, additionally, bares the risk of overlooking the respective terminals or codes. In addition, the algorithm used for load balancing is executed on a central computing system which collects all information in order to get a global view. This server poses a potential single point of failure which can be disastrous in case it breaks down during an emergency. In terms of its structure, the evacuation system proposed by Filippoupolitis et al. [66] is similar to OBESS presented in this thesis. It consists of an SSN and a dynamic network of mobile devices which are carried by people and guide their users to nearby exits. The static sensors collect information about risk values in the environment, such as smoke or heat. The sensors are connected to each other and exchange the measured risk values with their communication neighbors. When evacuees pass by such a sensor, they are sent to the next sensor which is closest to the building's exit and reports the lowest risk value. In contrast to OBESS, the system lacks the possibility to incorporate user input such as preferences for path planning. Secondly, there is no localization method provided that supports navigation. Thirdly, the evacuation planning does not take into account the current distribution of evacuees in the building or potential congestions resulting from this distribution. Using GPS-less localization in MANETs for building evacuation, is suggested in Inoue et al. [106]. The research presented, however, remains on a conceptual level. In contrast to OBESS, the proposed system architecture is not designed for controlled self-organization and it does not account for user preferences or input. Furthermore, incorporating information about other evacuees' positions in the evacuation planning is not considered in this research.

2.4 Localization

The art of localization and navigation is an inevitable prerequisite for seafaring and, thus, dates back a long time. Since the ancient days when people have used the positions of stars in the sky for localization and navigation purposes, a lot of research has been conducted in this field and many different navigation systems have been proposed since (cf. Fallah et al. [63], Hightower and Borriello [94]). Localization denotes the process of determining the location of a certain subject. When talking about a location, physical and symbolic locations as well as absolute and relative locations can be distinguished (cf. Hightower and Borriello [94]). While a physical location is described by precise coordinates, e.g., longitude and latitude, a symbolic location is more an abstract place, such as "in Germany", "at the University", "next to a street lamp", or the like.

Kröller et al. [127], for example, propose to determine symbolic locations in an SSN using cluster algorithms. A localization system can be used to provide both kinds of information, nevertheless, it is usually built to determine a physical location, which can then be mapped into a symbolic location using additional knowledge, for example a map of the environment. It holds for any type of location that the notion of location always needs a frame of reference to be meaningful. In other words, "all positions are relative. [...] assigning a set of coordinates to an object is meaningless without knowledge of the coordinate system with which those coordinates are associated" Savarese et al. [205]. These considerations lead to the difference between absolute and relative locations. While absolute locations share a common reference grid, relative locations do not. The relative location of an object makes a statement about the object's location with respect to a certain reference point. Knowing the relative location of an object with respect to a reference point, however, does not provide any information about the same object's relative location with respect to a different reference point. While any absolute location can be transferred to a relative one, as soon as the absolute location of the reference point is given, it does not work the other way around. Figure 2.9 illustrates the difference between absolute and relative locations. On the left-hand side, the absolute locations of five different devices are depicted, on the right hand side, a sample result of relative localization is shown. While the devices still have the same distance and orientation with respect to each other, the computed locations are different from their actual positions, namely mirror-inverted and rotated compared to the absolute locations. Prominent examples of common reference grids are geographic coordinate systems, which humans have globally agreed upon in order to exchange location information. Location information which refers to such a common reference grid is, for example described in terms of longitude and latitude. Because of the common understanding about the reference frame, everybody can point to exactly the same place on earth, when given such a coordinate. For a localization system to be as flexible as possible, absolute physical locations are the desired output. These can be mapped to symbolic or relative locations if needed.

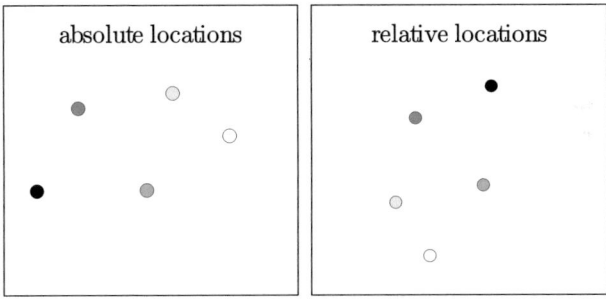

Figure 2.9: Comparison of exemplary results after applying absolute and relative localization methods in ad hoc networks. By using relative localization, the relationships between the devices stay intact, but the locations can be mirror-inverted or rotated when compared to the absolute locations.

The ability to determine the locations of devices plays an important role in SSNs. Examples are the localization of event reporting in a monitoring SSN (cf. Szewczyk et al. [226], Werner-Allen et al. [248]), location dependent routing (cf. Liao et al. [136], Maihofer [145]) or the assistance of group querying (cf. Gehrke and Madden [73]) in order to save energy, security enhancements to prevent wormhole attacks (cf. Hu et al. [98], Karlof and Wagner [117]),

41

and many more. Therefore, many localization methods for SSNs are proposed in the literature. SSNs differ from MANETs in the fact that the devices are stationary. However, most algorithms developed for SSNs are transferable to MANETs by constantly repeating the localization process in order to account for the devices' new locations. The simple application of algorithms which are developed for SSNs to MANETs is a viable approach. Neglecting the mobility aspect of the network, though, can have a major negative impact on localization results as demonstrated by a study presented in this thesis (cf. Section 5.1). Despite this drawback, this aspect has received surprisingly little attention by the research community up to this point.

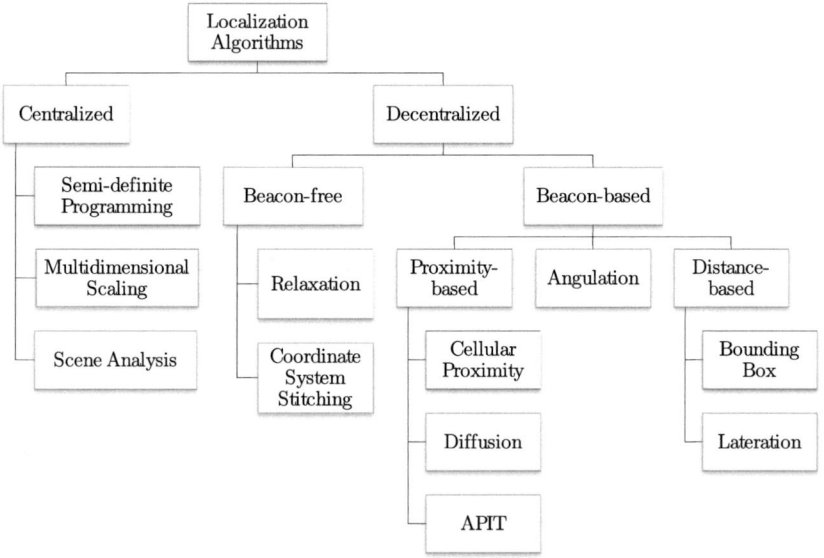

Figure 2.10: Classification of localization algorithms.

2.4.1 Algorithms

Localization algorithms can be classified according to the scheme shown in Figure 2.10. On the highest level, methods can be divided into centralized and decentralized approaches, depending on whether the location calculations are carried out on a central computing unit or in a decentralized way directly on the devices to be located. It should be noted, though, that decentralized algorithms can also be executed in a centralized way by sending all necessary information from the devices which are object of localization to a central server where all locations are computed. In this case, the disadvantages of centralized algorithms apply as well. Centralized algorithms, on the other hand, cannot be executed in a decentralized way because they require input data from numerous devices in order to compute their locations.

Centralized Algorithms

Two well-studied centralized algorithmic concepts for localization are *Semi-definite Programming (SDP)* presented by Doherty et al. [55] and *Multidimensional Scaling Map (MDS-Map)* from Shang et al. [215]. In SDP, geometric constraints, such as distances or angles between devices, are estimated by the devices in the network and sent to a central server. On the central server, the constraints are collected and represented as linear matrix inequalities, which are then solved in order to find locations for the devices in a way that the constraints are fulfilled. In MDS-Map, a technique from mathematical psychology is used (cf. Bachrach and Taylor [12]). The algorithm constructs relative positions based on distance estimates and applies concepts of linear algebra to calculate the coordinates. The main advantage of centralized algorithms is that information from all devices in the network can be used to compute locations which often results in a higher precision compared to approaches which use only local information. On the other hand, a major drawback is that they primarily stress devices close to the central station during information collection because these devices have to forward information from all other devices in the network (cf. Bachrach and Taylor [12]). Moreover, when central computation is used, the computation is usually a time consuming process because a lot of information has to be forwarded through the network, processed on the central server, and possibly be sent back to the devices in case they require the location information. This can pose problems, especially if the devices to be located are mobile, since the devices may have already changed their locations by the time the computation is completed. Apart from that, there is a lot of communication involved in the process since all devices have to exchange information with the central computing unit. These factors make centralized algorithms hardly scalable and unsuitable for dynamic networks.

Scene analysis, also called *odometry*, is a localization approach which requires the device which is object of localization to be able to perform odometry readings. Odometry readings are, for example, observations of the environment which can be used to draw conclusions about the current location. Such information can be obtained via sensors attached to the device, such as infrared sensors to measure the distance to nearby walls or barriers, photosensors, which measure the incidence of light, or even cameras, which record visual data from the device's surroundings. A set of odometry readings at a specific location is called *fingerprint*. This fingerprint is subsequently matched with entries in a database. This database consists of locations and corresponding fingerprint entries, which are measured preliminary for different locations in the application area of the system. A high storage capacity is required for the database and sufficient computing power has to be available to perform the pattern matching process, especially when cameras are used for the odometry readings (cf. Hightower and Borriello [94]). Hence, the database is usually located on a central server and queried via wireless communication. In theory, it is conceivable to have a copy of the database locally stored on the device which is object of localization. If this is possible, the approach belongs to decentralized localization methods. However, this is usually not feasible due to the restrictions of the devices to be located. Scene analysis requires a high configuration effort when collecting the database entries. Furthermore, the sensor data has to be different for any of the considered locations in order to distinguish them. This usually requires more than one type of sensor reading. For these reasons, this localization approach is rarely applied to SSNs in which the devices usually have only one sensor at their disposal and are limited in computing power, memory space, and power supply. Examples of localization using a scene analysis approach are described in Rajamäki et al. [188], Retscher [191], and Bahl and Padmanabhan [13].

Decentralized Algorithms

There are two types of decentralized localization algorithms depending on whether or not they rely on the existence of beacons. Beacon-based algorithms are required, whenever resulting coordinates have to relate to a common reference frame, i.e., when absolute locations are desired. In contrast, beacon-free or non-beacon-based algorithms can only perform relative localization, which can result in locations being rotated or mirror-inverted with respect to the actual coordinate system.

45

Beacon-free Algorithms There are two different approaches for beacon-free localization algorithms which compute physical, relative coordinates. The first concept is called *relaxation-based localization* which uses a coarse algorithm to roughly determine the devices' locations and then iteratively adjusts each device's position in order to minimize some local error metric (cf. Bachrach and Taylor [12]). An example of such an algorithm is the spring model presented by Priyantha et al. [184]. The second procedure is called *coordinate system stitching*. For this bottom-up approach, the network is divided into small overlapping subregions. In each subregion, a local map is created and then adjacent sub-regions merge their local maps iteratively until a single global map is formed. Examples of such algorithms can be found in Ji and Zha [112] and Meertens and Fitzpatrick [149]. Relative localization has the advantage that there is no need for specially equipped devices, i.e., beacons. In OBESS, however, the resulting coordinates should not be rotated or mirrored with respect to the building map. Still, such algorithms can be applied for refinement of coordinates produced by an absolute localization process.

Beacon-based Algorithms Beacons are devices which are equipped with similar or equal hardware as the devices to be located but possess knowledge of their exact positions a priori and can, therefore, support the computation of coordinates for all other devices in the network. A beacon can have a priori knowledge of its own location either due to manual configuration, because it possesses a working GPS-receiver, or because it has already computed its own location. In the latter case, the device is usually not denoted as a beacon, but can be used as such in any beacon-based algorithm. For precise calculation of two-dimensional absolute coordinates, the appropriate localization algorithm and at least three beacons are needed, which are placed in a non-colinear way. For three dimensions, four beacons are needed respectively. In a fully connected network and in the absence of any distance measurement errors, these three or four reference points yield a perfect solution and no improvement is observed from having additional reference points (cf. Savarese et al. [205]). However, localization hardware produces noisy measurements due to occlusion, collisions, and multipath effects (cf. Bachrach and Taylor [12]) and as a result, beacon-based localization normally uses several beacons to improve localization results. It is usually aimed at minimizing the number of beacons in a system because these devices can be expensive either due to their additional equipment with GPS-receivers, or in terms of preparation effort, when they have to be configured with their exact location information. With beacons available, there are three categories of localization algorithms which can be applied: proximity, angulation, and distance-based localization. These methods differ in the required hardware, number of beacons, accuracy of the derived results, and input parameters used for localization.

One group of localization approaches are algorithms which require knowledge about the *proximity* of beacons to the device which is to be located. Proximity knowledge means that a device is able to sort nearby beacons according to their distance from itself. In contrast to distance-based localization methods, the exact value of the distance, however, is not required. A method which is often used to decide about the proximity of beacons is to compare the quality of the communication signal received from different beacons (cf. Bulusu et al. [29]).

The most straightforward proximity based localization approach is the so-called *cellular proximity* method, which requires a vast number of beacons to achieve high accuracy results. In this method, beacons send a signal and their location information to nearby devices. The device receives these messages and determines its own location to be at the same location like the beacon which is closest to the device. The accuracy of the location system increases with the number of beacons in the system. A cellular proximity based localization system is, for example, proposed by Want et al. [244]. The *diffusion* method, sometimes also referred to as *centroid localization*, requires fewer beacons, but still comparatively more than angulation or distance-based localization techniques. With this method, a device derives its location at the center of the locations of a fixed number of beacons, which are closest to the device. In Figure 2.11, the localization of a device (grey dot) using diffusion and four beacons (black dots) is demonstrated. The center of the four beacons lies at the intersection of the dashed lines which is where the diffusion algorithm estimates the device's position. Exemplary implementations for the diffusion approach can be found in Almuzaini and Gulliver [7] and Kaseva et al. [118]. Meertens and Fitzpatrick [149] refine this concept further by determining a device's location not only in the center of their nearest beacons, but in the center of all neighboring devices after they have determined their locations. The appealing advantage of this algorithm is its simplicity since there is no estimate for the distance or angle information needed. Nevertheless, it is not always guaranteed that there are enough beacons to achieve the desired accuracy in localization. A more sophisticated proximity-based approach called *Approximated Point-in-Triangle Test (APIT)* is proposed by He et al. [86]. In APIT, each device divides its environment into different triangles, which are determined by all possible combinations of three nearby beacon locations. Subsequently, the device uses a point-in-triangle test to determine whether it is located outside or inside of each defined triangle. The latter triangles are then aggregated and the device's location is computed as the center of gravity of

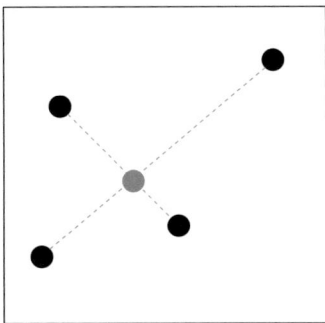

Figure 2.11: Location derived using the diffusion approach. The black dots represent beacons while the gray dot marks the location determined via diffusion at the center of the beacons.

the combined triangles. The basic idea of the point-in-triangle test is the following consideration. If there is a location next to the current location of a device which is further or closer to all beacons which define the triangle, the location of the device lies outside this triangle, otherwise it is inside. Since the devices are not assumed to be able to move in any direction in order to check whether this changes their proximity to the beacons, the authors propose to check whether the locations of the device's communication neighbors fulfill this condition. Figure 2.12 illustrates the localization process using APIT.

Angulation, as the name suggests, uses knowledge about the angles between the device to be located and the beacons. Examples of angulation can be found in Nasipuri and Li [173] and Zhang et al. [255]. To compute the angle between a device and a reference beacon, directed antennas or microphones are used which can distinguish the direction of an incoming signal. In addition, it is

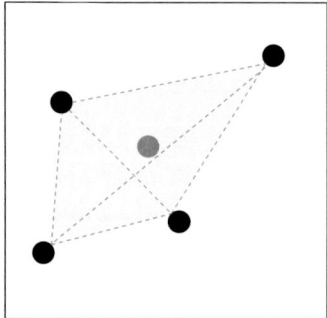

Figure 2.12: Example of localization using the APIT method. The black dots symbolize beacons and the gray dot represents the determined location. The triangles defined by the beacons' locations are indicated by dashed lines. In this example, the location lies inside all possible triangles, indicated by gray shaded areas, and is therefore determined to be at the center of gravity of the tetragon resulting from aggregation of all triangles.

possible to derive the *Angle of Arrival (AoA)* from optical communication (cf. Bachrach and Taylor [12]). The angles are estimated
using the time difference between the signals' arrivals at individual
microphones, or other receivers. The accuracy lies within a few degrees (cf. Priyantha et al. [183]). Since this method needs complex
installation and bulky hardware, the procedure is not commonly
applied to SSNs. Also, the need for spatial separation between
speakers is difficult with decreasing sensor size (cf. Bachrach and
Taylor [12]). In the work of Coore [44], an algorithm to compute
relative angles between network devices and a beacon without the
use of hardware is proposed. The computed angles are relative, i.e.,
they start at an arbitrary device with an angle value of zero and
estimate consistent angles from this point on. Niculescu and Nath
[178] suggest using AoA information in combination with distance
information to enhance localization results. From at least two
known angles, the unknown location of a device can be computed.
Figure 2.13 displays how angles between four beacons (black dots)
and the device to be located (gray dot) are used to determine the
unknown location of that fifth device.

While angulation is based on estimated angles, *distance-based
localization* methods require an estimate for the distances between
beacons and devices in the network. There are two algorithms
which use distance estimates to derive location information: the
bounding box approach and *lateration*. The bounding box method
is, for example, published by Savvides et al. [206] and Bachrach
and Taylor [12]. It assumes the position of a device to be in the
center of the overlap of square boxes which are drawn around the
beacons. The inradii of the square boxes correspond to the distance
estimates between the device and the respective beacons. Figure
2.14 illustrates how the location is determined with the bounding
box method as described. Although the bounding box procedure

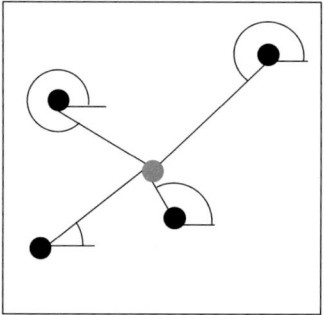

Figure 2.13: Example of localization using angulation. The black dots symbolize beacons, while the gray dot represents the unknown location. For each beacon the angle between the x-axis and the unknown location is determined. The unknown location is then assumed to be at the intersection of the lines radiating from each beacon at the predetermined angle.

has the advantage to be computationally relatively simple, the derived locations can be calculated more precisely using lateration, which requires the same kind of information as the bounding box procedure and is, therefore, used more often.

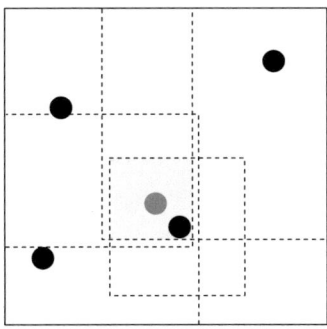

Figure 2.14: With the bounding box method, the position estimate (gray dot) is at the center of the bounding boxes with inradii equal to the respective distance estimates between the device and the beacons (black dots).

Lateration is the most well-known localization technique (cf. Nagpal et al. [171] and Bachrach and Taylor [12]). Although it is often referred to as triangulation, the notion of triangulation actually includes angulation and lateration (cf. Bachrach and Taylor [12]). In contrast to angulation, lateration is based on determining distances to beacons instead of angles. Using lateration, the position of a device is assumed to be in the overlap of circles around beacons with radii equal to the estimated distances between the device and the respective beacons (cf. Figure 2.15).

In the work of Nagpal et al. [171], an iterative version of the lateration algorithm is proposed. The method iteratively improves

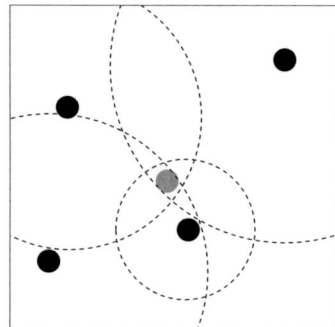

Figure 2.15: With lateration, the unknown position (gray dot) lies within the overlap of circles around the beacons (black dots) with radii equal to the respective distance estimates.

an initial location estimate, for example random coordinates, by stepwise minimizing the error between the estimated distances to all beacons and the distances of the coordinates in the current iteration.

In addition to the previously presented methods for localization, several hybrid approaches have been suggested over time, for example in Chintalapudi et al. [40], Sun et al. [223], and Eren [60]. They usually combine some of the localization methods mentioned previously in order to benefit from their various advantages and to compensate for their drawbacks.

2.4.2 Distance Estimation

As mentioned in the preceding section, the determination of distances between devices and beacons is a crucial element of distance-based localization algorithms. However, since the devices to be located usually have no means to explicitly measure distances, numerous methods for distance estimation have been proposed over time to overcome this problem. Figure 2.16 gives an overview of these techniques, which can generally be categorized into *range-based* and *range-free* methods. Range-based methods rely on the analysis of physically transmitted signals. In contrast, range-free methods abstract from the signal and derive information about the distances of devices from the content of messages which devices exchange in a network. The following two sections describe these two kinds of distance estimation methods in detail.

Range-based Distance Estimation

The most common approach to distance estimation is to analyze the strength of a transmitted radio frequency signal. This method is commonly referred to as *Radio Signal Strength Indication (RSSI)* (cf. Kai and Chun [114], Patwari and Hero [180]). The signal strength $p(d)$ decreases with increasing distance d. Hence, the strength of a communication signal on receipt provides information about the distance between sender and receiver. Equation 2.1 shows the underlying theoretical model:

$$p(d) = \overline{p(d_0)} - 10 \; \alpha \; log\left(\frac{d}{d_0}\right) + X \qquad (2.1)$$

d_0 denotes a reference distance, α represents the path-loss exponent, $X \sim \mathcal{N}(\mu, \sigma)$ denotes a normally distributed random variable with mean (μ) zero and variance σ, which describes the shadowing effect. Although widely studied in the literature, there are some drawbacks to this approach. RSSI ranging measurements contain noise in the order of several meters (cf. Bahl and Padmanabhan [13]) and radio propagation tends to be highly affected by barriers such as walls or

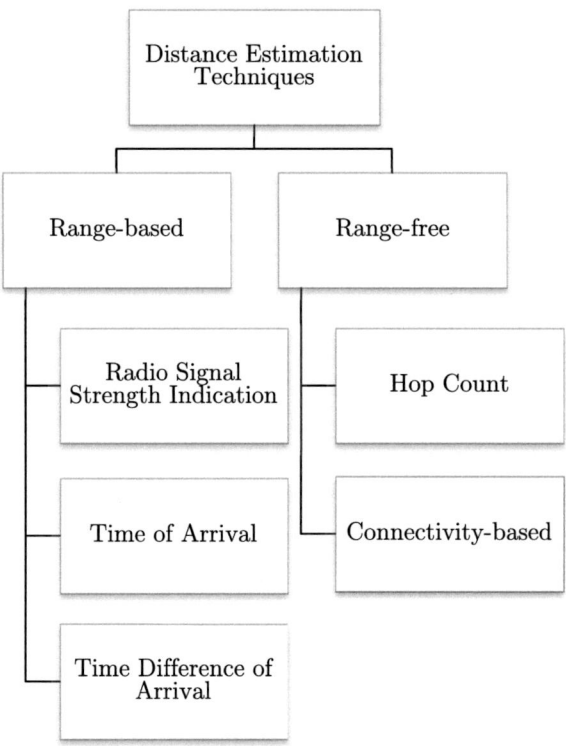

Figure 2.16: Classification of distance estimation techniques.

furniture since they tend to reflect or absorb signals (cf. Bachrach and Taylor [12]).

Another prominent method for distance estimation is called *Time of Arrival (ToA)*, also often referred to as *Time of Flight (ToF)* (cf. Girod and Estrin [77], Meghani et al. [150]). In ToA, the time for a physical signal to be transmitted from one device to another is measured. ToA can be performed in a one-way or two-way version. In the two-way version, a transceiver sends a signal to the receiver which, in turn, sends an answer. The sender measures the time t between sending and receiving the signal and, together with the velocity v of the signal and the expected delay t_{reply} which occurs between receiving a signal and answering, the distance estimate $\bar{d}$ between the two devices can be computed using Equation 2.2. For the one-way version, the system clocks of the transmitting and receiving device have to be synchronized. This is usually done using radio and ultrasonic signals. The radio signal has almost zero propagation speed indoors when compared to the ultrasonic signal and is used for synchronization purpose (cf. Meghani et al. [150]). Every device is equipped with a speaker and a microphone. The transmitter (beacon) first sends a radio message, waits for a fixed time period, and then sends a chirp sequence over its speaker. The receiver gets the radio signal, turns on its microphone and hears the chirp sequence. It notes the time t of the transmission of the ultrasonic signal and uses this information together with the transmission speed v of the audio signal to calculate its physical distance from the transmitter using Equation 2.3. While ToA is impressively accurate for some scenarios, it has the major drawback to require line-of-sight conditions and extensive hardware. In addition, the speed of sound in the air varies with air temperature and humidity (cf. Bachrach and Taylor [12]). Furthermore, relatively fast processing capabilities are required in order to be able to resolve small time differences. Kwon et al. [131] show that the precision can be improved by checking for reflexivity and the triangle inequality.

$$\bar{d}_{ToA} = v \cdot \left(\frac{1}{2}t - t_{reply} \right) \tag{2.2}$$

$$\bar{d}_{ToA} = v \cdot t \tag{2.3}$$

A similar distance estimation technique is called *Time Difference of Arrival (TDoA)* (cf. Gustafsson and Gunnarsson [80], Mao et al. [146], Meghani et al. [150]). The device to be located sends signals to the beacons in the network and these beacons each measure the ToA of their signal. From each set of differences between ToAs and the known distance between the respective beacons, unique hyperbolic curves around the respective beacons are defined. The intersections of these curves determine the unknown location of the device (cf. Bucher and Misra [27]).

All range-based distance estimation methods have in common that they require special hardware in order to be able to analyze physical signals. Since such hardware can be large and expensive, range-based distance estimation is unsuitable for some applications. However, range-free distance estimation methods are able to overcome this drawback.

Range-free Distance Estimation

Estimating distances in a network without having to rely on the interpretation of the physical signal is called range-free distance estimation. Instead, range-free distance estimation is based on messages which are exchanged between the devices in a network. There are two types of range-free distance estimation algorithms, *hop count based* and *connectivity-based* distance estimation algorithms.

The hop count based algorithm is the more established approach of the two. A hop count denotes the minimum number of relay devices a device needs to be able to communicate with a beacon. The *Gradient Algorithm (GA)*, proposed by Nagpal et al. [171], is an algorithm for networks used to determine each device's hop count with respect to a beacon. It is the basis for all distance estimation algorithms based on hop counts. With GA, each beacon initiates a so-called gradient wave by sending a message including an integer value of 0 to its neighbors. Each neighboring device takes the minimum value it receives, increments it by 1, and propagates it to its neighbors. This process is repeated in fixed intervals, such that the value can be updated regularly, especially, in dynamic networks. Figure 2.17 illustrates the concept of hop counts. Devices which are able to communicate with each other are connected by straight lines. The beacon, displayed as a black dot on the left side, initiates the process by communicating a value of zero to its neighbors. All devices in the network take the minimum value they receive and add one to compute their own hop count, which is represented by the number inside the respective dots. Figure 2.18 shows an example of the result achieved by the GA when applied to an ad hoc network. All devices with the same hop count value are colorized in the same shade of Grey. All devices with the same hop counts are located in symmetrical rings around the beacon and each ring has approximately the width of the communication range r (cf. Nagpal et al. [171]). Therefore, the most basic idea for hop count based distance estimation is to use r as an approximation for the length of each hop and r times the hop count as an estimate for the distance between a device and beacons. However, this estimate is only valid for perfectly dense networks, which rarely occur in reality.

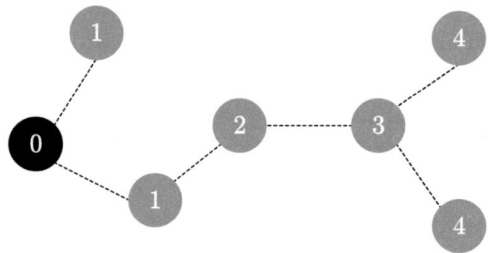

Figure 2.17: Hop count determination with GA initiated by the beacon (black dot) which sends a value of zero to its neighbors (connected by dotted lines), which compute their hop count as minimum value received plus one (numbers inside the dots).

Figure 2.18 displays the perfect gradient rings, i.e., the rings centered at the beacon with radii of multiples of r, drawn as black circular rings. It is easy to see that the gradient rings which result from GA differ from these perfect gradient rings. Kleinrock and Silvester [122] show that the expected length of a hop in uniformly random distributed networks is given as a function of the local neighborhood density, i.e., the number of communication partners. A similar, but somewhat simpler principle is used by Wong et al. [249] for networks with varying density. Here, density dependent reduction rates are chosen manually depending on the local density and applied to the naive estimate r before multiplying it with the hop count. A different method to estimate the length of a hop is provided by an approach called *DV-HOP* (cf. Huang and Selvakennedy [102], Niculescu and Nath [177]). DV-Hop uses the fact that Euclidean distances between beacons are known because their location information is available. By comparison of the Euclidean

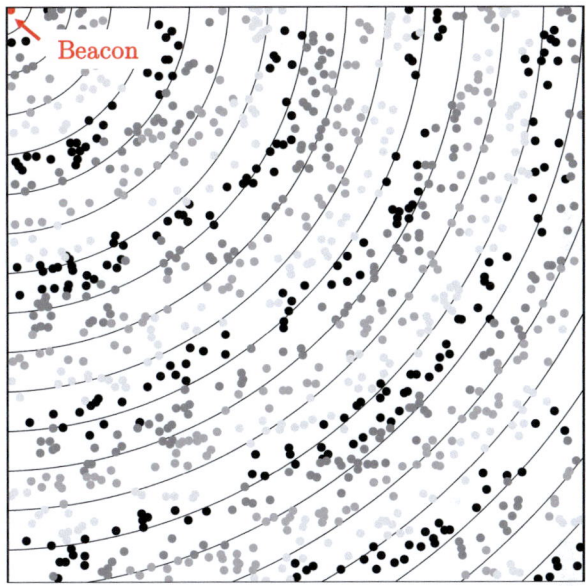

Figure 2.18: A network situation after application of GA. Devices with the same hop counts are displayed in the same shade of Grey. Black rings are centered at the beacon and have radii of multiples of r, with r being the communication range of the devices.

distances with the respective hop counts between beacons, the average length of a hop is calculated as a fraction of Euclidean distance and hop count. Apart from improving the hop length estimate, various methods are developed to determine the position of a device within its own gradient ring. For example, in the work of Nagpal et al. [171], an average of all hop counts in a device's neighborhood is calculated before multiplying it by the hop length estimate, following the principle that devices which are closer to the inner border of their gradient ring have a higher number of neighbors with lower hop counts. Conversely, a node which is closer to the outer border of its gradient ring has a higher number of neighbors with higher hop counts. Liu et al. [140] refine this approximation further by using the exact proportions of neighbors with lower, equal, or higher hop counts in order to improve the estimate and Wang et al. [242] propose to refine distance estimates through weighted interpolation.

The second type of range-free distance estimation algorithms is called *connectivity-based* distance estimation. It relies on the number of shared communication partners between two devices with respect to the total number of communication partners. The idea behind this concept is that devices which are close to each other share more communication neighbors than distant devices (cf. Figure 2.19). This approach was first presented by Fekete et al. [64] and Buschmann et al. [33]. Later on, it was refined by Aslam et al. [10], Villafuerte et al. [236] and Huang et al. [99]. While Fekete et al. [64] and Buschmann et al. [33] use only the number of shared neighbors for distance estimation, Aslam et al. [10], Villafuerte et al. [236], and Huang et al. [99] expand the concept by using the ratio of shared to total communication partners. The mapping between this ratio and the distance estimate is generally designed as a lookup table derived through an a priori empirical study. However, Huang et al. [99] apply a first order Taylor series expansion to approximate the mapping function. The method is tested on real hardware and is shown to deliver more precise estimates compared to an RSSI-based distance estimation approach.

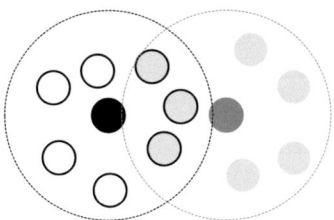

Figure 2.19: Two devices and their communication ranges. The distance between the devices and the number of shared communication partners (gray dots with black border-line) is correlated.

2.4.3 Mobility

As mentioned before, there is little research about the effects mobility has on the accuracy of localization algorithms. A common argument for why mobility is not considered explicitly is that the execution of the respective localization algorithm can be repeated constantly in order to update location information. However, localization requires input data, such as distances or angle information, usually derived by various estimation techniques, which are prone to error under mobile conditions. This is, for example, shown by Bergamo and Mazzini [17], where the accuracy of distance estimation based on radio signal strength is investigated in dynamic networks. Experiments reveal that Rayleigh fading due to the motions of the sensors can introduce significant errors to the estimates. Similar to these findings, mobility can be expected to have an impact on range-free distance estimation. Range-free distance estimates are derived from a device's communication neighborhood which is affected by the mobility of devices in the network. Potential influences on range-free distance estimation are not primarily hardware related and have to be examined individually. This is, for example, done by Lim and Rao [139], who identify the mobility of some devices in the network to have a positive impact on the accuracy of hop count based localization. However, the underlying assumption of the performed experiments is that the mobile devices know when they are moved and, if so, immediately update their hop count values and distance estimates. This leads to a general improvement of distance estimation within the network as it resembles a scenario in which new devices are placed in the network at all locations, where the devices move to. Therefore, the network density is virtually increased. Liu et al. [140] show that mobility affects the probabilistic density of devices in a communication range which can influence the computed hop count values. The authors provide a method to account for mobility when calculating distance estimates based on hop counts. It has to be noted, though, that for the proposed compensation of mobility-induced density distortions, knowledge about the underlying mobility model is required. The question how the devices can attain knowledge about their own mobility pattern stays unanswered though. At least for devices which are either carried or moved by external forces and do not move actively, the answer to this question is not straightforward. One solution to this problem is proposed by Kumar and Das [130]. The authors derive the movement pattern from a sequence of previously computed locations. However, the assumption that mobility in a network follows a certain pattern is not always valid.

In contrast to localization techniques, dead-reckoning methods, or deduced reckoning, are specific methods to locate, or better, track the positions of mobile objects over time. Originally, dead-reckoning was used by seafarers in the fifteenth century before more accurate celestial navigation techniques were developed. A ship's current location was determine using its previous location and an estimate for the direction and distance it has sailed since (cf. Kumar and Das [130]). The estimate of an object's current location using dead-reckoning is based on previously determined locations, a model which describes the object's dynamics, and frequent corrections by odometry readings, for example the object's speed and direction. For odometry readings, sensors such as accelometers, magnetometers, compasses, and gyroscopes are used. Kalman Filters (cf. Bartlett [15]) or Particle Filters (cf. Ristic et al. [197]), which take into account that sensor values are usually prone to error, can be used to compute the location estimate. Examples of localization systems that use dead-reckoning can be found in Fischer et al. [67], Höllerer et al. [96], Koide and Kato [123], and Retscher [191]. If the mobile device is carried by a human user, information about the user's specific walking behavior, such as his average speed, can be used instead of odometry readings in order to direct the search towards the most likely locations (cf. Wu et al. [250]). Hu and Evans [97] use the location of newly detected beacons, which come into range when the device moves, as odometry readings to derive location estimates. A major drawback of dead-reckoning systems is the necessity for odometry readings and the required model of the object's dynamics. Moreover, dead-reckoning is subject to cumulative errors up to the point where it receives new extrinsic location information, hence this approach is best used in combination with other localization techniques for error correction. A great advantage is the possibility to extrapolate locations in case there is not enough information available to apply a localization algorithm, for example due to a temporary absence of beacons or due to the failure of distance estimation. Additionally, dead-reckoning allows for the prediction of likely future locations of mobile devices, which can come in handy for several applications. Apart from research which deals with the mobility of the devices to be located, some researchers attend to the potential improvement of localization by employing mobile beacons (cf. Li et al. [133], Wang et al. [243], You et al. [253], Zhang and Yu [254].

2.4.4 Indoor Localization Systems

In the literature, numerous localization systems specifically developed for indoor applications can be found. This section aims at providing an overview of the proposed solutions. Apart from the localization method applied, localization systems can be distinguished with regard to various criteria (cf. Hightower and Borriello [94]). One criterion is the wireless data transmission technique in the system, which is usually infrared, radio frequency, or ultrasound. Data transmission by means of radio frequency signals can further be classified according to the implemented communication protocols, such as Bluetooth [20], Zigbee [257], or the IEEE 802.11 standards, which are commonly used in *Wireless Local Area Network (WLAN)* technology [104]. There are localization systems where the devices to be located perform the necessary computations locally and systems in which the localization is undertaken by an external, mostly centralized computing unit. The latter approach is associated with all disadvantages that characterize centralized localization algorithms (cf. Section 2.4). In addition, these systems bear the risk of privacy infringement since the location information is computed on an extrinsic server. Localization systems, in general, can further differ with regard to their costs and installation expenditure, the accuracy and precision of obtained locations, or the kind of locations they deliver, i.e. physical versus symbolic, absolute or relative locations. There are also some indoor localization systems which use entirely different localization methods than those presented in Section 2.4.1. Two examples of alternative localization systems are the *Smart Floor* introduced by Orr and Abowd [179] and the *MotionStar* concept presented by Raab et al. [187]. SmartFloor is a localization system for buildings which derives the locations of people from embedded pressure sensors in the floor. In MotionStar, devices which generate axial DC magnetic-field pulses are installed at fixed locations in the building. Magnetic sensors in the devices to be located are used to determine the orientation of the magnetic field and derive their locations from this information. Table 2.1 gives an overview of various indoor localization systems. Except for the *SpotOn* localization system, none of the proposed indoor navigation solutions listed in Table 2.1 specifically exploits ad hoc network connections between the devices to be located. This is probably due to the fact that localization systems are desired to work even if there is only a single device to be located in the building. In localization systems based on ad hoc networks, the quality of the locations correlates positively with the number of devices in the building. However, in an evacuation scenario, a small number of devices imply a reduced danger of congestions during the evacuation process. Hence, the importance of the drawback that there are few devices available for localization is dampened because the reduction in evacuation time which can be achieved by the navigation system is negligible. Nevertheless, localization systems based on ad hoc networks can significantly reduce the requirements of the localization infrastructure, which in turn reduces hardware costs, as well as installation and maintenance expenditure. High costs and effort have, so far, been a major hindrance in the prevalence of indoor localization systems, a trend which could be overcome by the use of ad hoc network based localization systems. Since dynamic evacuation support systems should be available in as many buildings as possible, enhancing localization support by exploiting ad hoc network connections could advance this vision and bring it closer to reality. For this reason, this thesis concentrates on the investigation of ad hoc network based localization methods for mobile devices.

Table 2.1: Overview of indoor localization systems, their applied localization algorithms, and the wireless communication technique in use.

Localization	Communication	System
Scene analysis	Computer vision	Wearable computers [78] Indoor navigation for the blind [103] NAVIO [191] Easy Living [128]
	IEEE 802.11	LaureaPOP [188] NAVIO [191] RADAR [13]
Lateration	RFID tags	Virtual leading blocks [8]
	Infrared	Navigation aid system [16]
	Ultrasound	Cricket [182] Drishti [189]
	UHF	Navitime [9]
	IEEE 802.11	Semantic navigation system [232] RADAR [13]
	3G	NAVIO [191]
	Magnetic pulse	MotionStar [187]
Proximity	RFID tags	RadioVirgilio/ SesamoNet [48] RG-I [129] Wearable way-finding computer [201]

		Blind navigation system [54] Space-identifying infrastructure [18] SpotOn [95]
	Infrared	Active Badge [244]
	Ultrasound	ActiveBats [85] Cricket [182]
	Bluetooth	Smart navigation environment [101]
	Barcode scanning	E-scavenger hunt game [227] Context-aware wayfinding [37] Metronaut [218]
Dead-reckoning	RFID tags	Human navigation system [123]
	3G	NAVIO [191]
	Ultrasound	Ultrasound Indoor Navigation [67]

CHAPTER 3

ORGANIC BUILDING EVACUATION

Organic Computing deals with the design of complex, self-organizing technical systems in order to make them flexible and trustworthy at the same time. According to the definition provided by Muehl et al. [166], a system is self-organizing when it is self-managing, structure-adaptive, and employing decentralized control. A system is denoted as being self-managing if it can adapt to changes in its environment without outside control. Structure-adaptive means that the system has to maintain a certain kind of structure which can be spatial, temporal, or of other kind. The O/C Architecture developed in Organic Computing supports self-organization by feedback and learning mechanisms as explained in Section 2.2.1. In contrast to the previously given definition of self-organization, the O/C Architecture explicitly allows for external control in order to make the system trustworthy and robust against failure. Especially for such a dynamic environment as a building evacuation scenario, adaptability plays an important role since it is impossible to consider all potentially arising situations at design time of an evacuation system. However, it is even more important to make such an evacuation system controllable, since relying completely on a technical system in case of a life-threatening situation is undesirable for most humans. In the following, a concept for OBESS is introduced, which is designed according to the paradigm of controlled self-organization from Organic Computing. The main system components and their respective functionalities are described. Furthermore, it is noted how the O/C Architecture can be used in OBESS in order to achieve the desired system behavior.

3.1 Concept of an Organic Building Evacuation Support System

OBESS consists of three main components, which are displayed in Figure 3.1. There is a *CCU*, i.e., a central server for each building, which is used to configure the sensors in the SSN. The SSN is the second component of OBESS and consists of numerous sensors distributed throughout the building. These sensors are able to communicate with each other and the CCU. The third system component is a MANET, established by wireless communication between mobile devices carried by potential evacuees. Mobile devices in the MANET can communicate with sensors of the SSN and vice versa. The functionalities of all three system components are explained in detail in the following.

3.1.1 Central Control Unit

One important aspect of OBESS is its decentralized structure. As emphasized before, the lack of a single point of failure is crucial, especially in emergency systems. Nevertheless, there is a CCU in

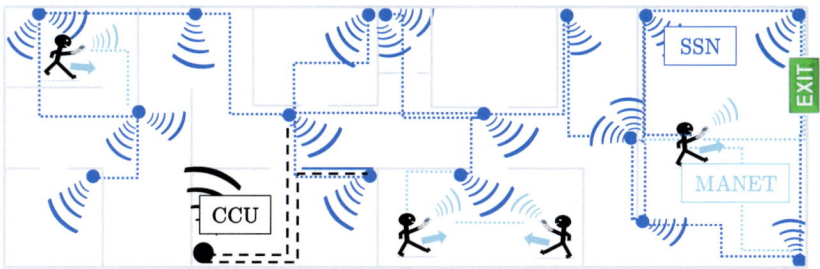

Figure 3.1: Structure of OBESS, its main elements (CCU, SSN, and MANET), and the communication links between the components.

OBESS and it is important to note that this control unit does not play any part in the evacuation planning process and is, therefore, not fatal for the evacuation support service in case of failure. The main task of the CCU is to configure the static sensors. For example, providing the building layout and corresponding information or assigning the respective location information to each sensor in the building, such that they can be used as beacons for localization of the mobile devices. In order to accomplish this task, the CCU offers an interface for the user, which can be used to configure and control OBESS. Apart from that, the CCU collects information from the mobile devices using the sensors in the SSN in order to optimize and adjust OBESS to the building's specifics over time. Such information could be the average number of mobile devices in the building at specific times and days, the most frequented rooms and paths, or others. The CCU can learn building-specific characteristics and adapt the evacuation system over time in order to improve its effectiveness. For this, the two-level learning mechanism of the generic O/C Architecture can be used which is described in Section 2.2.1. An example for such a building-specific optimization of OBESS is described in Section 5.4, where the placement of the sensors is improved in order to achieve better results during the localization process of the mobile devices.

3.1.2 Static Sensor Network

The most obvious task of the SSN is to monitor indicators for dangerous situations, such as heat, smoke, or similar properties, perceivable by technical sensors. In case any of the measured values exceeds a certain threshold, an alarm can be triggered or a human user, who is responsible for the alarm, can be notified. The SSN, therefore, serves as a monitoring and alarm system, similar to the ones that can be found in certain buildings today. In Section 4.2, an algorithm is presented which relies partly on such sensor information. The sensors in the SSN are assumed to have knowledge of their exact locations in the building due to an a priori configuration via the CCU interface. Hence, the static sensors serve as beacons to support the localization of the mobile devices in the building as detailed in Section 2.4. In addition, sensors can provide useful information as a download to the mobile devices, for example a layout of the building and its representation as an evacuation graph model (cf. Section 2.3.1). Normally, sensors in the network communicate wirelessly with each other. Nevertheless, it is conceivable that the SSN is set up as a so-called small world network. Small world networks are characterized by having mainly local communication links between nearby devices but occasionally feature certain devices which are connected over longer distances by wire. It is shown that, in small world networks, a small number of wired long distance connections can speed up the spread of information significantly (cf. Watts and Strogatz [245]). As a consequence, providing some wired connections between the sensors can enhance the information exchange between distant mobile and static sensor devices. Another task for the SSN is to collect information from the mobile devices which can be used to evaluate the current status of the evacuation system in this specific building. Such information could be available input data for localization or trajectories of the devices' movements through the building. Sensors in OBESS are not required to have an extensive computing capacity, and there is no need to implement a complex O/C Architecture on these devices.

3.1.3 Mobile Ad Hoc Network

The devices in the MANET are assumed to run software enabling their usage for building evacuation. Whenever such a device enters a building which is equipped with OBESS hardware, it receives a message from a nearby sensor, including all necessary information about the current building. In particular a possibility for downloading the building's layout and the respective evacuation graph model is provided. In case of an emergency situation, the sensors inform all nearby mobile devices about this situation. The device then calls the attention of its user by ringing and vibrating. On the display of the device, the building's layout and the current location of the user are shown and the device indicates navigation instructions to an exit door, for example by pointing out the direction on the screen or via voice instructions.

The mobile devices in OBESS are each assumed to belong to a specific person who carries the device. This provides the opportunity to collect information about the human user's preferences and characteristics. These preferences or characteristics can be used to personalize the evacuation support service offered by the

75

device. For example, the device can collect information about the age of its user or whether he has any handicaps in order to adjust the navigation instructions accordingly. Also, rescue forces can be informed about certain health conditions to improve the help they can provide. Whether such personal information is manually entered by the user himself or is even learned by the mobile device from observing its user's behavior, i.e., visited websites, social networks, et cetera, is open for discussion and future research. Of course, an important aspect in this context is the protection of the user's privacy.

The main focus of this thesis lies on the mobile devices in OBESS. In order to design the software for these devices, two main algorithmic challenges have to be mastered. Firstly, the device has to be able to compute an evacuation path from its current position to an exit of the building, thereby integrating knowledge about the current evacuation situation. Two algorithms which can generate navigation instructions are presented in Chapter 4. The second challenge is that the devices have to be capable of determining their locations inside the building. Chapter 5 addresses exemplary ways to master this task. An implementation of the O/C Architecture for the mobile evacuation devices in OBESS is described in the following.

3.2 Observer/Controller Architecture for Mobile Devices

As described in Section 2.2.1, the O/C Architecture is a design framework for organic technical systems, i.e., systems which are self-organizing and exhibit life-like properties, such as being adaptable to unforeseen changes, while at the same time being trustworthy, robust, and controllable by human users. Hereafter, an exemplary implementation of this generic architecture for mobile devices used in OBESS is presented.

In OBESS, each mobile device and the CCU is designed according to the O/C Architecture. However, the resulting system structure is not hierarchical because there are no means for the CCU to control the mobile devices in the system. Hence, the structure is rather a decentralized one as depicted in Figure 2.4(b). The SuOC of the mobile devices is different from the standard structure in the way that the devices cannot only observe themselves, but also all devices located in their communication ranges. Nevertheless, only the devices' own actions are controllable. Figure 3.2 illustrates this structure.

The software of a mobile device in OBESS has three modes of operation. Firstly, it can simply display the layout of the building on its screen without providing any further functionality. Secondly, it can run in *localization-mode*, in which the software determines the device's location within the building and shows it on its screen. Thirdly, the device can switch to *evacuation-mode*, in which it additionally computes navigation instructions in order to support the evacuation of its user from the building. Since all devices have limited resources and constrained energy supply, it is reasonable to turn-off the evacuation functionalities if they are not needed. To do so, the O/C Architecture provides the concept of observation models which determine what kind of data is currently being monitored and processed. The controller can switch between these observation models depending on the current requirements. For example, if the device is notified of an emergency situation either by the sensors in its environment or directly by its user, evacuation-mode can be switched-on; otherwise it is turned off and only localization or simply the building's layout is available to the user. Both kinds of operation modes can have numerous different sub-

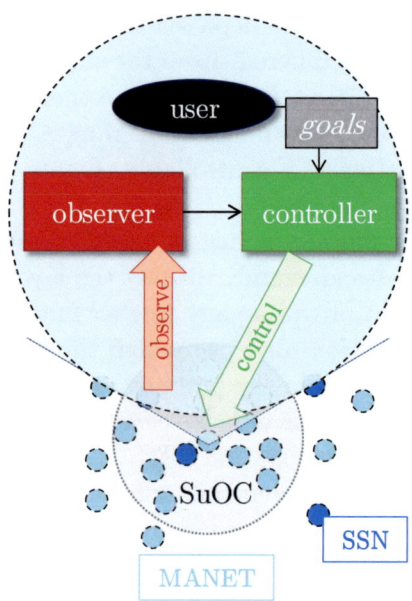

Figure 3.2: Structure of the O/C Architecture for mobile devices in OBESS.

level observation models, one for each evacuation or localization algorithm which is available to the mobile device. The main purpose of the O/C Architecture is to observe and characterize the device's environment and switch between different algorithms for evacuation planning and localization in order to select the most suitable one for the current situation of the mobile device. Furthermore, changes in the environment are meant to be detected which trigger an update of the evacuation route. In the following, the O/C Architecture is described for both, the evacuation-mode, as well as the localization-mode. It should be noted that the evacuation-mode requires location information, which is why the evacuation-mode constitutes an enhancement of the localization-mode observation model.

3.2.1 Observer

The observer's task is to provide for a characterization of the current system situation as well as a prediction of probable future system states to the controller. These characterizations are used as a basis for making decisions in the controller, i.e. selecting the most suitable localization and evacuation algorithm. Figure 2.2 illustrates the observer part of the generic O/C Architecture. The monitor unit is responsible for observing all data specified by the observation model. In case of the evacuation-mode, all necessary input data to perform evacuation planning has to be monitored and the same holds for localization. For evacuation planning, the locations of other evacuees in the building could be of interest, as well as sensor data about dangerous areas. As mentioned before, there is one observation model for each available evacuation or localization algorithm. Hence, depending on the selected algorithm, different input data is monitored. For example, when beacon-based localization is applied (cf. Section 2.4.1), any beacon location communicated by a nearby device is monitored. In case of distance-based localization, hop count information from surrounding devices could be monitored, or other data depending on the selected distance estimation technique (cf. Section 2.4.2). In addition, information about the current environment of the device is observed, such as indicators about the network topology, for example how many beacons are within reach. This environmental information can be used in the controller to decide about a necessary change of the selected algorithm. Section 3.2.2 explains this in detail. The pre-processor computes derivative data for the algorithms by processing or filtering the monitored data. For example, if the device receives multiple messages with contradictory content, the pre-processor decides which message contains the most up-to-date information by comparing age-values of the messages received. Another example would be to find the minimum hop count value from a set of hop count messages received by neighbors or to evaluate a potential evacuation route by summarizing sensor information from rooms along this path. In the data-analyzer, meaningful attributes which are able to characterize the current system state are derived from the pre-processed data. Examples for such attributes are the average speed with which nearby devices are moved and their direction of movement. These parameters could be used to characterize the mobility in the network. For evacuation planning, the average concentration of evacuees in the building is an example for a computed value which characterizes the evacuation situation. The prediction module of the generic O/C Architecture is meant to forecast the most likely future system state. For evacuation planning, it is conceivable to assess the emergence of congestions, for example from an increasing concentration of devices in parts of the building. In case of an active localization-mode, this is the place where dead-reckoning methods, as described in Section 2.4.3, could be used in order to predict the next location of a device. The observer's aggregator module passes all this information to the controller.

3.2.2 Controller

The controller's main function in the O/C Architecture is to choose an appropriate action, given a certain situation assessment and a prediction of a future system state by the observer. In the presented implementation of the O/C Architecture for mobile evacuation devices in OBESS, choosing an appropriate action is equivalent to selecting a suitable evacuation planning and localization algorithm. For evacuation planning, there are two evacuation planning approaches proposed in this thesis which differ in the information required and deliver evacuation routes of different quality. Depending on the device's state-of-charge, it might be advisable to choose an evacuation planning algorithm which requires fewer messages to be exchanged, even though the computed navigation instructions are suboptimal. Furthermore, replanning of an evacuation instruction can become necessary when there is new information about the situation in the building available to a device. In Section 2.4, the broad variety of localization methods for ad hoc networks is demonstrated. The sheer quantity of different approaches to the problem suggests that there is more than one optimal method to find the location of devices in a network. In fact, each algorithm has its own advantages and disadvantages and it is not always easy to choose which localization algorithm is preferable for a given situation. Fortunately, the organic O/C Architecture offers a solution to select between multiple evacuation and localization algorithms at runtime, respecting the current network situation and the device's system conditions. Figure 2.3 illustrates the controller part of the generic O/C Architecture, its elements, and their interactions. The controller takes actions in order to achieve desired and prevent unwanted system behavior. Undesired evacuation behavior occurs when an evacuation instruction is not optimal anymore with respect to current objectives. One reason for this can be a deviation of the user from the suggested evacuation path or because a newly available situation characteristic implies that another escape route is superior in terms of current optimization objectives. In case of localization, an undesired system behavior appears when locations which are computed by a chosen localization algorithm deviate too much from real locations of the device and when there is another localization algorithm which is expected to deliver more accurate results. The available control actions are to change the applied evacuation or localization algorithm and to trigger replanning of evacuation instructions. In the O/C Architecture, there are two types of control mechanisms. An intrinsic control, where the controller chooses an action depending on the situation characteristics and prediction of the future system state which it receives from the observer. These characteristics are matched in the action selection module and the situation-action mapping which has the highest reward is chosen as described in Section 2.2.1. Alternatively, it is also conceivable that a control action is triggered by the user of the O/C system. In the generic O/C Architecture, the user is intended to control the system by setting and adapting the system's objectives and goals. The most obvious change in system objectives is a switch between the modes of operation, such as turning the evacuation procedure on or off. Another conceivable change of system objectives is to set other optimization objectives for the escape route planning in the evacuation-mode. It could be desired to search for an escape route with minimum risk exposure instead of travel time. However, in the O/C Architecture for mobile devices in OBESS, a direct interaction between user and mobile device is also allowed. For example, the user can correct computed locations by tapping on the screen of the device or by choosing a different evacuation route than the suggested one simply by walking in another direction. In addition, it is conceivable that the user selects a compulsory localization algorithm, which has to be used by the system, or inserts a priori available information about the building in order to facilitate the controller's selection of an appropriate algorithm. The O/C Architecture is, furthermore, particularly suited for respecting user preferences and characteristics during operation. The user can provide personal information which influences the objectives for evacuation planning in the evacuation-mode. Such information could be the need for accessible paths or the avoidance of stairs in case the user is handicapped or of high age.

In the generic O/C Architecture the situation to action mapping is intended to be learned using the two-level learning infrastructure provided. While the first-level learning, also called online learning, is a feedback mechanism, which evaluates results achieved by control actions at runtime, the second-level learning, or offline learning, is based on a simulation, in which potential control actions are tested before they are made available to the system. While the first-level learning is often based on a *Learning Classifier System (LCS)*, as described by Richter [193], the second-level learning can be implemented as an EA (cf. Section 2.2.1). For online learning, the LCS assigns a reward to each mapping. From different matching situations, it applies the action with the highest reward value. After applying an action, the system receives positive or negative feedback, evaluates the applied mapping accordingly, and updates its reward. In OBESS, receiving feedback for evacuation planning or localization is not straightforward since the mobile devices have no possibility to know whether they computed the right locations or whether the determined evacuation route is optimal. However, active interventions of the user can be interpreted as a negative feedback and, hence, used to evaluate the quality of the current localization and evacuation algorithms. Additionally, feedback can be derived from situation parameters provided by the observer. If a change in the environmental situation is detected, for example a recomputation of the evacuation instruction can be triggered, which integrates this newly available information. A sample situation for changing the applied evacuation planning algorithm is when the observed state-of-charge of the device's battery falls below a certain threshold and an evacuation algorithm which requires fewer messages to be exchanged is chosen in order to save energy. One way of evaluating a localization algorithm is to perform consistency checks. Usually, two consecutively computed locations should not lie far apart from each other. If this is the case, the currently selected localization algorithm does not deliver high quality results in the current network situation and the corresponding fitness value is decreased. Moreover, the computed locations of the device's neighbors should lie within its communication range, and so forth. Feedback for an evacuation route is obtained whenever the device receives new information about the current situation in the building. The device could receive information that there are more evacuees located in rooms along the currently chosen route than expected, in which case a replanning of the evacuation instruction is triggered. Apart from the online learning described above, the O/C Architecture provides for offline learning. For this, the situation parameters from the observer can be used to configure a simulation, which reflects the actual network situation and evacuation and localization algorithms can be tested offline in this simulation before they are made available for usage during runtime. This mechanism reduces the probability of choosing unsuitable actions, i.e., inappropriate localization algorithms, for a given network environment. It is also conceivable to use the generic O/C Architecture's capability for offline learning in order to improve evacuation planning. The simulation environment can be based on any of the evacuation models presented in Section 2.3.1 and it is initialized by choosing parameter values that reflect the situation currently observed in the building. With this simulation, the consequences of following a specific evacuation instruction derived by an evacuation planning algorithm can be assessed and evaluated. Evacuation instructions which lead to a slow evacuation time in the simulation can be substituted by instructions which result in quicker evacuations. This procedure ensures that evacuation instructions are thoroughly evaluated before they are shown to the user.

3.3 Summary

In this chapter, a concept for a building evacuation support system using mobile devices is introduced. This concept is based on the principles of Organic Computing and called OBESS. OBESS consists of mobile devices carried by potential evacuees, who organize in a MANET, a stationary SSN installed in the building, and a CCU mainly used for configuration purpose. The sensors are meant to be able to observe danger indicators in the building and support the localization of the mobile devices as beacons. The mobile devices guide their users to safe exits by performing localization and subsequent evacuation planning. This chapter proceeds with presenting an exemplary application of the generic O/C Architecture to mobile evacuation devices. The O/C Architecture supports an adaptive behavior of the mobile devices to changes in their environment by a two-level learning mechanism. Such a behavior is crucial in an evacuation scenario, which is unpredictable and dynamic. At the same time, the system becomes trustworthy, robust, and controllable by human users via intrinsic and direct control mechanisms. This is an important characteristic in order to make a technical system trustworthy, which humans are supposed to depend on in life-threatening situations. Apart from that, this generic architecture provides for several further advantages, such as the possibility to select the data that is currently monitored and to easily integrate user preferences into evacuation planning. The main objective of the O/C Architecture for mobile evacuation devices is to select an appropriate localization and evacuation planning algorithm from a set of available methods or to trigger a new evacuation path planning. The selected actions are chosen in the controller depending on the currently observed situation in the building and a prediction of its likely future state. To do so, a two-level learning structure is used which consists of an online learning mechanism based on feedback from the user and the device's environment and a simulation-based offline learning approach. It is discussed what kind of feedback can be used for online learning and how this information is used to choose an appropriate localization and evacuation planning algorithm at runtime. Offline learning offers the possibility for simulative testing of localization algorithms in realistic network scenarios as well as the evaluation of a specific evacuation instruction before admitting it to productive utilization. The main advantage compared to standard simulative based approaches, is that the simulation can be parameterized according to the currently observed situation inside the building instead of being based on expected values derived from past experiences.

CHAPTER 4

SWARM EVACUATION PLANNING WITH MOBILE DEVICES

If a building has to be evacuated, the evacuees, ideally, leave the place in the shortest time possible. According to Daniels et al. [46], the time evacuees need to escape is composed of the time until the emergency is detected and the alarm is triggered and the time for evacuees to react and leave the building. Apart from the reaction time of the evacuee, all other components can be subject to optimization in an evacuation support system. Nevertheless, in the following, only the time for leaving the building is considered. This time can be influenced directly by the quality of navigation suggestions provided by mobile devices. The time which an evacuee needs to find his way out of a building depends on several factors. The knowledge about a building's layout and the right choice of directions towards an exit have the highest impact. In today's buildings, the layout is usually provided by stationary emergency evacuation maps. Apart from that, standard evacuation signs as well as markings on the evacuation map point out the shortest path from a certain location to a nearby exit. Although knowing the shortest path is helpful, the shortest path does not always correspond to the quickest path leading outside the building. The main reason for this is that congestions often arise when a huge crowd tries to leave the building on the shortest path. Other causes can be fire or gas which block passages that are part of a shortest path. As a consequence, evacuation planning should concentrate on finding the quickest rather than the shortest path leading outside a building. Currently, evacuation research tackles this problem by performing simulations and, subsequently, trying to avoid congestions by either making modifications to the building or to the recommended exit routes (cf. Section 2.3.2). This procedure, however, does not guarantee good results for situations which differ strongly from the simulations, for example, if there are far more or less evacuees inside the building compared to the scenario it has been optimized for. This is the point at which OBESS begins to develop its full potential. Due to the ability of the mobile devices to communicate over ad hoc network connections, the opportunity arises to gain insights into the current situation inside the building at the time of evacuation. Using communication, knowledge about the number of evacuees inside the building, potential congestions, or other useful information can be distributed over the ad hoc network. This allows for the devices to get a view of the evacuation situation, which extends beyond their own limited range of communication. This knowledge can, subsequently, be integrated into evacuation path planning, enabling not only the optimization of the distance but also of the time it takes to reach an exit. Of course, questions arise whether the information gathered via local communication in a MANET has enough quality to really improve evacuation planning since it is potentially incomplete, delayed, or error-prone and how evacuation planning can be performed in a decentralized way without central coordination. This chapter addresses these questions and proposes two algorithms, which are evaluated in a simulative evacuation scenario. In order to be able to realize a decentralized evacuation system like OBESS, the mobile devices have to be enabled to compute reasonable evacuation routes towards a building's exit without central control. Furthermore, it is desirable to integrate available knowledge about the current situation from localization communication into this process.

Definition 4.1 (Swarm Evacuation Planning). *Swarm Evacuation Planning (SEP) denotes the process of finding an optimal evacuation route for users of mobile devices without the help of a central computing unit by integrating information about the current evacuation situation gathered via local communication.*

SEP receives its name due to its similarity to the concept of Swarm Intelligence (cf. Section 2.2.3). In Swarm Intelligence, a global behavior, which is not achievable by an individual alone, arises as an emergent effect from the interactions between the individuals in the swarm. The same holds for SEP. Only a swarm of mobile devices is able to collect enough information about the global evacuation situation to be able to assess congestion potentials and guide evacuees on optimal routes.

For computation of the optimal route, information about the global situation is collected via local communication. The result of SEP is an evacuation route for the individual user of each device such that the overall evacuation time is minimized. Another conceivable objective is to optimize each individual's evacuation time. This could possibly lead to a higher acceptance of the evacuation device but certainly could also increase the overall evacuation time.

OBESS, so far, optimizes the overall evacuation time because this objective is more reasonable from a social perspective. Nevertheless, changing this objective to a more egoistic one could certainly be up for discussion.

A great advantage of such a decentralized evacuation system is that the information exchange works, even in case of failure of certain devices. Such a network is robust and lacks a single point of failure, which makes its deployment attractive, especially for emergency situations. To avoid that each user fully depends on his mobile device, the system can easily be complemented by installing some static digital devices inside the building, which can serve as a fallback in case a user does not have a portable device or if it is broken or run out of battery. The approaches proposed hereafter and the corresponding experimental results have been published partially by Merkel et al. [155, 158].

4.1 Macroscopic Swarm Evacuation Planning

As introduced in Section 2.3.2, macroscopic evacuation models are the common basis for evacuation planning. Macroscopic models regard groups of homogeneous evacuees, i.e., evacuees who are equal in terms of speed, size, and behavior. Such a graph model is usually assumed to be constructed manually by experts and can be provided to the devices beforehand. The environment is modeled as a graph $G = (N, E)$ with nodes, $n \in N$, representing rooms or corridors of the building, and edges, $e \in E$, representing doors or similar connections between the areas represented by nodes. Nodes are typically modeled to have a capacity and a number of initially allocated evacuees, which corresponds to the number of evacuees currently located in that room. An edge has two weights, c and l, with c referring to the number of evacuees who can travel simultaneously on this edge and l representing the length of the edge. The edge length can, for example, be measured as the average time needed for one evacuee to traverse it or as the distance between the centers of the connected rooms. Figure 2.6 shows an example of a building and its corresponding macroscopic graph model G.

The goal of traditional macroscopic evacuation planning is to determine how many evacuees (flow size) have to be sent on which path in order to optimize the given objective. This objective can be to minimize the overall travel time, maximize the flow size in a certain time period, and so forth (cf. Section 2.3.2 for a detailed description). The problem with such macroscopic evacuation planning is that it only computes how many evacuees located in a room have to use a certain path towards the exit. There are no means to decide which evacuee is sent on which path. Since the different paths have different evacuation times, the allocation of evacuees to paths is a challenge in SEP. In addition, macroscopic evacuation planning algorithms require global information about the number of evacuees and their locations in the building, which is not provided in a scenario without a global observer. Nevertheless, for a first attempt to develop an SEP algorithm it seems reasonable to take a traditional evacuation planning approach as a role model. Thus, a macroscopic evacuation planning approach serves as a basis for the following capacity constrained SEP algorithm. The algorithm is modified in order to work in a distributed and decentralized way, i.e., to be executable on each device in the network, and to deliver an optimal evacuation route for each evacuee.

4.1.1 Capacity Constrained Swarm Evacuation Planning

The evacuation scenario considered consists of m mobile devices, which have the evacuation graph model G of the building at their disposal. For simplicity, each device has perfect information about its own position in the building. In order to compute an optimal evacuation route for each individual, the mobile device uses the *Capacity Constrained Swarm Evacuation Planner (CC-SEP)*, which is shown coarsely in Algorithm 4.1. Firstly, the device collects information about the position of other evacuees in the network via local communication. This information is then used to compute a global evacuation plan with an appropriate macroscopic evacuation algorithm. As a final step, one of the evacuation instructions from the evacuation plan is selected. This instruction can be used by the device to guide its user, for example by displaying the respective directions on its screen. In the following, the realization of each step in this algorithm is described in detail.

Algorithm 4.1 Capacity Constrained Swarm Evacuation Planner

Require: Evacuation graph $G = (N, E)$
Ensure: Evacuation instruction i
1: $G = InformationCollection\,(G)$
2: Evacuation plan $I = EvacuationPlanning\,(G)$
3: Evacuation instruction $i = InstructionSelection\,(I)$
4: **return** i

Information Collection

In order to compute the global evacuation plan, initial allocations of evacuees in the evacuation graph have to be known, i.e., how many evacuees are currently located at each node. This knowledge is gathered via local communication. Since the optimization is done on the abstract graph level, the exact position of each evacuee is negligible and only the number of evacuees located at a certain node is required. To obtain the initial allocation, each evacuee's device periodically sends a message containing its identification number (ID), the information about the node n where the device is currently located at, and two lists, which are referred to as *local-count* and *global-count*. The *global-count* list maintains the number of devices located at each node in the evacuation graph, which is the required information for the evacuation planning process. In order to compile this data, an auxiliary list called *local-count* is used. It contains IDs from all known devices which are located at the same node as the device to which this list belongs. Each entry in these lists has an age-value assigned to it and all age-values are increased by 1 before a device sends a message. Due to asynchronous message forwarding in the network, it can happen that a message which contains more up-to-date information is transmitted subsequently to a message with outdated information. The age-value ensures that each device knows which message contains the most recent information. The lower an age-value is, the more recent the respective information. Each device generates an entry for its own node in the *global-count* list by counting the IDs in its *local-count* list. The exact procedure is described in the following. The *local-count* always contains the device's ID with an age-value of 0 assigned to it. When a device communicates with another nearby device at the same node, it adds the ID of its communication partner to the *local-count* list and assigns an age-value of 0 to this information as well. In addition, it compares the entries from its own *local-count* list with the ones in the *local-count* list of its communication partner. It adds all IDs which are unknown to its *local-count* list and assigns the same age-values which the entries have in the communication partner's list. If two different messages contain the same ID, the device takes the one with the more recent age-value. As a next step, the device counts all entries in its *local-count* list and adds an entry to its *global-count* list which contains the node information n, the number of entries $a\,(n)$ and an assigned age-value of 0. Further, the device compares the entries in the *global-count* list of its communication partners with its own and adds the missing entries with the age-values they have in the communication partner's list. If the device receives a message with an entry in the *global-count* list that is already stored in its own *global-count* list, it overwrites the information only in case the age-value of the received information is lower. If the age-value of an entry in the *local-count* or *global-count* list exceeds a predefined threshold t_{max}, the entry is removed from the list. This expiration date is necessary because it is impossible to determine whether an evacuee has already left a room or not. An increase in the age-value for a certain entry in the *local-count* list between two updates can have two reasons. Either, the evacuee is not in the room anymore and, therefore, there is no device which resets this age-value, or the device receiving the information is moving away from the source of information. In this case, the number of devices it takes to forward the message increases and, as a consequence, the age-value is higher when the information arrives at the device. The right choice of the expiration date is crucial. If the value is too small, it can happen that the information is not passed on to all devices before it is recognized as obsolete. If an expiration date is set too high, information about other evacuees' whereabouts are assumed to be up-to-date, although the devices may have already been moved somewhere else. In order to determine an appropriate value for the expiration date, the characteristics of the building's layout should be taken into account. Using knowledge about the building's layout and the communication range r of the devices, the expiration date for information on the *local-count* list is set as

$$max_{n \in N} \frac{SpEx\,(n)}{r}$$

where $n \in N$ represents each room in the building, i.e. node in the macroscopic graph, and $SpEx\,(n)$ refers to the spatial expansion of that room. In case of rectangular rooms this can, for example, be the diagonal of the room. For values in the *global-count* list, the expiration date is computed based on the spatial expansion of the whole building. In case of a building with multiple floors, the expansion of one floor would be the best reference value to compute the expiration date.

By using the algorithm described above, the devices are able to collect information about the number of evacuees in different rooms (nodes) and, with time, build a local view of the evacuation situation. This view can then be used in a macroscopic evacuation planning approach, in the same manner as if the device had global information. As soon as the initial allocation of evacuees is known, the evacuation planning can be initiated. There are two conceivable implementations for the evacuation planning. It is either performed only once by using all the information collected up to this point, for example right after the alarm is triggered, or the evacuation planning is constantly repeated, hence, adapting to new information which becomes available during the evacuation process. Both versions are tested in simulative experiments.

Evacuation Planning

In order to compute the global evacuation plan, any macroscopic evacuation planning algorithm can be used. As detailed in Section

2.3.2, most of these algorithms require a time-expansion of the evacuation graph, making evacuation planning a time and space consuming task. Lu et al. [143] introduce a heuristic algorithm called *Capacity Constrained Routing Planner (CCRP)*, which does not rely on a time-expansion of the evacuation graph and provides solutions of similar quality (cf. Sangho et al. [204]). However, the algorithm can also be replaced by other macroscopic planning methods, for example, the multi-objective optimization approach proposed by Cheng [39], Zong et al. [258], or evacuation planning based on EA as described in Garrett et al. [72] and Saadatseresht et al. [202].

CCRP returns an evacuation plan I which consists of a set of evacuation instructions i. Each instruction contains a path p in the evacuation graph, i.e., a sequence of nodes, a flow size f, i.e., the number of evacuees who are sent on this path, and a sequence of starting times t. The starting times denote at which time the corresponding node on path p is entered by evacuees who follow this evacuation instruction. The basic idea of CCRP is to model the used capacities of each node and each edge as a time series. This time series can then be used to derive waiting times at certain nodes and edges in order to find an optimal path with respect to traveling time, while taking into account all previously scheduled evacuees and the capacity constraints of the graph. The algorithm used for optimization is taken from network routing theory and assumes a homogeneous speed of the evacuees involved. CCRP is an iterative method, which computes evacuation paths for all evacuees located at one node before processing the next node. The priority with which the nodes are processed decreases with their increasing distance to an exit. In other words, firstly, all evacuees located on the node which is closest to an exit are scheduled for evacuation, after which the next node is processed and so forth. For each node, path p is determined as the path closest to an exit with minimum travel time. The travel time includes the time needed to cover the distance as well as the waiting times for released capacities which are occupied by previously scheduled evacuees. After the quickest path is found, the number of evacuees f which can be sent simultaneously on this path is computed. In the next step, the time series for all nodes on this path are updated and respective capacities are reserved for the evacuees at times t when they pass the respective node or edge. The reserved capacities are then taken into account in the next iteration when waiting times are computed. The set of p, f, and t form one evacuation instruction i and are added to the global evacuation plan I. The evacuation planning terminates when all evacuees are scheduled. Algorithm 4.2 describes the operating principle of CCRP (a fully detailed description can be found in Lu et al. [143]). As explained before, nodes $n \in N$ have an initial allocation $a(n)$ and a maximum capacity $c(n)$. The capacity of an edge $e = (n_i, n_j)$ is denoted by $c(e)$. Each edge in an evacuation graph represents the connection between the center of two rooms. An edge, therefore, has a length $l(e)$ which is comprised of the two parts $ls(e)$ and $le(e)$, with $ls(e)$ representing the travel distance inside the starting room and $le(e)$ the travel distance which corresponds to the target node of the edge. It holds that $ls(e) + le(e) = l(e)$. This is important for computing the reserved capacities in each room at the time evacuees are assumed to enter them. The evacuation graph G contains a set of exit nodes $D \subset N$, which represent the exits of the building. In order to find evacuation instructions with CCRP, an additional super source node $suSo$ and an additional super sink node $suSi$ are added to the evacuation graph, both with infinite capacities. The super source node $suSo$ is connected via edges with infinite capacities and zero lengths to all nodes in the graph, except

97

Table 4.1: Evacuation instructions obtained by applying CCRP to the example graph in Figure 2.6.

Instruction		
Index	Flow Size	Path and Timing
1	$f = 2$	$p = \; < n_3, n_4 >$ $t = \; < 0, 1 >$
2	$f = 1$	$p = \; < n_3, n_4 >$ $t = \; < 1, 2 >$
3	$f = 1$	$p = \; < n_1, n_3, n_4 >$ $t = \; < 0, 1, 2 >$
4	$f = 3$	$p = \; < n_2, n_4 >$ $t = \; < 0, 2 >$
5	$f = 2$	$p = \; < n_1, n_3, n_4 >$ $t = \; < 1, 2, 3 >$
6	$f = 1$	$p = \; < n_2, n_4 >$ $t = \; < 1, 3 >$

for the super sink node. Similarly, all exit nodes are connected to the super sink node via edges with infinite capacities and zero lengths. This is an auxiliary construction, which ensures that there is only one source and only one sink node in the graph and, hence, simplifies the wayfinding procedure. Table 4.1 shows an example of a list of evacuation instructions produced by the CCRP given the example graph shown in Figure 2.6 as input. It should be noted that the evacuation instructions returned by CCRP are sorted in ascending order with respect to their evacuation time and that it is possible to have more than one evacuation instruction for a specific starting node n.

Algorithm 4.2 Capacity Constrained Routing Planner [143]

Require: Evacuation graph $G = (N, E)$
Ensure: Evacuation plan I (set of evacuation instructions i)
    // Initialize capacity time series for all nodes and edges:
1: $\forall n \in N$: $freeCap(n, *) \leftarrow c(n)$,
    $freeCap(n, 0) \leftarrow c(n) - a(n)$
2: $\forall e \in E$: $freeCap(e, *) \leftarrow c(e)$
3: **while** $\exists n : freeCap(n, 0) < c(n)$ **do**
4:     $prev(n) \leftarrow null, minT(n) \leftarrow \infty$
5:     $\forall n \in N, minT(suSo) \leftarrow 0, Q \leftarrow \{suSo\}$
    // Find next best path:
6:     **while** $Q \neq \emptyset$ **do**
7:         Node $u \leftarrow min_{n \in Q}(minT(n))$
8:         **for** Node $v \in neighbors(u)$ **do**
9:             **if** $(u \neq suSo) \vee (freeCap(v, 0) < c(v))$ **then**
10:                 $arrT \leftarrow minT(u), waitT \leftarrow 0$
11:                 Edge $e \leftarrow (u, v)$
12:                 $nCap \leftarrow freeCap(v, arrT + waitT + ls(e))$
13:                 $eCap \leftarrow freeCap(e, arrT)$
14:                 **while** $eCap = 0 \vee nCap = 0$ **do**
15:                     $waitT \leftarrow waitT + 1$
16:                     $eCap \leftarrow freeCap(e, arrT + waitT)$
17:                     $nCap \leftarrow freeCap(v, arrT + waitT + ls(e))$
18:                 **end while**
19:                 **if** $(arrT + waitT + l(e)) < minT(v)$ **then**
20:                     $minT(v) \leftarrow arrT + waitT + l(e)$
21:                     $prev(v) \leftarrow u$
22:                 **end if**
23:             **end if**
24:         **end for**
25:     **end while**

	// Create path p time schedule t and flow size f:
26:	Node $n \leftarrow prev\,(suSi)$
27:	**while** $n \neq suSo$ **do**
28:	$p.add\,(n),\ t.add\,(minT\,(n) - l\,(e))$
29:	Edge $e \leftarrow (prev\,(n)\,,n)$
30:	$f \leftarrow min\,(f, freeCap\,(e, minT\,(n) - l\,(e)))$
31:	$n \leftarrow prev\,(n)$
32:	**end while**
33:	$reverse\,(p),\ reverse\,(t)$
34:	Source node $s \leftarrow p.getFirstNode\,()$
35:	$f \leftarrow min\,(f, c\,(s) - freeCap\,(s, 0))$
	// Allocate capacities on path:
36:	$freeCap\,(s, 0) \leftarrow freeCap\,(s, 0) + f$
37:	Node $n \leftarrow prev\,(suSi)$
38:	**while** $prev\,(n) \neq suSo$ **do**
39:	Edge $e \leftarrow (prev\,(n)\,,n)$
40:	$schedT \leftarrow minT\,(n) - l\,(e)$
41:	$waitT \leftarrow minT\,(n) - minT\,(prev\,(n)) - l\,(e)$
42:	$freeCap\,(e, schedT) \leftarrow freeCap\,(e, schedT) - f$
43:	$startT = minT\,(n)$
44:	$endT = minT\,(prev\,(n)) + waitT + ls\,(e)$
45:	**for** $startT \geq time > endT$ **do**
46:	$freeCap\,(n, time) \leftarrow freeCap\,(n, time) - f$
47:	**end for**
48:	$m = prev(n)$
49:	$startT = minT\,(m) + waitT + ls\,(e),\ endT = minT\,(m)$
50:	**for** $startT \geq time > endT$ **do**
51:	$freeCap(m, time) \leftarrow freeCap(m, time) - f$
52:	**end for**
53:	$n \leftarrow prev(n)$
54:	**end while**

55:     Evacuation instruction $i \leftarrow (p, t, f)$
56:     Add instruction i to plan I
57: **end while**
58: **return** Evacuation plan I

Instruction Selection

The third step in CC-SEP is to select an appropriate evacuation instruction for the device's user from the global evacuation plan I. Valid candidates are all instructions with a path p that starts at the node where the device is located. The objective of the instruction selection is for the number of devices which select a specific instruction to approximately correspond to the instruction's associated flow size f. This is necessary in order get a close match between the real waiting times which occur during evacuation and the waiting times used for evacuation planning. To meet this challenge, each evacuee's device sorts the IDs in its *local-count* list in an ascending order and maps the instructions returned by CCRP successively to the IDs in the list. Thereby, the flow-size of each instruction determines how many successive IDs are mapped to that specific instruction before advancing to the next one in the evacuation plan. The mapping process can be stopped as soon as the device's own ID is mapped to an evacuation instruction which the device then uses to guide its user. In CC-SEP each device has its own local view of the evacuation situation, as a result, the computed evacuation plan I can also differ from one device to another. Nevertheless, it is safe to assume that devices which are located in the same room have a very similar information base and, thus, their evacuation plans are similar as well. Although sorting according to device identification numbers seems to be a very naive approach to assign evacuation instructions, there is a high chance for the selection process to result in a distribution of evacuation instructions amongst the devices which is proportional to the flow-sizes of the respective instructions without explicit coordination between the devices. Nonetheless, this selection process is a naive procedure, which is prone to manipulation. Because the instructions in the evacuation plan are in increasing order of evacuation time, there is a high incentive for the mobile device user to manipulate the device's ID in order to receive a faster evacuation path. For a first assessment on how distributed and decentralized evacuation planning in a MANET can be performed, however, this approach is sufficient.

4.1.2 Evaluation

For the experimental evaluations presented in this thesis, a Java-based simulation called *Swarm Simulation* is developed, which incorporates both, an evacuation simulation and a mobile ad hoc network simulation. The evacuation simulation is based on a simple time-discrete evacuation model similar to the two-dimensional cellular automaton described in Burstedde et al. [32]. For the mobile ad hoc network communication, the communication neighborhood of a device corresponds to its physical neighborhood on the plane within a fixed Euclidean distance r. This model corresponds to the so-called *unit disc* model which is described by Clark et al. [43]. Agents in the simulation are equivalent to evacuees and the mobile devices they carry around. The simulation runs in cycles and in each cycle, all agents are executed once sequentially in a specified order, which is also called scheduling. For the evaluations in this thesis, a random scheduling is selected. One execution denotes the process of first updating the list of neighbor's a device currently has, i.e. can communicate with. As a next step, the behavior of the agent is executed; this can, for example, be the computation of an evacuation instruction or the current location of the device. For such computations, the device can access any information from its neighbors as it is available at that point of time. After the behavior is finished, the configured movement of the agent is executed. Table 4.2 shows the main configuration parameters of the simulation. In addition to these parameters, there are several more configuration options depending on the selected behavior or movement. The simulation is built in a modular way, such that it can be easily extended to define new behaviors, movements, environments, agents, or scheduling-schemes.

For evacuation, a layout of the building is read from an XML-file, which is required to follow a specified standard. The building's layout has to be in form of a grid with variable dimensions and each patch in this grid can be marked to be accessible to the evacuees or to be part of a wall or barrier. Additionally, each patch of the discretized layout is assigned to a node in the macroscopic evacuation graph, which is also specified in the XML input file. Edges between nodes in the macroscopic evacuation graph are required to be specified manually in the input file. The capacity of a node $c(n)$ is computed as the number of patches in a room. The length of an edge $l(e)$ is calculated as the Manhattan distance between the two patches at the center of each room. The edge capacity $c(e)$ corresponds to the width of the connecting door, measured in the number of patches. If there is no passage, i.e. sequence of accessible patches, between two nodes which are connected via an edge in the graph, the simulation responds with an error. The same holds for an initial distribution of agents in rooms where there is not enough space.

Table 4.2: Main configuration parameters for the Swarm Simulation.

Parameter	Description
Behavior	Software program run on the mobile devices.
PopSize	Number of agents in the simulation.
SignalRange	Communication range as percentage of the side-length of the square environment.
SimCycles	Number of simulation cycles run before the simulation is terminated.
Torus	Whether the environment is a torus world.
NumInit	Number of beacons in the environment.
Positioning	Initial distribution of agents in the environment.
Seed	Random seed used in this simulation run.
Scheduling	Order in which the agents are executed.
Environment	Design of the simultion environment.
Colliding	Whether agents are colliding with each other.
Movement	The type of mobility model executed.

Experiment Settings

In order to evaluate the results achieved with CC-SEP, a simple evacuation scenario is simulated and the impact of several parameters, such as the number of evacuees or their distribution inside the building are investigated. The objective of this experiment is to examine the effectiveness of the proposed CC-SEP approach and to investigate whether evacuation planning can be improved by integrating information about other evacuees in the building, even though this information is potentially faulty, delayed, and incomplete. For this, the overall evacuation time is compared with the time needed in an uncoordinated panic-like situation and a situation in which all evacuees escape using the shortest path leading outside the building. Although one of the main motivations for OBESS is the construction of increasingly complex buildings, the investigated scenarios in this study are comparatively simple. It should be noted, though, that any building layout can be divided into small two-dimensional sections, which, for example, represent one floor. Therefore, the insights gained in this study can be directly transferred to more complex scenarios. Due to the general absence of central control, all algorithms presented in this thesis, including the CC-SEP, scale well to complex scenarios.

For the experimental study, an evacuation scenario is simulated in a simple building, which is shown in Figure 4.3. The environment is a square field, which is divided into 25 times 25 patches. One agent can occupy exactly one patch. Patches which are occupied by an agent or which are a-priori marked to be part of a wall or barrier are not accessible for the agents during the evacuation simulation. The simulation terminates when all agents have reached the exit. The devices start computing their evacuation instructions after a warm up time of 30 cycles, in which they are allowed to gather information through communication. When an evacuation instruction is available, the agent consequently follows this instruction by walking on the shortest path between its current patch and the closest patch belonging to the next room of the instruction. The shortest path in Manhattan distance metric between these patches is computed with the A^* *Algorithm* presented in Hart et al. [83]. Agents are only allowed to move to an accessible adjacent patch in their von-Neumann neighborhood (cf. Figure 4.1(a)), i.e. all adjacent patches without diagonal patches. This restriction ensures a constant traveling speed of the agent because the Euclidean distance traveled in each movement is constant. However, if there is no free patch in the von-Neumann neighborhood but in the Moore-neighborhood (cf. Figure 4.1(b)), i.e. all adjacent patches including the diagonal patches, and this patch is closer in Euclidean distance to the target patch than the patch where the agent is currently located, the individual moves in two time steps to this closer patch in the Moore neighborhood. This has the effect that agents cluster in front of doors in an arc-like shape instead of lining-up in front of it.

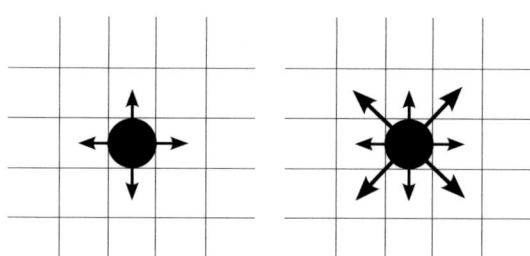

(a) Von-Neumann neighborhood   (b) Moore neighborhood

Figure 4.1: Different neighborhood models for movements in the evacuation simulation.

Two scenarios with different initial distribution of evacuees across two rooms are considered. In Scenario A agents are initially located at nodes 1 and 3 in the sample building shown in Figure 4.3. In Scenario B, evacuees are initially located in rooms 1 and 2. Simulations are run with 50 and 100 evacuees. In order to test the impact of evacuees' distributions in the building, different experiments are performed in which the percentage of agents located in room 1 is decreased from 100% to 0% and the remaining evacuees start in the second room of the considered scneario, respectively. Node 6 indicates the exit of the building and the communication range is set to 5%, 10%, and 15%. It is defined as a fraction of the side length of the square plane. With a communication range of 5% the agent's own patch and its von-Neumann-neighborhood is covered. Setting r to 10% and 15% increases the communication range by one patch each. Figure 4.2 illustrates the examined communication ranges. The communication range r is assumed to be equal for all devices. The influence of walls on the communication range is neglected in the simulation. Panic behavior is simulated by letting agents randomly select their next room, omitting doors which they have already passed through unless there is no other option. All experiments are repeated 40 times with different initial random agent placement according to the constraints and the results are averaged.

Scenario A

The first scenario serves as a basis for investigating the effectiveness of CC-SEP. The main focus lies on whether local communication can deliver enough information in order to improve the overall evacuation time when compared to a shortest path approach or panic behavior. In addition, the effects of different communication ranges, the total number of evacuees, and their distribution across

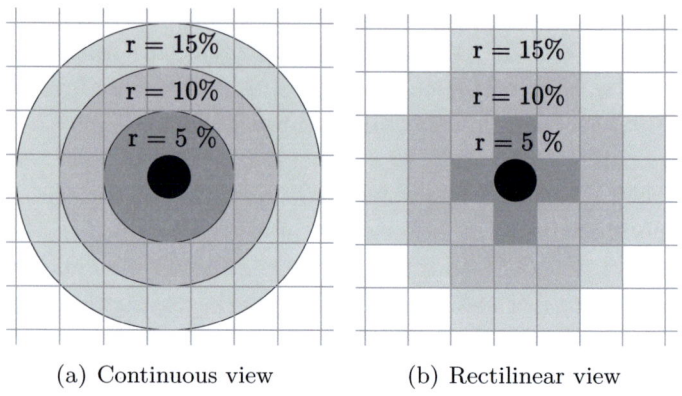

(a) Continuous view (b) Rectilinear view

Figure 4.2: Different communication ranges for the experiments.

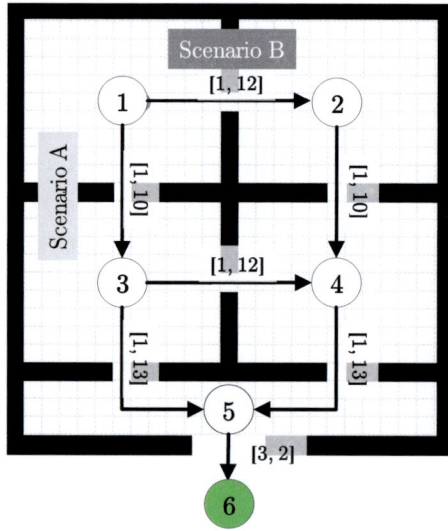

Figure 4.3: Building plan and corresponding macroscopic representation used in the experimental study.

the building are examined. In Scenario A, agents are distributed equally across the two rooms which belong to node 1 and 3 of the macroscopic graph. This way, each agent has two possibilities to reach the building's exit, with the shortest path being: node 1, node 3, node 5, and node 6. The alternative route is node 1, node 2, node 4, node 5, and node 6, or node 3, node 4, node 5, and node 6 respectively. In this experiment setting, CC-SEP is expected to deliver good results because the agents can switch to a slightly longer but less crowded evacuation route.

Figure 4.4(a) shows the average total time for evacuation in Scenario A using 50 agents and varying the occupation of the two rooms. For a communication range of 5%, the overall evacuation time is only slightly improved by CC-SEP compared to the shortest path behavior. This can be explained by the restrictive communication abilities and, as a consequence, the lack of information which can be used for CC-SEP. Due to the lack of information, most evacuees assume room 1 and 3 to be empty and, thus, choose the shortest path towards the exit. By increasing the communication range, however, the total time for evacuation decreases and CC-SEP starts to deliver significantly better results because evacuees now switch to the longer but less crowded paths. By setting the communication range to 15% the total time for evacuation can be reduced by up to 30% if all agents are located in either room 1 or 2, which are the scenarios with highest congestion potential. However, the reduction in evacuation time when increasing the communication range from 10% to 15% is not significant anymore, which implies that a communication range of 10% is already sufficient to gather most information about the evacuation situation. In this scenario, the panic behavior exhibits the worst evacuation time.

Figure 4.4(b) displays the results for 100 agents. From this experiment, it can be observed that the shortest path behavior produces

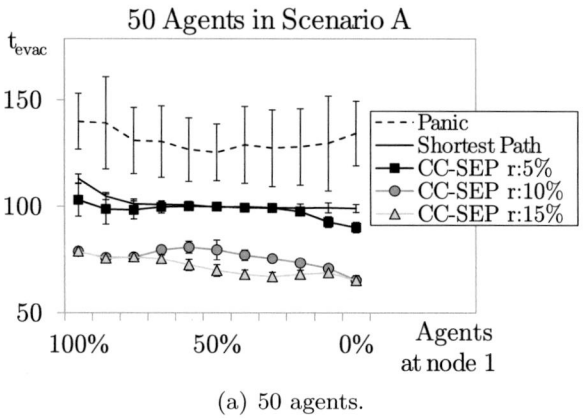

(a) 50 agents.

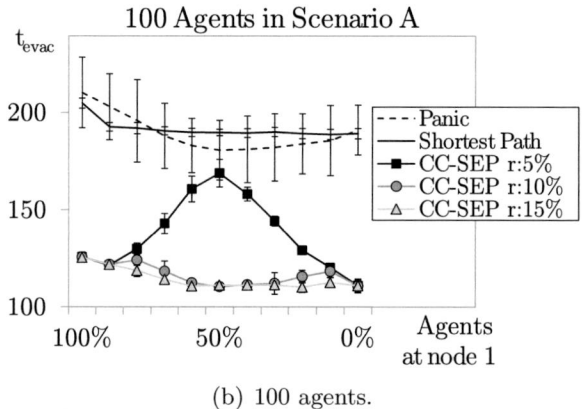

(b) 100 agents.

Figure 4.4: Comparison of the total time for evacuation with only 50 (a) and 100 agents (b) in Scenario A applying CC-SEP, shortest path, and panic behavior.

similar overall evacuation times when compared to the panic-like behavior. In the case of agents being quite equally distributed across both rooms at the beginning of the evacuation, a panic-like behavior can yield even lower total evacuation times. The reason for this effect is that with 100 agents in the building, the congestion on the shortest path has become so large that randomly searching for an exit results in a faster evacuation process when compared to enduring the waiting time in the congestion. With CC-SEP and a communication range of 15% the evacuation process is up to 40% faster than in the shortest path and the panic-like behavior, which is a higher improvement when compared to the same scenario with 50 agents inside the building. Here, the difference between shortest and quickest path, which is emphasized at the beginning of this section, becomes clearly apparent. So far, it can be concluded that providing information about the shortest path to the exit is better for most investigated situations when compared to evacuees blindly searching for their way out. Nevertheless, leading all evacuees on the shortest path can lead to congestions, which can result in an evacuation performance which is even worse than the one in a panic situation. It is shown that CC-SEP, on the other hand, is able to collect and use information about other evacuees' locations in the building and, thus, reduce the overall evacuation time, even though this information has to be collected over uncertain links of an ad hoc network. Similar to the scenario with 50 agents, the difference between evacuation times produced by CC-SEP with 10% communication range and a 15% range is not significant, however, the results for a 5% communication range are noticeably different. With 5% and a high concentration of agents in one of the two initial rooms, the performance of CC-SEP is similar to the results with 10% and 15%, but the more equally the agents are distributed, the worse the results get. When agents are distributed across both rooms, 50 agents are located in each room. Hence, the scenario is similar to the first experiment where all agents are concentrated in room number 1, except for the fact that now additional 50 agents are located in room 3. Due to the small communication range, the devices, again, assume that the shortest path is occupied by only a few other evacuees and choose this path for evacuation. The overall evacuation time is now even higher than for the scenario with 50 agents because of the additional 50 evacuees in room 3, who are the reason for the increase in the time it takes for evacuees in room 1 to reach the exit on the shortest path.

Scenario B

In Scenario B, the path options for some evacuees are reduced. When following the shortest path, agents in room 1 leave the building over node 1, node 3, node 5, and node 6, while agents on node 2 pass by node 4, node 5, and node 6. Agents from the room corresponding to node 2 have only one path leading to the exit, while agents in room 1 can still select between two choices. As a consequence, it depends on the amount of agents in room 2 whether or not it is advisable for agents of room 1 to switch to the route with a longer distance to the exit. With this scenario, it is examined whether CC-SEP is capable of recognizing the right choice for agents in room 1.

In Figure 4.5(a), the results for 50 agents are displayed, which basically confirm the observations from Scenario A. The shortest path behavior causes a slightly higher evacuation time compared to CC-SEP with a communication range of 5%. When using a wider communication range of 10% or 15%, the evacuation time is further reduced by up to 30%. When more than half of all evacuees are initially located in room 2, CC-SEP does not yield any additional performance improvement when compared to the shortest path.

The reason for this is that due to the accumulation of agents in room 2, the escape route node 2, node 4, node 5, and node 6 does not present an attractive path choice for agents in room 1. The shortest path route node 3, node 5, and node 6 is more attractive for agents in room 1. Since the design of the evacuation graph does not provide any other choice of route for evacuees in room 2 than the path over node 4, node 5, and node 6, CC-SEP does not bring any additional benefit compared to the shortest path behavior in case of such a distribution. This example shows how important the choice of the macroscopic building model is for the evacuation performance with CC-SEP.

In Figure 4.5(b), the experimental results with 100 evacuees are depicted. When 100 evacuees are distributed equally across the two starting rooms, CC-SEP becomes slightly worse than the shortest path behavior for a 5% communication range. To understand the reason for this effect, it has to be noted that any deviation from the shortest path increases the evacuation time in a scenario with precisely as many evacuees in room 1 and room 2. This is because any evacuee which deviates from the respective shortest path would block evacuees on the alternative path due to the symmetrical layout of the graph. With a 5% communication range, the chance for evacuees in room 1 to receive no information about evacuees in room 2 is higher when compared to a situation with a 10% or 15% communication range. Hence, evacuees are more likely to choose route node 2, node 4, node 5, and node 6 than with a larger communication range. In contrast to Scenario A, where the panic behavior received better results compared to the shortest path behavior, this is not the case in Scenario B. The reason for this is that in Scenario A, the shortest path always contains node 3 where the agents meet, while in Scenario B this happens the

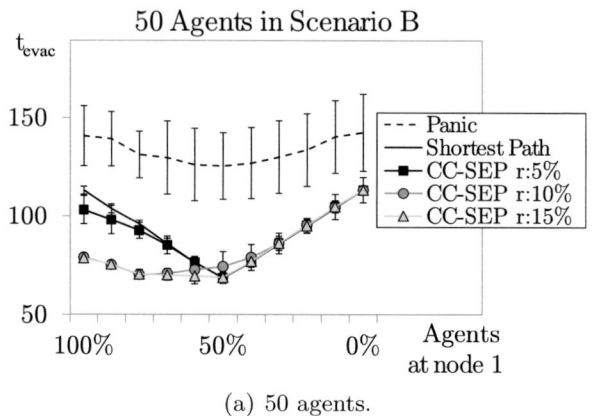

(a) 50 agents.

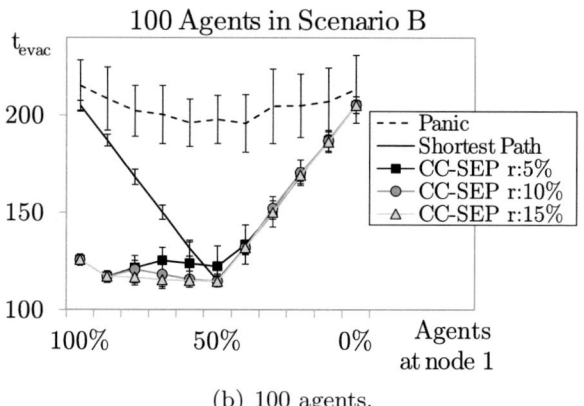

(b) 100 agents.

Figure 4.5: Comparison of the total time for evacuation with 50 (a) and 100 agents (b) in Scenario B applying CC-SEP, shortest path, and panic behavior.

earliest in the room associated to node 5, where the capacity is higher.

Initialization Time and Repetition

So far, CC-SEP is computed after an initialization time of 30 cycles, in which the agents are allowed to collect information. Although this is a sound presupposition, there could be scenarios in which such a time is not given, thus, it is interesting to investigate the influence of initialization time on the algorithm's performance. All following experiments are carried out with 100 agents and a communication range of 15%. The results for panic-like behavior are omitted since it has been shown that, on average, they are significantly worse than evacuation times achieved with CC-SEP or the shortest path following behavior. Figures 4.6(a) and 4.6(b) display the results with and without initialization time. If CC-SEP starts immediately, it means that information can only be gained from devices which are one hop away before the computation of evacuation instructions begins. The results confirm the intuitive expectation that providing for a time period to initialize and, thus, collect information, improves the overall evacuation time. Of course, this is not the case if there is no possibility to choose between paths, such as in Scenario B when most agents start at node 2. In addition, when agents are concentrated in one room, initialization time does not improve the evacuation time significantly because most information can be exchanged in few rounds.

When aiming at building an adaptive evacuation system, one has to allow for the computation of new evacuation instructions in order to include recent information. Such adaptive route planning is achievable when CC-SEP is computed repeatedly. Figures 4.7(a) and 4.7(b) show the results for experiments where CC-SEP starts

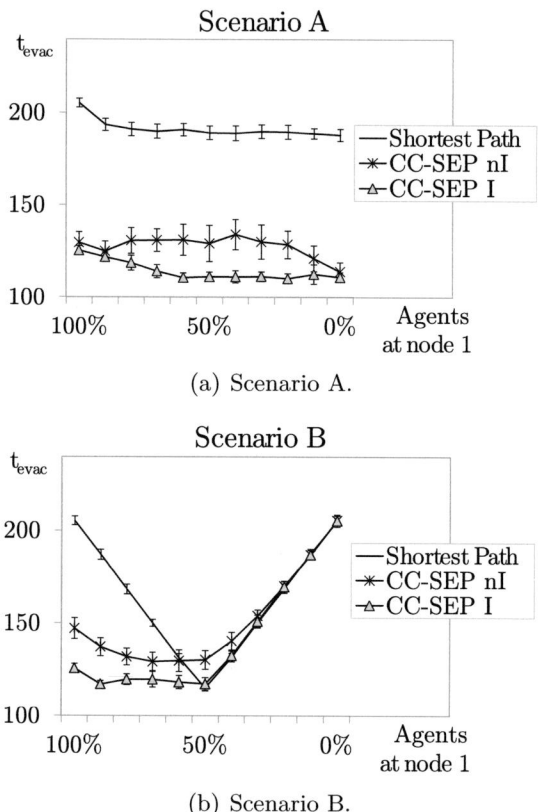

(a) Scenario A.

(b) Scenario B.

Figure 4.6: Results for evacuation time with (I) and without (nI) initialization time of 30 cycles.

without initialization time and is repeated in every simulation cycle, while taking the most current information into account.

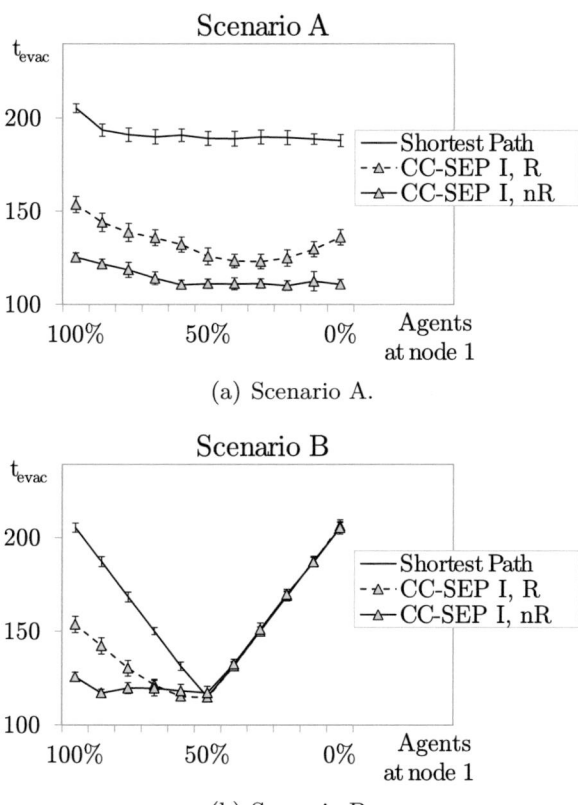

(a) Scenario A.

(b) Scenario B.

Figure 4.7: Results for evacuation time with (R) and without (nR) repetition of computing evacuation instructions when allowing for an initialization time (I).

Figures 4.8(a) and 4.8(b) illustrate the experimental results when CC-SEP is repeatedly executed after an initialization time of 30 cycles. It can be observed that, when there is little time to collect information before the instruction is computed, repetitions can help to reduce the evacuation time in certain cases. However, when many agents are located at node 1, repeating CC-SEP prolongs the evacuation process, especially, when time for information collection is given to the agents before the evacuation starts. There are two reasons why repeated execution of CC-SEP can worsen the results. Firstly, agents often change between evacuation instructions and lose time in doing so. The second reason lies within the design of the information exchange procedure. In CC-SEP, only the number of evacuees in each room of the building is exchanged over the network and not the IDs of the respective evacuees. Hence, information about other rooms in the building is only available in an aggregated and anonymized manner. Because of this design decision, it can occur that evacuees which change rooms are counted multiple times in different rooms before the age-value of the obsolete information expires and the number of known evacuees in the respective previous rooms is reduced. Although this is an undesired effect, repetition of evacuation planning is necessary for an evacuation management system to be adaptive. Consequently, it is a positive observation that the evacuation time is still well below the evacuation time needed when all agents take the shortest path.

Approaches for Reducing Frequent Decision Switching

While the problem of obsolete information is hard to deal with, a high frequency of target changes caused by repeated execution of CC-SEP can be counteracted. To do so, two variations of CC-SEP are being tested subsequently. Agents are, now, only allowed to recompute instructions after a certain patience period after a target

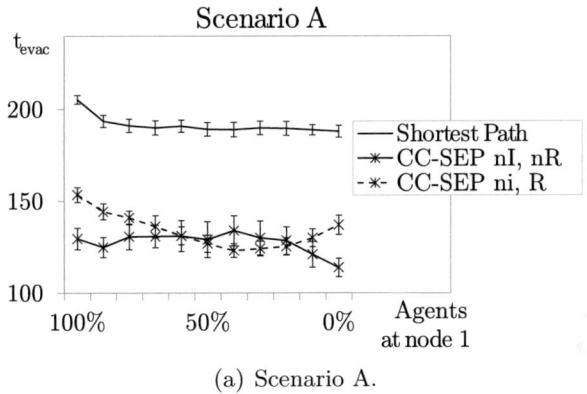

(a) Scenario A.

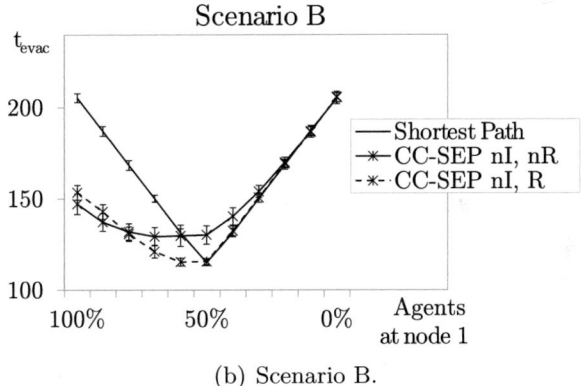

(b) Scenario B.

Figure 4.8: Results for evacuation time with (R) and without (nR) repetition of computing the evacuation instructions without allowing for initialization time (nI).

change or if they are more than a maximum distance away from their current target. The patience period prevents agents from changing targets too frequently and the maximum distance avoids target changes shortly before the current target is reached. The results for a set-up in which 100 agents start in the room belonging to node 1 are depicted in Figure 4.9(a) and 4.9(b). As previously defined, distances are denoted as a fraction of the side length of the square test environment. The patience period does not have a significant impact on the overall evacuation time, which indicates that frequently switching targets is not the main problem when executing CC-SEP repeatedly. Nevertheless, it might be helpful to introduce a certain patience period before rule changing is allowed not only to reduce total evacuation time, but also to avoid creating mistrust and frustration with the system amongst the users due to a high frequency of decision changes. It is shown that prohibiting changes in evacuation instructions for agents which are close to their next target leads to an improvement of evacuation time if the maximum distance is sufficiently large. However, if the maximum distance is chosen too large, this can lead to a situation where agents do not change instructions anymore. As a consequence, the adaptability of the system is lost. It can be concluded from these results that the slight performance decrease when computing CC-SEP repeatedly is likely to be caused by the design of the information exchange as aggregated, anonymized numbers.

To conclude the experimental study, the robustness of CC-SEP is tested. For this, 100 agents are located in room 1 and the amount of rule following agents is reduced gradually. Evacuees who do not follow the instructions provided by CC-SEP are assumed to be taking the shortest path to the exit instead. In addition to this robustness test, the evacuation behavior with CC-SEP is investigated in a more complex environment. Figure 4.10 depicts

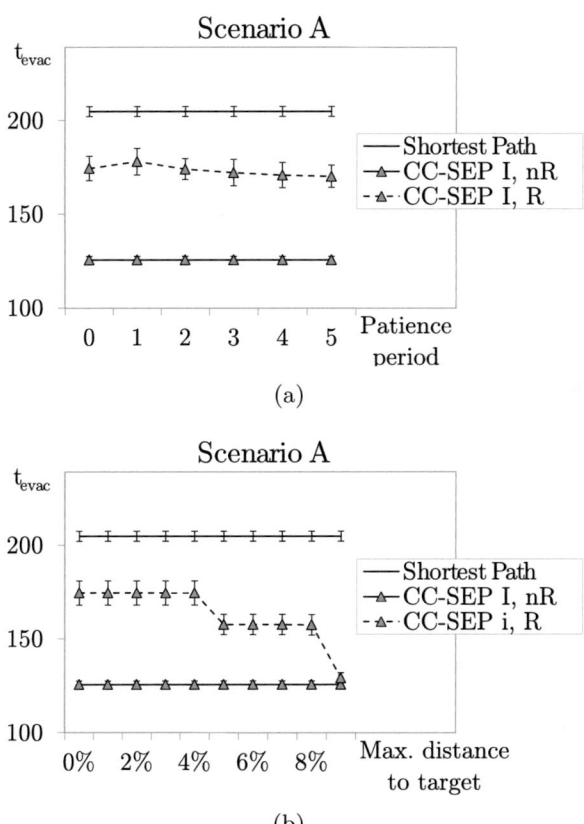

(a)

(b)

Figure 4.9: Total evacuation time when repeating CC-SEP after a certain patience period after changing targets (a) and when limiting repetitions to agents which are a maximum distance away from their target (b).

the more complex and realistic Scenario C, in which 100 evacuees are distributed according to a uniform random distribution across all rooms of the building. Node 16 represents the exit of the building.

Robustness

Figure 4.11(a) shows the results of the robustness test in the simple scenario. Without repeating the computation of evacuation instructions, evacuation time increases linearly with a decreasing number of rule-following agents until it is reduced to the performance of the shortest path behavior. For repeated computations, the evacuation time even decreases slightly with a higher percentage of non-followers and there is a tolerance for up to only 40% of rule-following agents before the overall evacuation time is worse than the scenario in which all agents follow the instructions provided by CC-SEP. Unfortunately, a similar behavior cannot be observed in Scenario C, which indicates that this result is most likely due to the concentration of agents in one room or due to the construction of the macroscopic evacuation graph. However, the important result is that in both scenarios evacuation time does not increase over proportionally when the number of rule-followers is reduced by less than 30%. This shows that CC-SEP is quite robust even when some evacuees deviate from the evacuation instructions. Furthermore, these results suggest that the deterioration of performance due to a repeated execution of CC-SEP is limited to few specific cases. With a uniformly random initial evacuee distribution and the more realistic Scenario C, the deterioration of performance when CC-SEP is executed repeatedly is negligible compared to the previous test set-up.

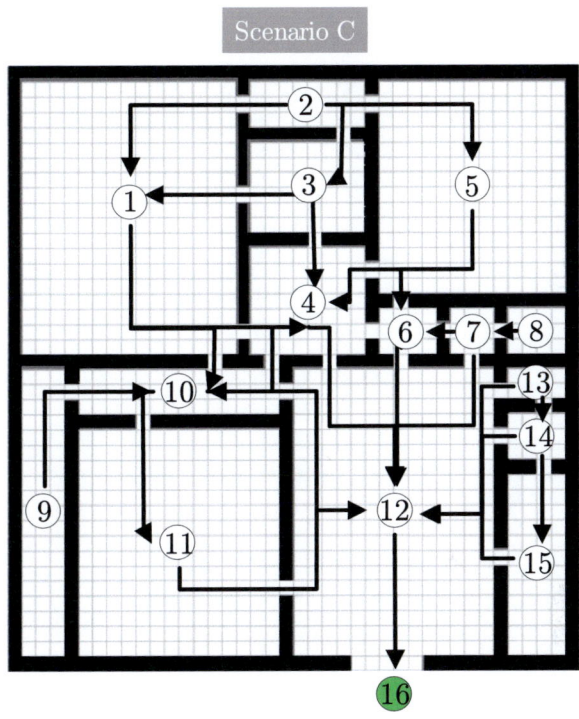

Figure 4.10: Building plan of Scenario C and the corresponding macroscopic graph representation.

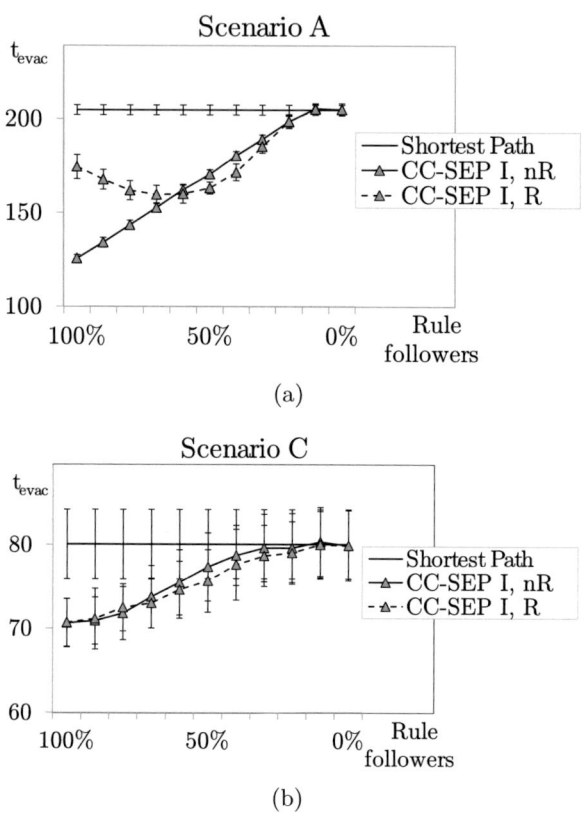

(a)

(b)

Figure 4.11: Robustness test of CC-SEP with 100 agents placed in room 1 of Scenario A (a) and with 100 agents placed randomly inside the building of Scenario C (b).

4.1.3 Conclusion

In this section, an SEP algorithm based on capacity constrained routing is presented, which can be used to estimate the quickest evacuation path based on uncertain information. Information about the distribution of evacuees in the building is gained via local communication by using ad hoc network connections between mobile devices. A modification of the CCRP algorithm published by Lu et al. [142, 143] is introduced, which estimates waiting times on each path using a time series model in order to evaluate the different path options for each evacuee. The main challenge for any SEP algorithm is the lack of certain global knowledge. Hence, experiments are performed in order to determine whether CC-SEP is able to improve the total evacuation time when compared to simply offering the shortest path as a navigation instruction to each evacuee. In experiments, varying communication ranges (5%, 10% and 15%), different numbers of evacuees in the building (50, 100), as well as variations in their initial distribution over the rooms of the building are investigated. Additionally, two different building layouts are considered. The first layout is specifically designed to cause congestions and the second layout is a more realistic and complex building layout with a large number of different rooms and valid paths towards the exit. The performance of CC-SEP is compared to a shortest path following behavior of evacuees and a panic model, in which evacuees are assumed to have no knowledge about the building's layout. Furthermore, different variations of CC-SEP are subject to examination, such as the introduction of an initialization time where mobile devices are allowed to collect information, an iterative repetition of evacuation planning, as well as a patience period and a maximum target distance which have to be fulfilled in order to allow for changes in evacuation instructions.

Finally, the robustness of CC-SEP against rule deviating evacuees is considered. The results confirm that knowledge collected via ad hoc network connections significantly improves evacuation time in almost all scenarios considered by up to 40% when compared to the shortest path behavior, even though the local view on the real evacuation situation is mostly incomplete and sometimes even incorrect. When comparing the results with the panic-like behavior of evacuees, the improvement is even higher. Increasing the communication range from 5% to 10% provides significantly more information for CC-SEP and, hence, improves the evacuation time, while an increase from 10% to 15%, yields only slightly better results. The positive effect of CC-SEP on the evacuation time is stronger when there are more evacuees in the building, when they are concentrated in few rooms, and when there are multiple alternative paths towards the exit. This is due to an increased congestion potential, which CC-SEP successfully avoids. Evaluation of Scenario B reveals that the right choice of a macroscopic evacuation model is crucial for good performance of CC-SEP and that it is important to provide many alternative paths in order to exploit the full potential of CC-SEP. Especially the direction of edges in the graph is to be selected carefully. In this context, it can be useful to provide for the possibility to change directions of edges in the graph model dynamically depending on the expected distribution of evacuees across the building. In the work of Sangho et al. [204], an approach for reconfiguring macroscopic graph edges is presented, which could be applied to this problem. The O/C Architecture of the building's CCU (cf. Section 3.1.1) could be used to realize such a dynamic adaptation of the macroscopic graph model.

Providing for some initialization time in order to collect information is shown to improve the results of CC-SEP. When repeating evacuation planning in each cycle, however, evacuation time slightly increases. The reason for this is identified to be, most likely, the fact that information is disseminated over the network in an aggregated form, i.e. the number of devices in a room is communicated instead of their individual locations and, hence, outdated information is used in the evacuation planning process. However, the performance still exceeds the shortest path behavior in a vast majority of the considered scenarios. It is further shown to yield even better results compared to the scenario without repetition when there is no initialization time given to the evacuees. While introduction of a patience period does not lead to significant improvements, limiting the allowed route changes to situations in which evacuees are a certain distance away from their current target is shown to overcome slightly deteriorated results with planning repetitions. Furthermore, performance reductions resulting from a repeated execution of the evacuation planning are negligible in the more realistic scenario. Finally, CC-SEP is shown to be robust against up to 30% of rule deviators and the induced performance decrease does not increase overproportionally with the number of rule deviating evacuees. A possibility to further improve results of CC-SEP could be to distinguish between having no information about a path and having the information that the path is empty. The latter case could be deduced from knowing that there are many evacuees close to the respective path which do not report about anybody using it. Additionally, introducing a reliability measurement based on message delays, which are encoded in the age-value, could lead to potential improvements of CC-SEP.

4.2 Dynamic Multi-objective Swarm Evacuation Planning

Distributed and decentralized evacuation planning on mobile devices with CC-SEP, presented in the previous section, is shown to work effectively in speeding-up the evacuation process compared to a situation in which the devices do not use a MANET for exchanging information. However, taking a macroscopic evacuation graph model as a basis for optimization and using the presented information model has several constraints:

1. Locations of evacuees are abstracted to be at the center of the corresponding room.

2. Edges in the macroscopic graph model are unidirectional, excluding feasible evacuation routes from planning.

3. Evacuees are assumed to be homogeneous and individual characteristics of the evacuees are not considered.

4. Waiting time on a path is assumed to be increasing linearly with an increasing amount of evacuees using the path.

5. The communication model in CC-SEP does not keep track of the locations of specific evacuees, but rather operates on aggregated and anonymized data.

These restrictions can lead to amendable path planning due to the high level of abstraction and loss of information. Due to the abstract nature of the macroscopic graph model, for example, different locations of evacuees within a single room are neglected by evacuation planning. Furthermore, unidirectional edges in the graph can lead to path planning which ignores potential escape routes even if they are short and empty. Additionally, homogeneous evacuees, as well as linearity of waiting times in congestions are far from reality (cf. Helbing et al. [90]). Another problem with CC-SEP lies within its communication model. The reduction of the exchanged information to the number of evacuees per room instead of their exact locations has the advantage that messages are kept short. However, the drawback of this feature is that the locations of single evacuees are untraceable. This can lead to multiple counting of the same evacuee in different rooms and can distort the information input for evacuation planning. This has shown to have a slightly negative effect when CC-SEP is executed repeatedly. This is not desirable since evacuation planning is supposed to be adaptive to new situations, such as blocked passages or the emergence of congestions for which repeated computations of paths are essential. For these reasons, it is worth looking into alternative possibilities to perform SEP on mobile devices.

Inspiration for an alternative approach to the evacuation planning presented in the previous section can be found in the area of robotics, where path planning, or motion planning as it is often referred to, is a well-studied task (cf. for example Choset [41] or LaValle [132]). Motion planning is often performed on the basis of a grid-like, discretized map of the environment, which is made available to the robot. The patches of this grid correspond to the size of the robot and represent nodes in a graph and neighboring patches are connected via edges. The resulting graph model is more detailed when compared to the macroscopic graph evacuation model used in CC-SEP. In addition, locations and distances are represented more realistically. This graph model is used for motion planning by applying a shortest path algorithm. In the work of König and Likhachev [125], for example, an algorithm for robot motion planning is presented, which can be used to compute lowest cost paths based on such a discretized map. This approach is especially interesting for evacuation path planning, since it is specifically designed for dynamic environments, where changes in traveling costs become available to the robot while it moves towards its target. Evacuation planning on the basis of information from communication in an ad hoc network has similar characteristics. The mobile devices constantly receive new information during the evacuation process. This newly available knowledge should, ideally, be integrated in the path planning process in order to adjust the evacuation instructions if reasonable. Only under these circumstances can the evacuation planning be adaptable to changes in the environment, such as blocked passages or emerging congestions. Apart from the constraints mentioned previously, another limitation of CC-SEP has to be addressed. Since the path planning is based on the CCRP algorithm (cf. Lu et al. [143]), it only optimizes for evacuation time and is inflexible to integrate other objectives. While the circumvention of potential congestions is an obvious goal when choosing an evacuation route, there are other criteria that should be considered. For example, the avoidance of risky areas can be crucial for the safety of evacuees. Moreover, the personal preference for such evaluation criteria can be different for each evacuee. For example, people with physical disabilities would probably prefer to take a shorter path or may be willing to take a longer path if it is better accessible. Evacuation planning should, ideally, be capable of respecting individual characteristics and preferences, as well as multiple objectives. The *Dynamic Multi-objective Swarm Evacuation Planner (DMO-SEP)* introduced hereafter overcomes some of the aforementioned limitations of CC-SEP and respects user preferences during path planning. It is designed to optimize for multiple criteria simultaneously when searching for an optimal escape route for a specific evacuee. DMO-SEP is based on the pre-

viously described dynamic robot motion planning algorithm, called
D^* *Lite*, which is introduced by König and Likhachev [125]. The
algorithm is described briefly in the next section, before DMO-SEP
is presented in detail and tested in an experimental study.

4.2.1 D* Lite

D^* Lite is based on a graph representation $G = (N, E)$ of the
environment which differs from the macroscopic evacuation graph
model. The environment is divided into square patches in a grid-like
fashion, such that each patch corresponds to the expansion of an
average person, and each patch represents a node $n \in N$ of graph
G. Neighboring patches in the von-Neumann neighborhood (cf.
Figure 4.1(a)) are connected via edges $E : (N \times N)$ in the graph
representation and each edge has traveling costs $c(n, m)$ assigned
to it, representing the costs for traveling from patch $n \in N$ to
$m \in N$. D^* Lite computes the path with minimal total costs from
a specific starting patch $n_s \in N$ to a target patch $n_t \in N$. The
starting patch corresponds to the current location of the robot.
The algorithm starts at the target patch and from there looks for
surrounding patches with minimal traveling costs to the target
patch similar to the well-known Dijkstra algorithm. The search is
directed towards the starting patch by means of a heuristic value
$h(n)$, which denotes the Euclidean distance between each patch n
and the robot's current position. Patches with a lower value for
$h(n)$ are preferred in the search for the lowest cost path, which
can reduce computational costs due to a faster termination of the
search. This approach was first proposed by Hart et al. [84] in
form of the A* algorithm designed for static path finding.
Let $Adj(n)$ return all adjacent nodes of a node $n \in N$ with respect to its von-Neumann neighborhood and $d(n)$ denote the

minimal traveling costs from n to n_t, $\bar{d}(n)$ is an auxiliary variable. In D* Lite, patches which have to be processed in order to find the lowest cost path are added to a sorted set U. All nodes in this set are sorted in ascending order with respect to $key_1(n) = min\left(d(n), \bar{d}(n)\right) + h(n)$ and, subsequently, $key_2(n) = min\left(d(n), \bar{d}(n)\right)$. Let $first(U)$ denote the first element in the set U, i.e., the element with the smallest key value. The complete procedure of D* Lite is described in Algorithm 4.3.

If a change in traveling costs is detected for an edge $e(n, m)$, for example because one of the corresponding patches is blocked, the update procedure is called for nodes n and m and for all nodes which are subsequently added to U, recursively, until U is empty or the starting patch is updated and consistent. Consistent means that the values for $d(n)$ and $\bar{d}(n)$ are equal. The consistency check in line 5 of the update procedure limits the propagation of cost changes to affected nodes and reduces the computational costs of the algorithm when compared to replanning from scratch. Figure 4.12 illustrates the update process with a simple example. The top row displays the discretized environment consisting of 9 patches; the start patch of the robot is marked with a circle and the target with a cross. The bottom row shows the corresponding graph representations using nodes (dots) and connecting edges. The traveling costs are assumed to be 1 for all edges in the graph and the numbers in the nodes denote the minimum travel costs $d(n)$ from that node to the target node. In the second state of the environment, the center patch is discovered to be blocked, therefore, the connected nodes are updated according to the procedure described in Algorithm 4.3. The gray nodes are found to be consistent, i.e., their distance costs are not affected by the change, whereas the shaded, red node is inconsistent and requires an update. Since the red node is the

---

Algorithm 4.3 D* Lite

Require: graph $G = (N, E)$, start node n_s, target node n_t, heuristic $h(n)\ \forall n \in N$, costs $c(e)\ \forall e \in E$

1: $d(n) \leftarrow \infty, \forall n \in N$
2: $\bar{d}(n) \leftarrow \infty, \forall n \in N, \bar{d}(n_t) \leftarrow 0$
3: $U.add(n_t)$

4: **procedure** COMPUTEPATH
5:   **while** $(key(first(U)) < key(n_s)) \vee \left(\bar{d}(n_s) \neq d(n_s) \right)$ **do**
6:     Define $u \leftarrow first(U)$
7:     **if** $d(u) > \bar{d}(u)$ **then**
8:       $d(u) \leftarrow \bar{d}(u)$
9:       $update(u)$
10:     **end if**
11:     **for** $p \in Adj(u)$ **do**
12:       $update(p)$
13:     **end for**
14:   **end while**
15: **end procedure**

16: **procedure** UPDATE(n)
17:   **if** $n \neq n_t$ **then**
18:     $\bar{d}(n) \leftarrow min_{\forall s \in Adj(n)}(c(n,s) + d(s))$
19:     $U.add(n)$
20:     **if** $d(n) = \bar{d}(n)$ **then**
21:       $U.remove(n)$
22:     **end if**
23:   **end if**
24: **end procedure**

---

starting node and it is consistent after the update, the process terminates and the new cost minimal path is found by following the nodes which have the lowest costs assigned. In this example, there are two valid lowest cost paths, of which one is selected at random and depicted. From this example, the advantage of D* Lite becomes apparent. In contrast to updating all nodes in the graph after a change in the environment is detected, only the nodes which are affected require an update.

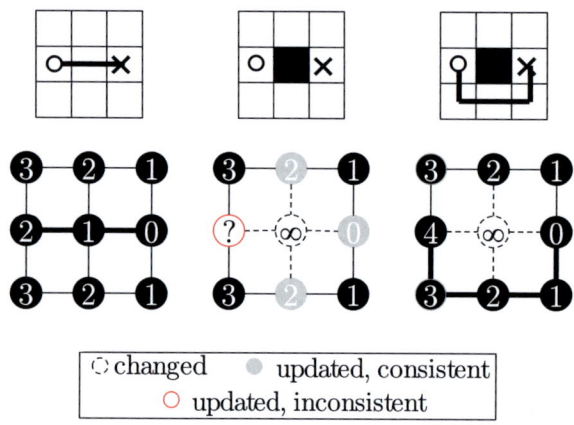

Figure 4.12: Update process of D* Lite when a patch is discovered to be blocked.

4.2.2 Dynamic Multi-objective Swarm Evacuation Planning

For DMO-SEP, each device is assumed to possess knowledge of its current location and of the building's layout, e.g., by downloading it upon entering the building. Similar to CC-SEP, DMO-SEP relies on an exchange of information between mobile devices via ad hoc network links and performs decentralized path computations on each device. It, therefore, belongs to the family of SEP algorithms as defined in Section 4.1. The information from local communication is used to assign costs to the edges of the graph model before applying the dynamic path planning algorithm D* Lite (cf. Section 4.2.1) to find an optimal path towards the exit. Since route planning with D* Lite is solely based on costs instead of an estimation of traveling and waiting times, the approach is flexible to incorporate multiple objectives. This can be achieved by using a complex cost function which consists of multiple components $o \in O$, such as risk, distance, or waiting time, each representing a different optimization objective. These components are weighted and summarized in order to derive the total traveling costs for evacuee a, which can then be used for D* Lite:

$$c^a(e) = \sum_{o \in O} \left(w_o^a \cdot c_o^a(e) \right) \tag{4.1}$$

with weights $w_o^a \in [0, 1]$ and $\sum_O w_o^a = 1$. The weights can be defined according to the characteristics and preferences of each evacuee. After the costs for all edges in the discretized layout have been computed, D* Lite finds the minimum cost path, which is a sequence of patches $< n_s, ..., n_t >$. From this path, a sequence of rooms is generated, by analogy with the evacuation instructions in CC-SEP, and a navigation path can be displayed to the user on the screen of the mobile device. The transformation from patches to a room-based path is not necessary, but it ensures that the displayed path is easily conceived by the user in contrast to a path which assembles a winding sequence of patches.

To illustrate and test the functionality of DMO-SEP, three optimization criteria are considered. Since a straightforward objective for evacuation planning is to reduce the traveling distance, the distance traveled constitutes one of the cost components. These costs $c_{distance}(e)$ arise for each edge $e \in E$ in the graph model G and represent the distance between the patches which are connected by the respective edge. They can be made available to the mobile devices along with the download of the building's layout. Although they are initially equal for all devices, it is conceivable that an evacuee detects a blocked passage during his escape, reports this to his mobile evacuation device, and this information is then spread to other mobile devices using the ad hoc network communication. In such a case it is possible that, due to the delays and potential network link breakages, distance costs for the patches in the graph model diverge between mobile devices. Apart from traveling distance, two other objectives are considered when choosing evacuation routes, the minimization of risk and the minimization of waiting time on the paths. Since jamming queues in front of narrow passages or doors are the main reason for waiting time, the minimization of waiting time is considered equivalent to congestion avoidance.

Risk Minimization

In order to be able to avoid risky paths, the devices need to know which areas are dangerous. It is reasonable to assume that there are sensors installed inside the building which can measure potential danger indicators, such as gas or heat, and forward this information to mobile devices nearby. Such a scenario is, for example, examined by Filippoupolitis et al. [66]. For simplicity reasons, it is assumed that the sensors communicate a certain risk level $risk(R) \in [0, 1]$ for room R instead of empirical measurement data which would require a certain degree of interpretation. The corresponding costs are assigned to all edges $e(n, m), n \in R$ connecting nodes in the respective room:

$$c_{risk}\left(e\left(n,m\right)\right) = risk\left(R\right) : n \in R \qquad (4.2)$$

By assigning a risk value to each patch in a room, it becomes comparatively more expensive to cross a larger room with the same risk level. The information about the risk level of a room is shared with other devices using ad hoc network connections. To do so, each message contains an age-value which is set to zero at the moment at which a risk level is reported from a sensor to a mobile device. Then, the age-value is increased according to the system clock of the mobile devices. When the information is forwarded to other mobile devices, the age-value is included in the message. Whenever a device receives contradictory information about the risk level of a room from two different sources, it can identify and adopt the most recent information.

Congestion Avoidance

Congestion avoidance is a well-known task in the research area of traffic optimization. However, there is a major difference between traffic and evacuation scenarios. While traffic jams are usually rather well-organized situations, in which cars are lined up behind red traffic lights or other barriers, evacuation is often accompanied by panic. In panic situations, however, the time needed for evacuees to traverse a narrow passage is not easy to estimate. Firstly, it does not increase linearly with the number of waiting evacuees or the size of the door, but is rather dependent on many other factors which affect the forces that act on the evacuees and, hence, determine the time needed for a congestion to dissolve (cf. Helbing et al. [90]). This kind of situation is further aggravated when information about the locations of all evacuees is uncertain. Similar to CC-SEP, the mobile devices in DMO-SEP are assumed to communicate their own location to other nearby devices and spread such information in the ad hoc network. However, the main difference is that now all known locations of other devices are reported as opposed to solely reporting the total number of observed devices in each room. Analogously to the exchange of risk messages, each message concerning location information has an age-value assigned to it, which is zero if the device's own location is being reported and which is increased in accordance with the device's system clock in any other case. Due to the delays and link breakages, which are likely to occur in the communication network, the knowledge about other evacuees' positions is uncertain. As a consequence, predicting waiting times on this basis is prone to error. Fortunately, it is sufficient for evacuation planning to be able to compare two routes with respect to their potential for congestion emergence, which is why a precise prediction of waiting times for each path is not necessarily required. In order to measure a route's potential for congestion emergence, two indicators are proposed. These can be computed from the locations of evacuees in the building, and are intuitively suitable to evaluate congestion potentials on evacuation paths. Both indicators are introduced hereafter and tested for their effectiveness in a subsequent experimental evaluation.

Load The first congestion indicator is based on the idea that jamming queues are more likely to occur when a large number of evacuees are located in a relatively small room. The potential for such a situation to occur is measured by a parameter called *load*, which is constituted of the number of devices $d \in D$ in relation to the size of the room R in which their location is determined. The associated costs for each edge $e\,(n, m)$ between nodes n and m in room R are computed as:

$$c_{load}\left(e\left(n,m\right)\right) = \frac{|\{d \in D : n\left(d\right) \in R\}|}{|\{n \in R\}|} \qquad (4.3)$$

with $n\left(d\right)$ denoting the node on which device d is located. One could argue that using the number of devices in relation to the size of the room's doors as an indicator would be more effective, but a room can have multiple doors and yet usually only one of them determines the room's flow rate. Since it is hard to tell which doors will be used by how many evacuees, load as defined above seems the more general indicator for congestions.

Entropy Congestions are so-called emergent phenomena, i.e., formations of order from disorder based on self-organization. Emergence can be measured by applying the concept of *entropy*, a metric to measure the amount of order in a system, as suggested by Mnif and Müller-Schloer [162]. A system with high order corresponds to a low entropy value and vice versa. When congestions arise in an evacuation situation, it is usually because evacuees jam up in front of doors or narrow exits. As a consequence, the distribution of the locations of mobile devices in the affected room is concentrated in front of the cause for congestion. Entropy can be used to describe this degree of concentration as explained in the following. Patches in a room can be organized in rows and columns reflecting their horizontal and vertical order respectively. Let a room R contain $x \times y$ patches, i.e., x columns and y rows. Let further $num\left(i\right)$, $num\left(j\right)$ denote the number of devices $d \in D$ located on column i or row j respectively. The entropy of a room R is computed as shown in Equation 4.4 and 4.5, with $x\left(n\right)$, $y\left(n\right)$ denoting the row and column of a patch n, respectively. The value $p\left(n\right)$ denotes the relative frequency of evacuees on patch n of room R.

$$e(R) = -\sum_{n \in R} p(n) \ \mathrm{ld} \ p(n) \tag{4.4}$$

$$p(n) = \frac{num(x(n)) + num(y(n))}{\sum_{i=1}^{x} \sum_{j=1}^{y} num(i) + num(j)} \tag{4.5}$$

Figure 4.13 shows an example of the calculation of a room's entropy. The locations of devices are marked with four rings inside the respective patches. Firstly, the devices in each row and column are counted. Then, the sum of the corresponding values is assigned to each patch. In the second step, the relative frequencies $p(n)$ are computed for each patch and the entropy value $e(R)$ of room R is derived. The entropy value can vary significantly for different room sizes. To make rooms comparable, the entropy is normalized as follows. The maximum entropy $e_{max}(R) = ld(x \cdot y)$ for a room R is reached when each patch is occupied by one evacuee since the size of each patch corresponds to the expansion of an average person (cf. Section 4.2.1). The minimum entropy value $e_{min}(R) = ld(x+y) - \frac{2}{x+y}$ is achieved when only one single evacuee is located somewhere in the room. Since entropy decreases with increasing concentration of devices, the entropy based cost component for edge $e(n,m)$ with $n \in R$ is computed as:

$$c_{entropy}(e(n,m)) = 1 - \left(\frac{e(R) - e_{min}(R)}{e_{max}(R) - e_{min}(R)} \right), n \in R \tag{4.6}$$

4.2.3 Evaluation

In order to assess whether DMO-SEP can accelerate the evacuation process, a simulative experimental study is performed. By analogy with the evaluation of CC-SEP, agents correspond to evacuees

140

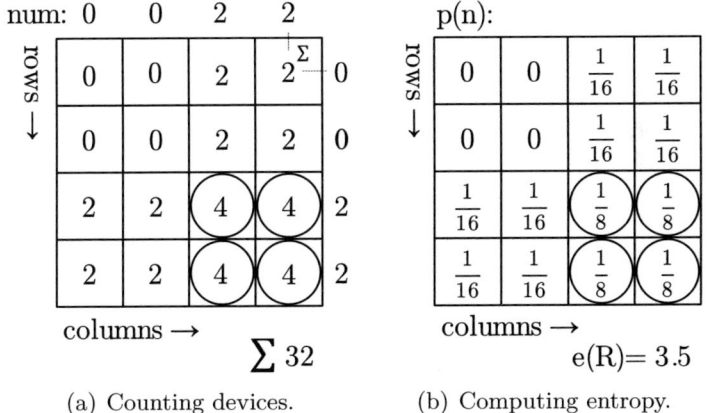

(a) Counting devices.   (b) Computing entropy.

Figure 4.13: Example of computing the entropy of a room with sixteen patches and four evacuees (patches with rings).

and their mobile devices. The first aim is to verify whether the reduced abstraction of the underlying evacuation model helps to improve evacuation time compared to the macroscopic graph based CC-SEP. Furthermore, the proposed risk avoidance mechanism is to be tested and it is subject to investigation whether the presented congestion indicators are suited to compare routes with respect to their congestion potential and, hence, to avoid jamming queues and to facilitate a faster evacuation of the building. The simulation environment used in the experimental study is the same as described in Section 4.1.2. The investigated building layout is the same as Scenario C used for evaluation of CC-SEP, which is the more complex building layout shown in Figure 4.10. The rooms with number 4, 6, and 10 connect the other rooms behind to the room with number 12, which leads directly to the building's exit. Hence, agents initially located in rooms behind these potential bottlenecks are likely to get caught up in congestions. Due to this characteristic and because there are various valid escape routes, this layout is suitable to test the effectiveness of the congestion indicators. Unless stated otherwise, all experiments are performed with 60 agents and are repeated 40 times, randomly varying the initial distribution of agents in the building. The initial locations are chosen randomly according to a uniform distribution. The communication range is set to $r = 15\%$, which covers the agent's current patch plus three patches in horizontal and vertical direction respectively (cf. Figure 4.2). Walls or barriers do not interfere with the communication range. For evaluation, total and average evacuation time is measured as well as the average time spent in risky areas or without movement. The latter is denoted as waiting time. Naturally, a significant difference between total and average evacuation time is to be expected in most scenarios because total evacuation time reflects the maximum time any agent needs to leave the building. Hence, one outliner can significantly influence this result.

Evaluation of Reduced Abstraction

Firstly, the performance of DMO-SEP is compared to CC-SEP in a sample scenario where agents are distributed over the building according to a uniform random distribution. In this scenario, congestions are expected to be minimal, since there are only few agents located initially in each room. Hence, the impact of the reduced abstractions in DMO-SEP compared to CC-SEP becomes clearly visible. Figure 4.14 displays the results. It becomes apparent that the differences between DMO-SEP and CC-SEP are only marginal when there is no congestion avoidance necessary. Nevertheless, a slight improvement in the total evacuation time by one round on average is achieved by DMO-SEP when compared to CC-SEP. Since congestions are unlikely in the considered scenario, the reason for this can be found in the reduced abstraction of the evacuation graph model. While the macroscopic graph measures all distances from the center of the rooms, DMO-SEP takes into account the agents' actual locations. In addition, DMO-SEP allows for bidirectional edges which increases the number of available evacuation routes for planning. The results of this first experiment indicate that DMO-SEP computes slightly faster evacuation instructions for situations in which congestions are unlikely due to several reduced abstractions in the planning process. Subsequently, the integration of different objectives in DMO-SEP is investigated, starting with risk avoidance.

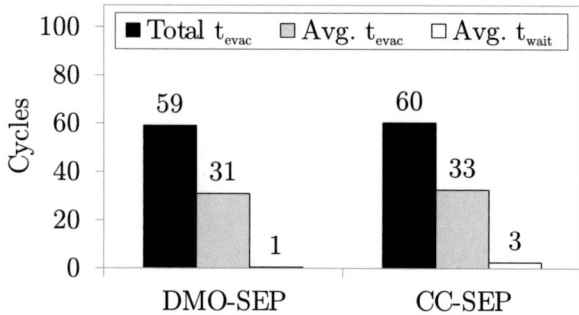

Figure 4.14: Comparison of the two proposed SEP approaches without congestion indicators.

Evaluation of Risk Minimization

The next experiment is performed in order to evaluate the impact of risk avoidance on the total evacuation time and the average evacuation time per agent, as well as on the time agents spend waiting in congestions or are exposed to risk. To accomplish this, two classes of evacuees are defined, one class consisting of risk aversive agents, and another class which consists of agents who prefer short ways even if they lead through risky areas. In this experiment, rooms 4 and 10 are assumed to have a risk level of 1 and agents which enter these rooms are informed about their current risk exposure. Risk aversive agents optimize path costs with weights $w_{risk} = 0.9$, $w_{distance} = 0.1$ and less careful agents assign weights $w_{risk} = 0.8$ and $w_{distance} = 0.2$ to the respective costs. Figure 4.15 shows a sample situation which occurred during an experiment run. Here, the different reactions to the detection of higher risk levels for both agent classes can be observed. A risk aversive agent, depicted as a blue square, chooses a path with a longer traveling distance in order to avoid the risky area in room 4.

Agents with a higher tolerance for risk, on the other hand, refrain from taking a detour and pass through rooms with higher risk levels. This exemplary situation also demonstrates how ad hoc network communication is employed in order to reduce the time needed for evacuation. The risk aversive device does not enter room 4 in order to realize that it is an area of high risk, but, instead, is informed about it by other agents via communication over the ad hoc network. Therefore, the agent starts walking directly on the alternative path instead of wasting time checking the condition of room 4 by himself.

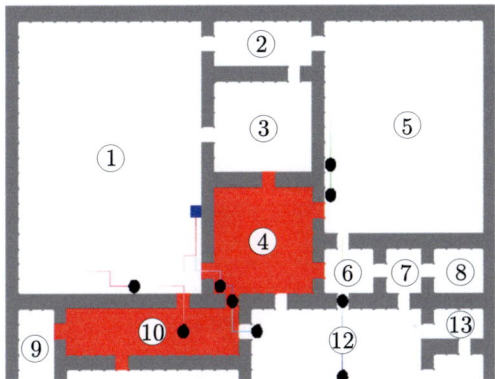

Figure 4.15: Risk avoidance for two different agent classes. More risk aversive agents are depicted in black, rooms 4 and 10 represent areas of high risk.

In Figure 4.16, findings about the impact of risk avoidance on evacuation time are presented. In this experiment, there are only risk-aversive agents in the environment. The numerical results of the experiment described previously reveal a quite intuitive effect. The reduced average time an agent spends in risky areas comes at the cost of an increased evacuation time. Additionally, the average waiting time per agent is increased because more evacuees take the less risky routes and, thereby, the congestion potential is increased on these paths.

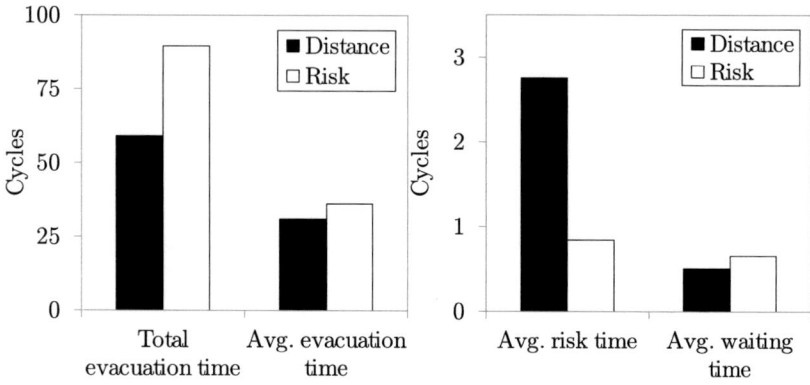

Figure 4.16: Experimental evaluation of risk avoidance.

Evaluation of Congestion Avoidance

The third experiment aims at testing the effectiveness of the proposed congestion indicators. Figure 4.17 displays a sample situation in which 40 agents are initially located in rooms number 3 and 4. This setting provokes congestions in both rooms when minimizing traveling distance is the only optimization objective. The integration of load, as well as entropy based costs, is expected to dissolve these jamming queues. Scenario (a) shows the situation in which only traveling distance is being optimized, while scenario (b) optimizes distance and load costs and scenario (c) distance and entropy costs. The weights for scenarios (b) and (c) are chosen as $w_{load} = w_{entropy} = 0.8$ and $w_{distance} = 0.2$. The depicted experimental results confirm the initial expectations. For both congestion indicators, the jamming queues in rooms 3 and 4 are reduced. The snapshots also show the different effect both congestion indicators have on the evacuation situation. When agents optimize entropy-based costs, they spread over various alternative paths, which reduces the concentration of agents in the building significantly. This effect is much less pronounced when load costs are being optimized. Figure 4.18 quantifies the evaluation of the three depicted scenarios which, generally confirms the previous observations. The integration of entropy and load costs reduces the overall evacuation time by 23% for the scenario with entropy costs and 19% for additional load costs respectively, when compared to evacuation planning where minimizing traveling distance is the only objective. A comparison with CC-SEP yields an even higher reduction in total evacuation time of 32% considering DMO-SEP with load costs and 26% when compared to DMO-SEP including entropy costs. This is a significant improvement when compared to the first experiment in which agents were distributed randomly over the building. This is due to the higher congestion potential. Furthermore, the average evacuation time per evacuee and the average waiting time, i.e., cycles without movements per agent, are reduced significantly with DMO-SEP when compared to CC-SEP. Achieving lower waiting times is an important criterion for the evaluation of an evacuation navigation support system. It seems natural that people in a panic situation are less patient and, if they are expected to wait often, are more likely to lose their trust in the navigation support system. CC-SEP navigation instructions obviously expect evacuees to wait more often at jammed doors compared to DMO-SEP. Even when the total evacuation time is similar for both approaches, it is more likely that evacuees follow navigation instructions which keep them moving during a panic situation in contrast to a system which expects them to wait either too frequently or for extended periods of time. It can be concluded that DMO-SEP is superior to CC-SEP in all considered criteria.

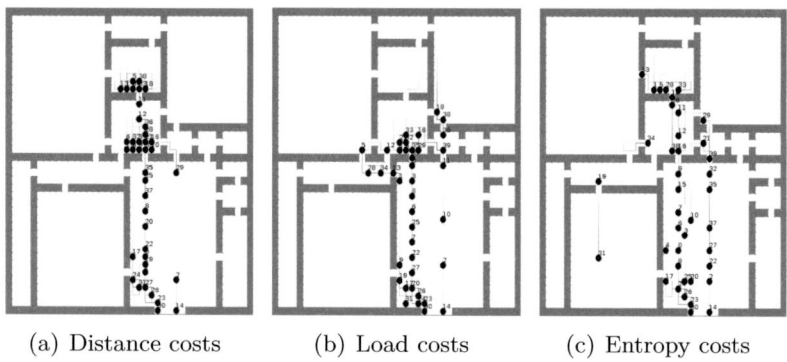

(a) Distance costs   (b) Load costs   (c) Entropy costs

Figure 4.17: Evacuation situation after 24 cycles when optimizing for distance costs only (a), distance and load costs (b), and distance and entropy costs (c).

4.2.4 Conclusion

In this section, DMO-SEP is presented. DMO-SEP is an alternative SEP approach for mobile devices which overcomes some of the drawbacks of CC-SEP. DMO-SEP is based on a less abstract environment model and collects precise location information from other mobile devices over the ad hoc network. Furthermore, DMO-SEP computes optimal evacuation paths with respect to several objectives at the same time and can take into account individual preferences and characteristics of the mobile device's user. The application of an incremental, heuristic search algorithm to find optimal paths allows for dynamic replanning of navigation

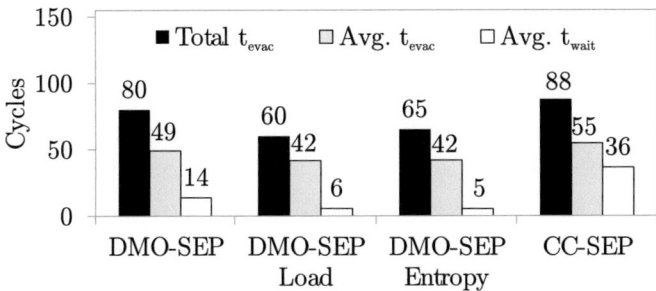

Figure 4.18: Experimental evaluation of congestion avoidance with DMO-SEP and comparison to the performance of CC-SEP.

instructions and reduces the necessary computations compared to a search from scratch. This is especially useful for SEP, where knowledge collected by devices via local communication changes constantly over time. Fast replanning and integration of newly available information makes the evacuation planning approach adaptable to detected changes in the environment, such as the emergence of congestions. DMO-SEP is able to evaluate paths with respect to multiple objectives by assigning a weighted sum of cost components to a path, such that each cost component reflects one optimization objective. Four cost components are proposed and evaluated in experiments. Two of these components are meant to capture the congestion potential on a path. One congestion indicator is based on the load of a path, i.e. the number of evacuees in relation to the size of the rooms on a path, the other is an entropy-based indicator, which assesses the concentration of evacuees within rooms along the considered path. Additionally, travel distance and danger indicators are proposed as cost components for optimization.

149

Experiments are performed in order to evaluate DMO-SEP. For this, a realistic scenario with various rooms in the building is taken as a basis, which is also used in the CC-SEP experiments. The performance of DMO-SEP is assessed by regarding the resulting total evacuation time, the average evacuation time per evacuee, the average time an evacuee spends in risky areas, and the average waiting time of each evacuee, i.e. the time it spends without moving. Firstly, DMO-SEP and CC-SEP are compared in a scenario with low congestion potential. It is shown that DMO-SEP produces better results in terms of total and average evacuation time, as well as waiting time than CC-SEP in this scenario, which is most likely due to the reduced abstractions in the evacuation model used as a basis for evacuation planning. The evaluation of DMO-SEP proceeds with testing the risk minimization objective and the integration of different preferences of evacuees. To do so, a sample scenario is analyzed in which two classes of evacuees are simulated, each of which representing different risk preferences. One class of agents is risk-aversive, the other is risk-friendly. The evacuation instructions produced by DMO-SEP are shown to respect these preferences and it is observable that evacuees are informed early about risky paths, such that they do not have to go near dangerous areas before they switch to alternative routes. Additionally, experiments with only risk-aversive agents reveal that risk-aversion comes at the cost of evacuation time, which is intuitively understandable. Furthermore, the impact of both congestion indicators is examined and it is shown that they reduce the overall evacuation time effectively, even in an uncertain and incomplete information situation. In a specific scenario, which provokes congestions, the total evacuation time is reduced with DMO-SEP and load-based congestion avoidance by up to 32% and with entropy-based congestion avoidance by only slightly less when compared to CC-SEP.

Furthermore, DMO-SEP is shown to improve average evacuation time and waiting timer per agent significantly when compared to CC-SEP. It can be concluded from the presented evaluation that DMO-SEP is superior to CC-SEP in terms of evacuation as well as waiting time and that DMO-SEP is, therefore, the better choice for evacuation planning than CC-SEP when the number of exchanged messages is not important. One remaining open question in context of DMO-SEP is the determination of optimal weights for the cost components. However, the O/C Architecture offers a solution to this problem. The online and offline learning mechanisms could be applied in order to learn the best weights for each optimization criteria depending on the current evacuation scenario in a building.

4.3 Summary

This chapter defines the process of SEP, which describes distributed and decentralized evacuation planning based on information which is collected via local communication in order to improve evacuation performance. The approach has its name from the characteristic that local communication and decision making is used to improve overall evacuation time for a swarm of mobile devices within a building. The main challenge for SEP is an uncertain information situation for each device, which arises from delays and link breakages in ad hoc network communication. This makes it hard to estimate waiting times on specific escape routes. Two specific SEP algorithms are introduced. The first approach is called CC-SEP and optimizes only total evacuation time. To achieve this goal, a routing algorithm is adapted, which uses capacity reserving strategies in order to find time-optimal routes for all evacuees in a building. Routing is based on an abstract graph model of the building, which is created from locally available information about other evacuees' locations. A suitable route for each specific mobile device is selected from the optimization result. An experimental study reveals that CC-SEP is able to improve total evacuation time significantly when compared to a situation where evacuees follow the shortest path towards the exit. Furthermore, results are shown to be robust even when some evacuees deviate from the evacuation routes suggested by CC-SEP. Slight drawbacks are identified when evacuation planning is executed repeatedly in order to adapt to new evacuation situations. However, the performance is still significantly better when compared to a simple shortest path following behavior and several methods are proposed and evaluated which can help to reduce this limitation. The second SEP approach, called DMO-SEP results in even faster evacuation times. The reason for this is partly due to a more detailed environmental model taken as a basis for path planning and an improved communication model. Apart from its improved performance, DMO-SEP has the advantage that it is based on a path planning approach instead of flow optimization in order to find escape routes. As a consequence, multiple objectives can be regarded for optimization and can be weighted according to evacuee-specific preferences. Apart from minimizing traveling distances, two other objectives are investigated, namely risk minimization and congestion avoidance. In order to avoid congestions, indicators based on the distribution of evacuees in the building are proposed, which evaluate routes according to their congestion potential instead of estimating waiting times, as it is done in CC-SEP. These congestion indicators improve the results of DMO-SEP even further and are shown to accelerate the evacuation of buildings by up to 32% when compared to CC-SEP in a scenario with high likelihood for congestions. This makes DMO-SEP more suitable for the computation of evacuation instructions. However, CC-SEP requires fewer configurations from the device's user since preferences do not have to be specified. This simplicity can be an advantage, for example, if the user is not willing to provide detailed information to the evacuation system. Moreover, exchanging the location information of each evacuee in the building increases the communication overhead when compared to exchanging only the observed number of evacuees in each room, as it is proposed for CC-SEP. Hence, CC-SEP could be the first choice for evacuation planning in case reducing energy consumption is an objective.

CHAPTER 5

LOCALIZATION IN MOBILE AD HOC NETWORKS

In OBESS, mobile devices in combination with a permanently installed SSN are intended to be used as navigation support for building evacuation. While the devices in the static network are assumed to possess knowledge of their positions in the building due to a priori configuration, the mobile devices have to be located first in order to be able to find suitable navigation instructions leading evacuees from their current positions to an exit. Since GPS is not available indoors, it cannot be used to localize mobile devices in OBESS. Furthermore, a single point of failure is to be avoided in the localization process in order to make it more robust against failure. As a consequence, decentralized computation methods for the mobile devices' locations are required. Because the static sensors are assumed to know their locations, beacon-based localization algorithms, which derive unknown locations of devices from several known locations, are applicable. Section 2.4.1 gives an overview of beacon-based localization algorithms which can be used for this purpose. Beacon-based algorithms allow for the computation of absolute locations with respect to a common reference grid, which corresponds to the building's layout in the scenario considered here. From the presented beacon-based localization algorithms, methods which require information about the angle between mobile and static devices are not suitable for usage in OBESS. As detailed before, the estimation of angles requires complex preparation and bulky hardware, which portable devices are usually not equipped with. This leaves the proximity and distance-based algorithms. While proximity-based algorithms are less complex in terms of computational effort, high quality localization results require numerous beacons in the network. Because the installation of sensors is costly, one objective in OBESS is to minimize the number of beacons in order to make its installation more attractive for building owners. Therefore, distance-based localization algorithms are generally the better choice. Nevertheless, proximity-based localization algorithms are a good fallback for the devices in case there are not enough beacon nodes for distance-based localization in certain areas of a building. Furthermore, proximity-based localization approaches are rather simple and, therefore, do not require complex computations to be performed on the devices. Hence, they could be the better choice when quality of localization results has to be traded for reducing energy consumption in case the mobile device runs out of battery. Although localization algorithms are studied widely in the literature, the impact of mobility has not yet been emphasized. As explained in Section 2.4.3, the focus of current research about the effects of mobility on localization either lies on examining the impairment of the physical signal or the mobility is assumed to be actively controllable by the device itself. In contrast to this assumption, mobile devices in OBESS are portable and do not autonomously move like robots, i.e. their mobility has a passive character.

Definition 5.1 (Passive mobility). *Passive mobility describes a state in which devices are carried by people, animals, or nature and in which the carrier, not the device, decides where and when to move.*

Distance-based algorithms use distance estimates between beacons and the devices to be located. These estimates can be derived by range-based or range-free distance estimation techniques (cf. Section 2.4.2). While range-based distance estimation requires specific hardware to analyze the physical communication signal, range-free methods use messages which are exchanged between the devices in a network. Since avoiding additional hardware for the mobile devices in OBESS is to be desired for making the devices more lightweight and less costly, range-free methods are the obvious choice for distance estimation in OBESS. Most range-free distance estimation techniques require a somewhat dense and uniform distribution of communication neighbors over a device's communication range. Since mobility of the devices influences the composition and structure of the network topology, it can be expected to have a significant impact on localization results. So far, there is little known about the influence of mobility on the results of range-free distance-based localization algorithms, hence, this investigation is subject to Sections 5.1, 5.2, and 5.3 of this chapter. In Section 5.1 localization algorithms based on hop counts are investigated while various mobility models are applied to the devices. The potential of synchronization for improving distance estimation based on hop counts in dynamic networks is examined in Section 5.2. Section 5.3 presents an alternative approach to distance estimation based on hop counts, which delivers promising results, especially in dynamic networks. As stated before, minimizing the number of beacons is an objective that has to be considered in OBESS as they are costly and need to be installed, configured, and maintained. On the other hand, the number and positions of beacons influence the quality of localization results. To address this trade-off, a method which optimizes the placement of beacons for localization of mobile devices, specifically during building evacuation, is presented in Section 5.4 of this chapter. Section 5.5 summarizes the findings of this chapter. Parts of the research presented hereafter are also published by Merkel et al. [152, 153, 154, 156, 157, 159].

5.1 Effects of Mobility on Hop Count Based Distance Estimation

A well-studied approach to estimate distances in ad hoc networks is based on so-called *hop counts*. A hop count denotes the minimum number of relay devices which two devices need to exchange messages with each other (cf. Ghosekar et al. [75]). Although this metric is mainly used in the context of routing (cf. Boukerche et al. [22], Chatterjee and Das [38], Chou et al. [42]), it can also be used to estimate distances. These distance estimates then form the basis for localization. In Section 2.4, some methods which transform hop counts into distance information are presented. This section, however, focuses on investigating the impact of mobility on hop counts and, consequently, on the quality of derived distance estimates. When investigating the influence of mobility, it is intuitively comprehensible that the characteristics of mobility play an important role. For example, distances between the devices do not change if all devices are moved with the same speed and in the same direction, whereas random mobility has a great impact on the distances. Furthermore, the number of moving devices, their speed, and direction of movement are important variables when it comes to examining the impact of mobility. As a consequence, a large spectrum of mobility models is examined in order to derive general statements about the influence of mobility on distance estimation based on hop counts.

5.1.1 Mobility Models

The mobility pattern in a dynamic network highly depends on its application and the environment it is deployed in. Therefore, in order to be able to make general statements about the impact of mobility on hop count based distance estimation, a variation of mobility models is analyzed. In the work of Camp et al. [34], some models for describing different kinds of mobility in networks are suggested and their impact on network connectivity and routing is investigated. These patterns are used hereafter as a basis for studying the effect of mobility on distance estimation based on hop counts. In addition, new mobility models, which are not considered by Camp et al. [34], are introduced.

Individual Mobility Models

Individual mobility models describe movements where the next position of a device is determined independently from any other device in the network. The *Random Walk (RW)* mobility model is one of the most widely studied mobility patterns in the literature, e.g., by Zonoozi and Dassanayake [259]. In RW, a random direction and speed are selected from predefined ranges and the device moves accordingly until a fixed distance is traveled or a specific time has passed. *Chaos Move (CM)* denotes an RW mobility model where a new speed and direction are selected at each step, i.e., the mobile device is kept in a small area around its starting position. The *Random Direction Walk (RD)* model defines a random target at the border of the environment and a speed value within a certain range and the device is moved accordingly until the target is reached. Once the device is there, it pauses for some time before a new target is selected. When using this model, there is a high likelihood that devices spend most of their time somewhere in the middle of the environment. *Bounded Random Walk (BR)* is similar to CM, but speed and direction are not varied completely at random but within a small range around the preceding values. Similar to this, the *Gauss Markov Move (GM)* selects the next direction and speed according to the following equations:

$$s_t = \alpha \cdot s_{t-1} + (1 - \alpha) \cdot \mu_s + \sqrt{(1 - \alpha^2)} \cdot s_{gr} \qquad (5.1)$$

$$d_t = \alpha \cdot d_{t-1} + (1 - \alpha) \cdot \mu_d + \sqrt{(1 - \alpha^2)} \cdot d_{gr} \qquad (5.2)$$

with s_t and d_t denoting the new values for speed and direction respectively, α being a random parameter ($0 \leq \alpha \leq 1$) and s_{gr} and d_{gr} being chosen from a Gaussian random distribution with zero mean and a standard deviation of one. μ_s and μ_d are constants. In *Probabilistic Random Walk (PR)*, the movement is defined by a finite state machine with fixed probabilities for state transits. The allowed states are *backward, forward* or *stop*, and turn *left* or *right*. The probabilities are chosen in a way that they emphasize continuous moves in the same direction (cf. Camp et al. [34]). Figure 5.1 shows trajectories of all individual mobility models considered above.

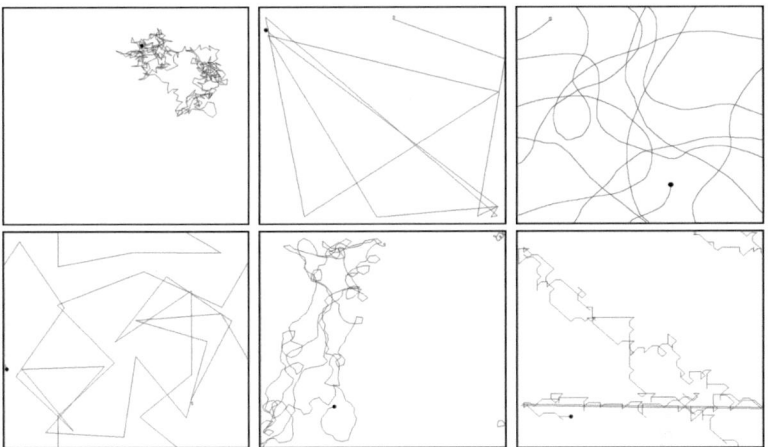

Figure 5.1: Trajectories. From top left to bottom right: CM, RD, BR, RW, GM, PR.

Coupled Mobility Models

Coupled mobility models are characterized by mutual influences between the mobile devices. The *Column Mobility (ColM)* model simulates children walking in a line behind their parents. Here, all devices move randomly (according to CM) except for some groups consisting of a leader and followers. All followers move approximately in a row behind the leading device. Furthermore, the *Nomadic Move (NomM)* model is defined in which all devices move according to CM except for some leaders that collect followers. Whenever a non-leader device comes within communication range of a leader, it starts following the leader while moving randomly within its communication range. When a leader has more than a maximum number of followers, a random follower leaves the group. In the *Reference Point Mobility (RefM)* model, each device is assumed to have a virtual reference point around which it moves randomly while never exceeding a maximum distance. The reference points are assembled in a grid and move according to CM, but share the same speed and direction as if they were connected to each other. The *Stream Mobility (StrM)* model simulates devices which are moved by regular forces such as wind or water. Each device remembers the direction of nearby devices and chooses its own moving direction within a certain range around the angle of the most recently moved neighbor, which is why the devices exhibit a stream-like movement. This mobility model was developed specifically for this study and does not belong to the models published by Camp et al. [34].

Beacon Mobility Models

Since the results of distance estimation based on hop counts depend on the position of the beacons in the network (cf. Bachrach and Taylor [12], Nagpal et al. [171]), beacon mobility models are defined additionally. Beacon mobility models define moves with a certain angle and speed around a beacon. Beacon mobility models can be further distinguished depending on whether individual or coupled movements are regarded. With individual beacon mobility models, a device moves with a predefined speed in the direction of α with respect to a beacon (cf. Figure 5.2(a)).

The coupled beacon mobility model is similar, except for the fact that the device is moved together with a fixed number of its neighbors in a specified direction with respect to the beacon (cf. Figure 5.2(b)). The same angle α is defined for all devices belonging to the coupled group. An angle of $\alpha = 0°$ indicates a movement leading away from the beacon, $\alpha = 180°$ directs the mobile devices towards the beacon. A movement at an angle of $\alpha = 90°$ means that the devices move along circular rings around the beacon. Figure 5.3 illustrates sample trajectories of the individual beacon mobility

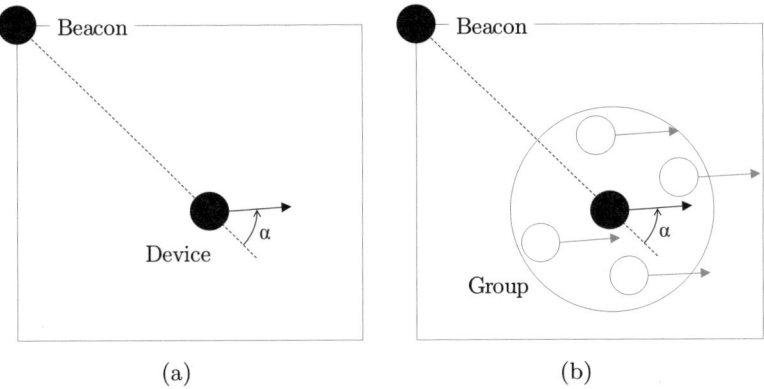

(a)   (b)

Figure 5.2: Illustration of the individual (a) and coupled (b) beacon mobility model.

model and Figure 5.4 of the coupled beacon mobility model for various directions of movements. From these trajectories, it can be observed that the density of devices in the environment is more regular for individual mobility than for the coupled mobility models. Table 5.1 summarizes the mobility models described before.

Table 5.1: Overview of mobility models investigated in this experimental study.

Type	Model	Short description
Individual	RW	Movement according to randomly chosen direction and speed until a fixed distance or time is traveled.
	CM	Similar to RW, but direction and speed are changed in each step.
	RD	Devices move towards randomly chosen target point at the environment's border.
	BR	Similar to CM but speed and directions are varied within a range around preceding values.
	GM	Speed and direction are selected according to Equations 5.1 and 5.2.
	PR	Next movements are defined by a finite state machine with fixed probabilities for state transits.
	Beacon Mobility	Movements with fixed speed and direction with respect to a beacon.

Coupled	ColM	Groups of followers which move approximately in a line behind a leading device.
	NomM	Groups of followers which move according to CM but stay within a leading device's communication range.
	RefM	Devices move around fixed reference points which are assembled like a grid and additionally moved according to CM.
	StrM	Directions of movements are chosen randomly within a range around the last observed directions of the most recently moved neighbor.
	Beacon Mobility	Leading devices and all devices in their communication ranges move with the same fixed speed and direction with respect to a beacon.

5.1.2 Hop Count Error Model

Hop counts relative to a beacon can be assigned to all devices in the network using the GA presented by Nagpal et al. [171]. As detailed in Section 2.4.2, there are various methods to derive distance estimates from hop counts. The basic idea is to multiply the hop count value by the communication range r in order to

165

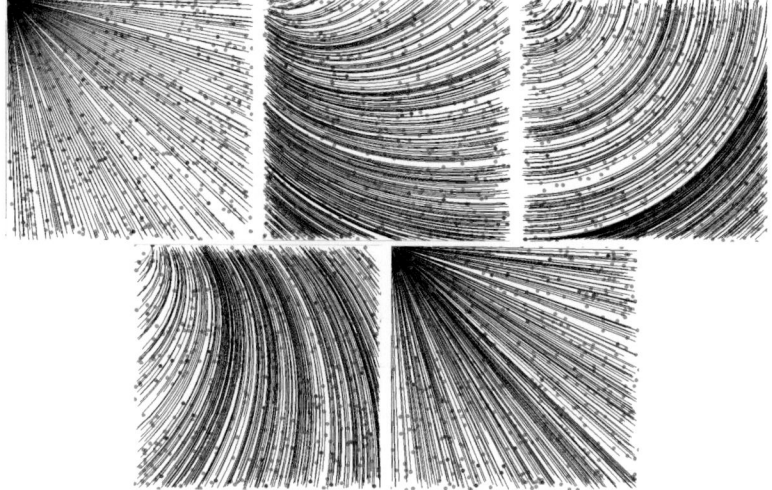

Figure 5.3: Trajectories of devices moved according to the individual beacon mobility model at an angle of $\alpha = 0°$, $45°$, $90°$, $135°$, $180°$ with respect to the beacon (left to right).

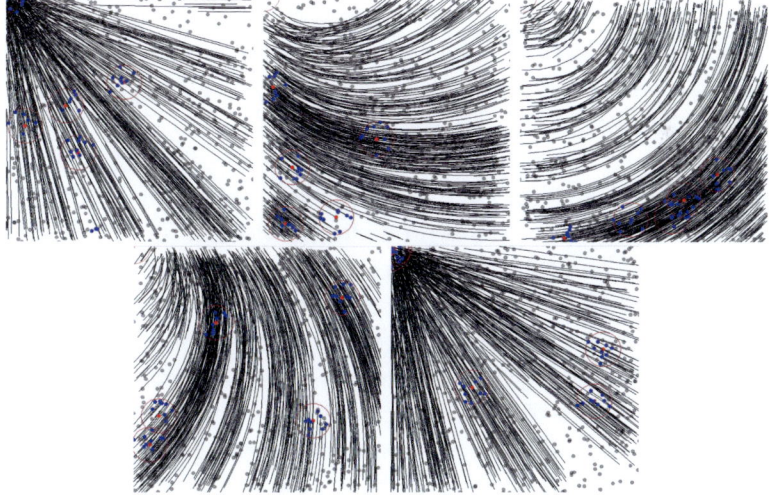

Figure 5.4: Trajectories of devices moved according to the coupled beacon mobility model at an angle of $\alpha = 0°$, $45°$, $90°$, $135°$, $180°$ with respect to the beacon (left to right).

get an estimate for the distance. However, because networks are usually not perfectly dense, this method generally overestimates the distances. As a consequence, refinements are proposed which adjust the estimates to the network density using statistical techniques. Such algorithms include the idea of applying a reduction rate depending on the local network density (cf. Kleinrock and Silvester [122], Wong et al. [249]), integrating information about the hop count distribution in the neighborhood (cf. Liu et al. [140], Nagpal et al. [171]), or computing the average hop length using knowledge about the distances between beacons (cf. Huang and Selvakennedy [102], Niculescu and Nath [176, 177], Savvides et al. [208]). It is notable that the distance estimation error is minimal for all estimation techniques in case the network is perfectly dense. This consideration offers the possibility of evaluating the impact of mobility on hop count based distance estimation independently from the specific estimation method. To achieve such an independent evaluation, the hop count of a device in the actual network is compared to the hop count a device at the same location would have if the network was perfectly dense. In order to do so, the concept of *ideal hop counts* is introduced, which denotes the hop count each device would have in a perfectly dense network.

Definition 5.2 (Ideal Hop Count Value). *Let $h_b^{ideal}(n)$ denote the ideal hop count value of a device n with respect to a beacon b. The ideal hop count corresponds to the smallest integer value which, multiplied by the communication range r, is not smaller than the distance between device n and beacon b. The ideal hop count is computed as shown in Equation 5.3, with $d(n,b)$ representing the Euclidean distance between device n and beacon b.*

$$h_b^{ideal}(n) := \lceil \frac{d(n,b)}{r} \rceil \qquad (5.3)$$

168

Considering a perfectly dense and evenly distributed ad hoc network, each device $n \in N$, with N being the set of all devices in the network, would be assigned a hop count value by the GA which corresponds to its ideal hop count. An area A in which $h_b^{ideal}(n)$ has the same value for all $n \in A$ represents one of the perfect gradient rings shown in Figure 2.17. Such a ring is called a gradient ring g_i, with i being the common value for $h_b^{ideal}(n)$ for all devices $n \in N$ which are located in g_i. The value i also corresponds to the ordinal number of the gradient ring when counting begins at the beacon. As explained, the deviation between the hop count values assigned to devices by the GA and the ideal hop count values is directly related to the quality of any hop count based distance estimation algorithm. Therefore, the *hop count error* is defined as follows.

Definition 5.3 (Hop Count Error). *The hop count error $E_b(n)$ of a device n is defined as the difference between the hop count value which a GA assigns to the device $h_b(n)$ and its ideal hop count ($h_b^{ideal}(n)$) with respect to a beacon b:*

$$E_b(n) = h_b(n) - h_b^{ideal}(n) \tag{5.4}$$

The average hop count error in a gradient ring $g_i(b)$ with respect to a beacon b can be computed as described in Equation 5.5 with $J = \{j \in N \mid \lceil \frac{d(j,b)}{r} \rceil = i\}$ referring to all the devices which are physically located in the gradient ring $g_i(b)$ with respect to the beacon b.

$$E_i(b) = \frac{1}{|J|} \sum_{j \in J} (i - h_b(j)) \tag{5.5}$$

Positive Hop Count Error

A positive hop count error means that $h_b(n)$ is larger than $h_b^{ideal}(n)$, i.e., the GA leads to an overestimation of the hop count. Overestimation occurs, for example due to low density, when the neighbor which is closest to the beacon is not located exactly at the border of a gradient ring (cf. Figure 5.5). Hop count overestimation is additive, since an overestimated hop count can serve as a basis for the hop count determination of subsequent devices. Figure 5.6 illustrates a simple example of a positive hop count error. The beacon is located at the top left corner and each device is labeled with its assigned hop count value $h(n)^1$. The error occurs in the gradient ring g_2 due to the gap in g_1. The device which is physically located in g_2 (marked in red) does not have any neighbor located in g_1 and, thus, its hop count has a value of 3. The hop count error in gradient ring g_2, hence, results in $E_2 = \frac{1}{4}$. A positive hop count error is common in static networks because they rarely are perfectly dense. This usually leads to overestimated distances, which the refinement techniques, described in Section 2.4.2, intend to compensate.

Negative Hop Count Error

In dynamic networks, density varies due to the mobility of the devices. In general, when a device is moved, the density of the network is decreased at its former position and increased at its new location. Consequently, at first sight such a movement does not seem to have any effect on the average hop count error in a network. At a closer look, however, it becomes apparent that movements towards the beacon increase the density in gradient

---

[1]In case of a single beacon in the network, the reference to the beacon is removed from the notations for better readability.

170

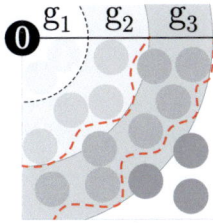 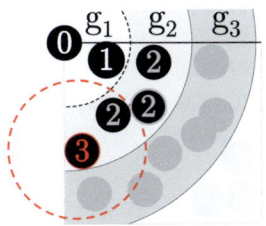

Figure 5.5: Shift of the gradient border towards the beacon due to low density in the network.

Figure 5.6: Illustration of the emergence of positive hop count error due to low density in the network.

rings which are closer to the beacon. Since hop count error is additive, the network's overall hop count error actually can be reduced by mobility. Figure 5.7 shows an example of a decreased hop count error due to density enhancement close to the beacon. This effect can reduce the positive hop count error.

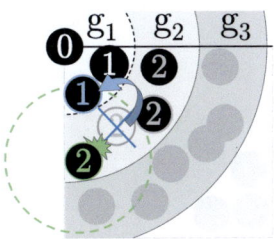

Figure 5.7: Illustration of hop count error correction due to mobility in the network.

171

Movements leading away from the beacon have the opposite effect. However, this is not the only effect they have. In MANETs, computations are usually assumed to be made asynchronously because the devices do not necessarily have synchronized system clocks. This fact, together with the assumption that the device does not know whether it is moved, can lead to a scenario where mobility is accompanied by a negative hop count error. When a device is moved to a gradient ring with a higher ordinal number, i.e., away from the beacon, it is possible that the device's new neighbors wrongfully adapt their hop count values according to the newly arrived device's hop count before that device itself updates its hop count. Since the newcomer has a lower hop count value, which serves as a basis for hop count computations of its new neighbors, the new neighbors are likely to underestimate their hop count and a negative hop count error can occur. Additionally, the negative error is additive to subsequent devices, similar to the positive hop count error. Figure 5.8 illustrates the emergence of a negative hop count error in gradient ring g_3 with $E_3 = -\frac{2}{5}$.

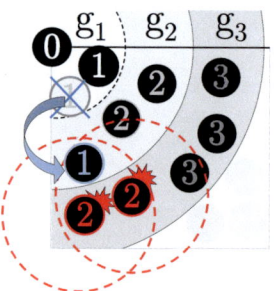

Figure 5.8: Illustration of the emergence of a negative hop count error due to mobility in the network.

Assessment of Hop Count Errors

In general, overestimation and underestimation of distances are undesired for localization algorithms, which is why, ideally, one should simply let both effects (density and mobility) compensate each other. But passive mobility cannot be controlled by the devices and, thus, the height of the negative error is not amenable to influence. As a consequence, natural overestimation of distances can turn into an unpredictably high underestimation and a balancing effect between mobility and density induced errors cannot be guaranteed. Furthermore, the density-induced overestimation can be counteracted with the statistical techniques for dealing with density-induced overestimation, described in Section 2.4.2, which are not valid anymore in dynamic networks. Due to its unpredictable character, mobility-induced underestimation is the more aggravating type of estimation error and should, therefore, be eliminated. In order to tackle this problem, a device has to be able to recognize whether and how it is moved. It has to be able to analyze the effect which the movement has on its hop count value and to be able to eliminate this effect by an appropriate adjustment of its hop count value. Since with passive mobility devices do not know whether they are moved, this objective is quite challenging.

Approaches to Reduce Hop Count Error in Dynamic Networks

To avoid the emergence of negative hop count errors, a modified version of the GA is proposed. The underlying assumption is that when a device moves towards a new neighborhood, it is more likely that, both, the minimum and the maximum hop count values in its neighborhood change. In contrast, a device which has not moved but detects a change in its neighbors' hop count values due to a newly arriving device, is likely to find either a new maximum or

173

a new minimum hop count value instead of both. As a result, it could be achievable to avoid that devices adapt their hop counts to newly arrived devices in their neighborhood which have not yet updated their hop counts and, thus, avoiding the emergence of negative hop count error.

Definition 5.4 (Maximum-oriented Gradient Algorithm). *The Maximum-oriented Gradient Algorithm (MoGA) is defined as an algorithm which is equal to the GA with the additional condition that a device updates its hop count only when the maximum hop count in its neighborhood has changed as well as the minimum hop count value.*

A second proposal to tackle the problem is that each device recognizes mobility and its characteristics by observing and analyzing certain changes in its neighborhood. Based on this analysis, the device subsequently makes reasonable adjustments to its hop count value. Since communication overhead is always an issue in mobile ad hoc networks, it is reasonable to aim at deriving information about movements from messages which are exchanged in the GA instead of defining additional messages required. In order to do so, two indicators *ID-change* and *HC-change* are proposed, which describe changes in a device's environment, i.e. its communication neighborhood, during certain time intervals.

Definition 5.5 (ID-change). *ID-change is defined as the percentage of changed IDs in a device's neighborhood in the time interval [t-1, t], with ID_t denoting the set of IDs in the device's neighborhood at time t:*

$$ID\text{-}change_t = \frac{|ID_t \setminus ID_{t-1}| + |ID_{t-1} \setminus ID_t|}{|ID_{t-1} \cup ID_t|} \qquad (5.6)$$

Definition 5.6 (HC-change). *HC-change is defined as the percentage change of the average hop count in a device's neighborhood in the time interval [t-1, t], with $\overline{HC}_t$ denoting the average hop count in the device's neighborhood at time t:*

$$HC\text{-}change_t = \frac{\overline{HC}_t - \overline{HC}_{t-1}}{\overline{HC}_{t-1}} \qquad (5.7)$$

Ideally, these change-indicators have conclusiveness about mobility characteristics in a device's neighborhood. In order to verify, whether this expectation is met, both indicators are examined in an experimental study in Section 5.1.3.

5.1.3 Evaluation

In order to quantify the impact of various passive mobility models on the average hop count error in a network and to evaluate the proposed containment techniques, a simulative model is used. In the first set of experiments, the impact of various mobility models on the hop count error is investigated. The second set of experiments evaluates the effectiveness of MoGA to avoid negative hop count errors and the ability of the two indicators ID-change and HC-change to capture mobility and its characteristics.

Experiment Settings

The ad hoc network model contains 1000 mobile devices, which are distributed according to a uniform random distribution on a two-dimensional, barrier-free plane. The communication neighborhood of a device corresponds to its physical neighborhood on the plane within a fixed Euclidean distance r. The communication range r is assumed to be equal for all devices and its default value is set to 7% of the square plane's side-length. This value corresponds to an

175

average neighborhood size of 14 devices, which is close to the critical minimum size identified by Nagpal et al. [171] needed to achieve good localization results. A static beacon, which initiates the GA, is located at the top-left corner of the environment (cf. Figure 2.17). With this setting, there are 21 gradient rings ($\lceil \sqrt{2}/0.07 \rceil = 21$). A simulation cycle is defined as $n = 1000$ randomly selected devices sequentially computing their hop counts. The hop counts are determined on the basis of available information from neighbors at the time of computation. This setting imitates the asynchronous environment in ad hoc networks. After computation of its hop count, the device is moved according to the mobility model examined. Collisions between devices, as well as communication deficiencies, such as interferences, shadowing, fading, or multipath effects, are not being considered. All experiments are repeated 50 times with different randomly chosen uniform distributions of the devices across the environment and the results are averaged for each gradient ring separately. Devices which are not able to compute a hop count because they are disconnected from the network are not taken into account. Since, due to the nature of the scenario, each of the gradient rings contains a different number of devices, only the middle hops (10-15) are considered because they contain a relatively high and similar number of devices. The simulation environment is a torus world, meaning that devices can leave the environment and enter again at the opposite side. When a device leaves the environment, its hop count is set to *unknown*, simulating a new device entering the environment on the other side. The speed range for each move is selected randomly between 3.4% and 3.6% of the plane's side-length traveled per cycle. This way, a device requires at least two cycles to leave its own communication range. For RW, the maximum moving distance is selected as 60%. In RD a move is paused for 10 cycles. For GM, α is set to 75% of the plane's side-length and an average angle of 0 degree measured from the x-Axis of the environment (bottom border) is selected. Angle tolerance for BR and StrM is set to 30 degrees, ColM and NomM are initialized with 10 leaders and 10 followers per leading device.

Average Hop Count Error for Various Mobility Models

In the first set of experiments, the error is calculated for 100 cycles starting with cycle 30, which is the minimum time required to elapse until hop count values are stable in a static network. A device is moved with a probability of $p_m = 0.5$ after each hop count update. At first, the hop count errors are calculated for a static network. The results are shown in table 5.2. Only positive hop count error values are obtained. These error values intensify as the index of the gradient ring increases, demonstrating the additive nature of the positive hop count error, which grows larger with increasing distance from the beacon.

Table 5.2: Error E_i for distance estimation based on hop counts in gradient rings g_1 to g_{10} in a static ad hoc network.

g_i	g_1	g_2	g_3	g_4	g_5	g_6	g_7	g_8	g_9	g_{10}
E_i	0.0	0.4	0.6	0.9	1.1	1.4	1.7	1.8	2.1	2.3
g_{11}	g_{12}	g_{13}	g_{14}	g_{15}	g_{16}	g_{17}	g_{18}	g_{19}	g_{20}	g_{21}
2.5	2.8	3.0	3.2	3.3	3.5	3.7	3.8	4.0	4.1	3.6

Figure 5.9 displays the average error for gradient rings from g_{10} to g_{15} when individual mobility models are applied. All individual mobility models overcome the positive error of a static network. PR shows a noticeably higher underestimation than the other mobility models. This can be explained by the nature of this model

as all devices are moved almost into the same direction leading away from the beacon. As an underestimation can only occur when movements are directed away from the beacon, the negative error induced by this mobility model is higher when compared to the other models. BR, GM, CM, RD, and RW show very similar tendencies in terms of error values. RD exhibits a slightly more positive behavior, which can be explained by the reduced mobility due to the pauses of devices. So far, underestimation does not become dominant for all individual mobility models under the selected settings, unless the movements are mainly directed away from the beacon.

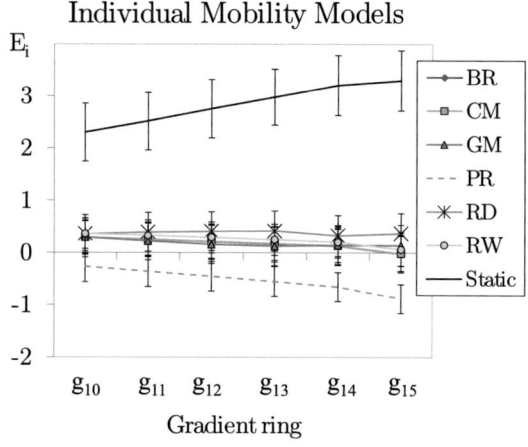

Figure 5.9: Hop count error with various individual mobility models.

Figure 5.10 shows the hop count error values for group mobility models. For StrM, as well as for NomM, the underestimation is less pronounced when compared to other coupled mobility models. One reason for this could be that similar movements in neighborhoods

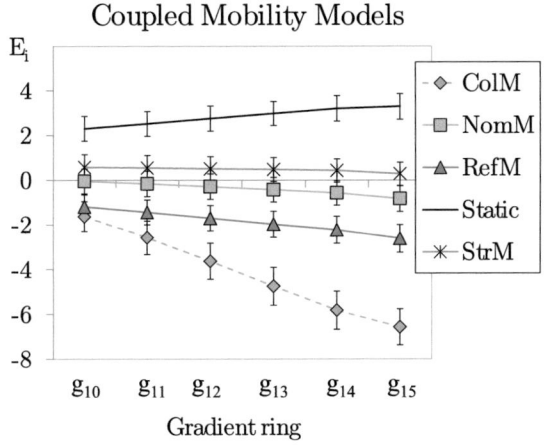

Figure 5.10: Hop count error with various coupled mobility models.

have a moderating effect on the mobility induced underestimation since both models generate different groups of devices, which move together through the network. As already shown for PR, another important factor for the development of negative hop count error is the direction of a move relative to the beacon. Both mobility models, StrM and NomM, cause random movements while ColM leads to movements in a more constant direction which are accompanied by higher negative error values. Apart from ColM, RefM also shows high negative error. This can be explained by the additional movement of the dynamic reference-point network supplementary to the individual movements of each device, which causes devices to move further in one time step when compared to other mobility models. This indicates that speed, i.e. distance traveled per unit time, is another influencing factor for the level of negative hop count error that arises with mobility. The experiment further confirms that mobility in the network can turn the inherent overestimation of hop counts in a static network into underestimation. Furthermore, the impact of mobility on the estimation error is strongly dependent on the characteristics of the specific mobility model. So far, the experiments indicate that there are three main characteristics of mobility which influence the hop count error:

- Direction of movements with respect to the beacon

- Speed of movements in terms of traveled distance between hop count updates

- Similarity of movements in a neighborhood

In order to be able to investigate these factors independently, the beacon mobility model is applied to 50 random devices in the network. For the coupled mobility model, 5 leaders are selected with 10 followers each. Figure 5.11 shows the average error in the gradient rings g_{10} to g_{15} for the individual beacon mobility model with varying values for angle α and speed. It is observable that both direction and speed are indeed relevant factors for the mobility induced hop count underestimation. Additionally, the results show that both parameters are interrelated and vary in the intensity of their impact. While speed is negatively correlated with the error value for an angle between 0 and 90 degrees as well as between 270 and 360 degrees, it has almost no impact when devices move at an angle between 135 and 225 degrees. In fact, movements towards the beacon hardly influence the hop count error at all and the hop count distribution in the network is almost the same as in a static network. Similar results can be observed for coupled mobility models as shown in Figure 5.12. A considerable difference between coupled and individual mobility models can be observed

around an angle of 180 degrees, where errors seem to decrease for
coupled movements when compared with individual movements.
This can be explained by the simultaneous increase in density close
to the beacon as described before. The reason why this effect does
not occur for individual movements is that the density does not
increase significantly at a specific point in time, i.e., the additive
effect is minor.

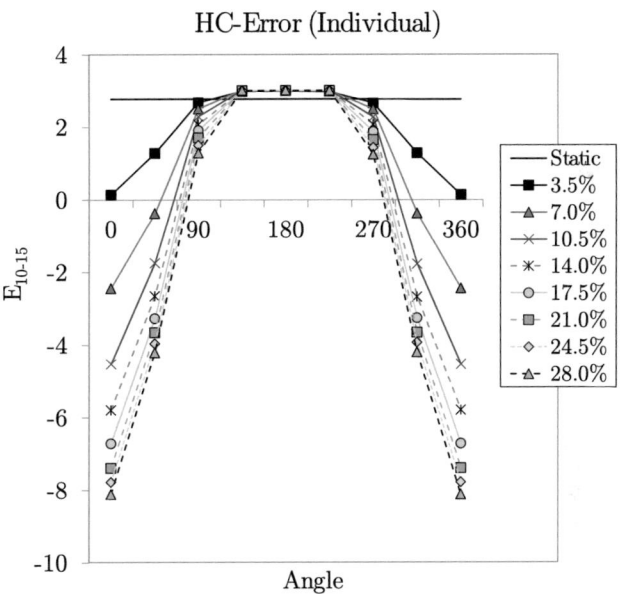

Figure 5.11: Hop count errors for individual mobility models with
different movement speeds and angles with respect to
the beacon.

Subsequently, the individual and coupled mobility models are compared for angles between 0 and 180 degrees only, due to symmetries
of error values. Figure 5.13 illustrates the hop count error averaged

181

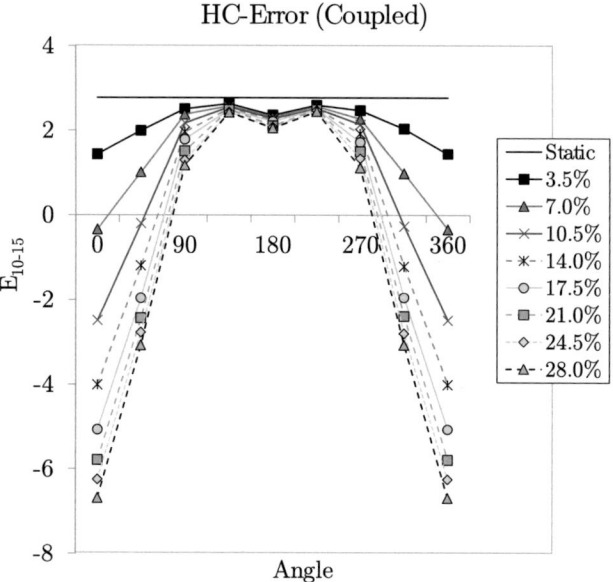

Figure 5.12: Hop count errors for coupled mobility models with different movement speeds and angles with respect to the beacon.

over experiments with different angles and Figure 5.14 averaged over experiments with different speeds respectively. In both experiments, with individual and coupled beacon mobility, the same total number of devices is moving in the same direction with the same speed respectively. The only difference is that in experiments with coupled beacon mobility, devices move in clusters. The results show that with coupled mobility, the negative hop count error is lower when compared to individual mobility models. This confirms the previously made observation that similar movements in a neighborhood mitigate the effect mobility has on the hop count error. For coupled mobility models and directions between 0 and 90 degrees, the effect of simultaneous density increase near the beacon becomes visible once more. The reason for the high dispersion of values lies in the fact that experiments with varying speeds and angles, respectively, are averaged.

Eliminating Mobility Induced Underestimation

While the previous section examines the influence of mobility on hop count estimation, this section investigates different solutions proposed for dealing with the problem of mobility induced underestimation. At first, the effectiveness of MoGA is being tested in the same experimental setup as described previously. Results are shown in Figures 5.15 and 5.16. A decrease in mobility induced underestimation when compared to GA can be identified in all examined cases. Nevertheless, negative error is not successfully eliminated and the reduction is almost constant relative to the error level. It can be concluded that MoGA has a mitigating effect on the negative error but does not solve the problem entirely.

In the next experiment, ID-change and HC-change (cf. Equations 5.6 and 5.7) are examined. These indicators' ability to recognize whether the device itself is moving or whether changing hop count

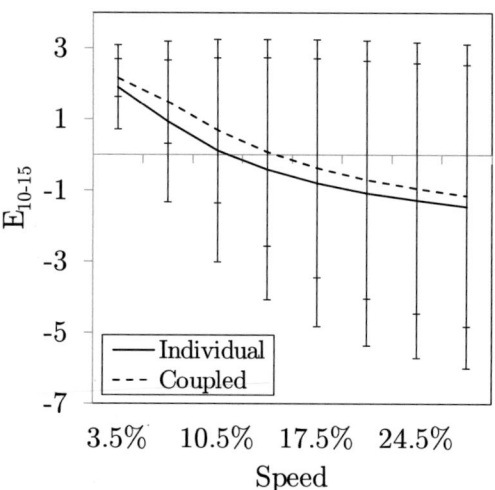

Figure 5.13: Hop count errors for individual and coupled beacon mobility models with different movement speeds.

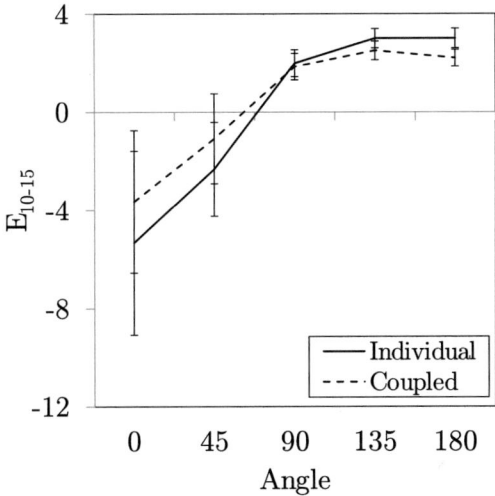

Figure 5.14: Hop count errors for individual and coupled beacon mobility models with different movement angles with respect to the beacon.

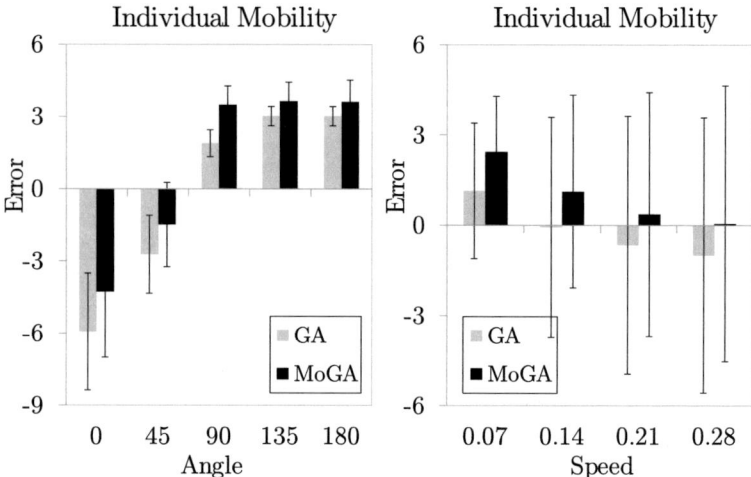

Figure 5.15: Hop count errors with and without the MoGA applied to networks with individual beacon mobility models.

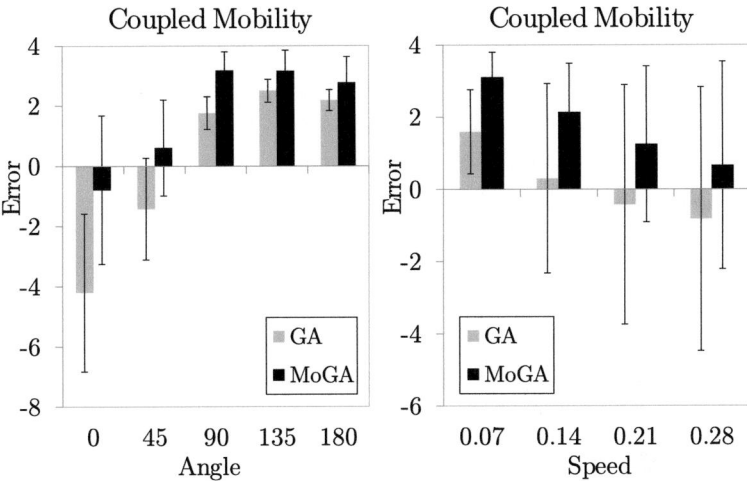

Figure 5.16: Hop count errors with and without the MoGA applied to networks with coupled beacon mobility models.

values are originated in movements of neighbors is subject to investigation. Also, it is desirable to characterize mobility and its impact on the hop count error values. If this can be achieved, it could be achievable to find an appropriate adaptation of the hop count values in order to reduce negative hop count errors in dynamic networks. Figure 5.17 shows the average values for both metrics for static and dynamic devices separately and averaged over all considered speed and angle values. It becomes apparent that ID-change is a strong indicator for whether a device has been moved or not. Although HC-change does not seem to be a good indicator to detect mobility, it is useful for its characterization. When considering Figure 5.18, where the average HC-change values are depicted for different angles and speeds, it becomes apparent that HC-change values display a similar pattern as the error values depicted in Figure 5.11. This suggests that there is a distinctive relationship between mobility parameters, such as speed and direction of movements, and HC-change values. Furthermore, it indicates that by applying an appropriate mapping method, HC-change can be used to characterize these parameters and to adapt the hop count values accordingly in order to avoid underestimation.

5.1.4 Conclusion

This section investigates the impact of mobility on hop count based distance estimation. In order to do so, a hop count error model is introduced, which is capable of assessing the deviation of hop counts from an ideal hop count distribution. This avoids examining the different hop count based distance estimation algorithms individually and facilitates the evaluation of mobility induced effects on hop count based distance estimation algorithms in general. A thorough experimental study is performed, in which hop count

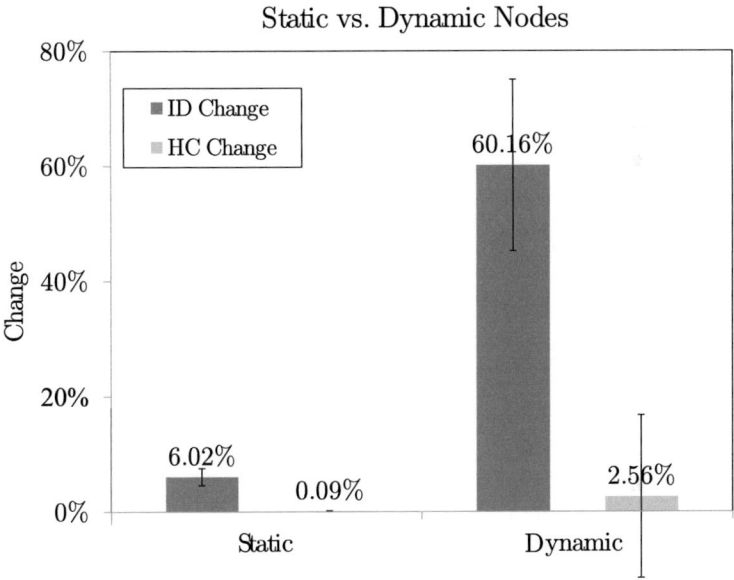

Figure 5.17: ID-change (5.17) for static and dynamic devices using the individual beacon mobility model.

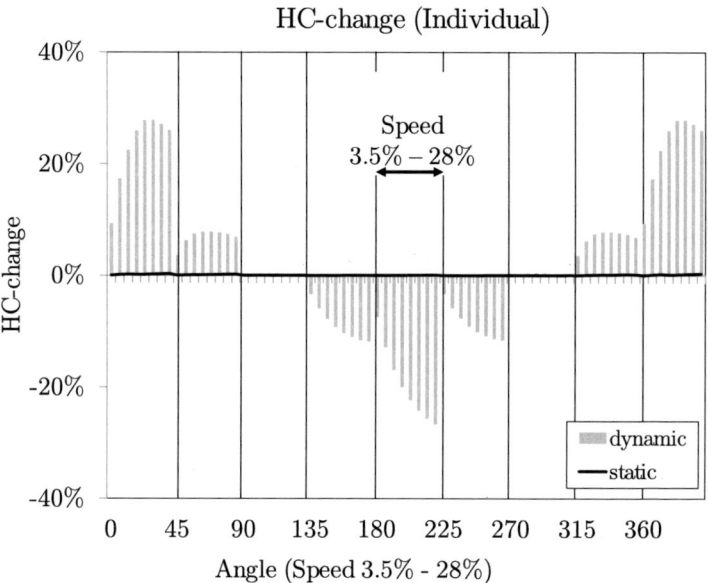

Figure 5.18: HC-change (5.18) for the individual beacon mobility model (the speed of the movement is increased from 3.5% until 28% for each angle).

errors are determined for networks where devices move according to different mobility models. The mobility models include some models proposed in the literature, as well as a set of mobility models designed specifically for this study.

From the experiments performed, it is revealed that mobility has the effect to turn a natural overestimation of hop counts and, thus, distances into an unpredictably high underestimation. Experiments indicate that mobility of a certain speed and direction with respect to beacons can compensate naturally positive hop count errors in a network. Nevertheless, for situations in which mobility in a network cannot be controlled, the overcompensation can negatively affect the accuracy of distance estimates. Furthermore, traditional heuristics to mitigate natural overestimation are not applicable to dynamic networks without further ado. Hence, it is concluded that the negative impact of mobility has to be contained. First experimental results with various mobility patterns suggest that direction, speed, and similarity of movements in neighboring regions not only affect the hop count error in different ways, but also display significant interdependencies, making their impact hard to predict. Each impact factor is investigated separately in further experiments and an increase in speed as well as movements leading away from beacon nodes are found to increase the negative hop count error, while movements directed towards beacons and a similarity of movements between nearby devices are found to have a positive impact on the hop count error.

Additionally, the concept of MoGA, an adapted version of the standard GA, is introduced and its performance is evaluated in an experimental study. The study shows that MoGA reduces negative hop count errors in dynamic networks. MoGA is demonstrated to reduce negative hop count error but does not eliminate it entirely. Moreover, the reduction is constant relative to the error level, such that a change in speed or direction still leads to a difference in hop count error values. Two indicators are proposed, which are able to assess characteristics of mobility in a network. Both indicators can be computed in a decentralized way using only information which is available locally from the messages exchanged in order to determine hop counts. These mobility indicators are shown to be able to help discovering and characterizing mobility in a network. Hence, they could be used in order to improve distance estimates by adapting hop counts accordingly. Such an adaptation could, for example, be implemented using learning mechanisms of the O/C Architecture in order to derive a mapping between these indicator values and the resulting hop count error in a network by training over time. This further emphasizes the need to integrate learning mechanisms in the localization process for MANETs.

5.2 Synchronized Hop Counting in Mobile Ad Hoc Networks

The previous section revealed that the accuracy of hop count based distance estimation and, hence, the accuracy of distance-based localization is influenced by passive mobility in the network such that underestimation of distances can occur. As discussed in Section 5.1.2, a negative hop count error is more aggravating than a positive error for the following two reasons: Firstly, it is hard to predict to what extent mobility causes a negative error, which makes it difficult to counteract it, for example by adjusting the hop count value. Secondly, most refinement techniques proposed in the literature deal with eliminating the positive hop count error due to low density and are not applicable to a network with mobility induced underestimation without further ado. As a result, a negative hop count error is undesired and should be eliminated if possible.

In the previous section, asynchronous computation of hop counts is identified to be the main reason for the occurrence of a negative hop count error. The logical consequence of this finding is to investigate whether a MANET can be synchronized and if this reduces negative hop count errors. These questions are addressed in the following. Furthermore, a procedure is introduced in order to encode hop count information in the timing at which a signal is sent instead of transmitting it as content of a message. This method assumes that the network is synchronized and that the mobile devices are able to send signals at any time. The proposed algorithm allows for the performance of distance estimation on devices which have only basic communication abilities. Additionally, the resource consumption while determining hop counts in MANETs can be reduced significantly.

Since MANETs lack a CCU, a decentralized synchronization technique has to be applied. As discussed in Section 2.2.3, nature is a good source of inspiration when looking for algorithms which can be applied to a distributed network without central control. For the task of synchronization, a natural role model can be found as well. In Southeast Asia, fireflies provide an impressive natural spectacle. Fireflies are also called "lightning bugs" due to their usage of bioluminescence. At dusk, thousands of these insects gather in trees and emit light-flashes to attract mates or prey, reaching almost perfect synchrony after some time (cf. Buck [28]). This phenomenon gives name to a class of algorithms called "firefly-algorithms", which can model the emergence of synchrony in distributed systems. Charles S. Peskin was the first person to mathematically describe this phenomenon of pulse-coupled oscillators in [181]. In his model, each oscillator emits a signal at the end of a fixed time period. This process is referred to as firing. When another oscillator observes such a firing signal, it reduces the remaining time until its next own firing. Figure 5.19 illustrates this mechanism. The gray and the black dots are two oscillators and the circle represents the fixed time period between the firings. The time period is equal for both oscillators but before synchronization, they start at different points in this time period. As time passes, the oscillators move along the circle and whenever they reach the point at the top of the circle, marked with a small line, they fire. Such firing causes the other oscillator to advance its phase by a certain value which is dependent on its current phase value. After two firings of the black oscillator and one firing of the gray oscillator, both oscillators are synchronized. Other examples of synchronization processes in nature following the same principle are heart pace-maker cells (cf. Peskin [181], Torre [231]), crickets chirping in synchrony (cf. Walker [240]), organized bursting in pancreatic beta-cells (cf. Sherman et al. [216]), and even female menstrual cycles, which tend to synchronize (cf. McClintock [148], Russell et al. [200]).

To transfer this concept to technical devices, it has to be noted that a device's system clock is usually equipped with an oscillator (cf. Sivrikaya and Yener [217]). This oscillator determines the clock's frequency by creating almost harmonic oscillations with period T. The state of an oscillator is described by its phase φ. When the phase is normalized between 0 and 1, it denotes the elapsed percentage of the oscillator's period and can, thus, be expressed in terms of time t (cf. Figure 5.20). Oscillators are said to be identical if their periods T have the same length. When, additionally, both periods start at the same time, i.e., their phase φ is identical for any point in time, the oscillators are called synchronous.

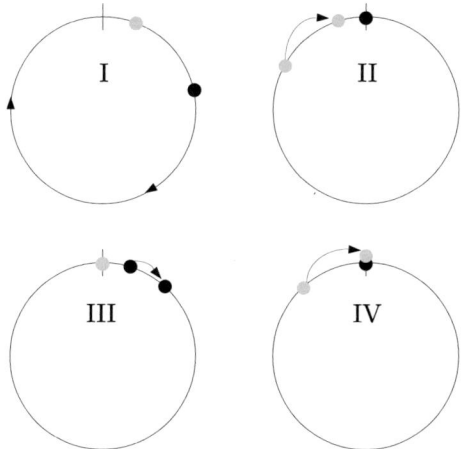

Figure 5.19: Illustration of the synchronization of two oscillators depicted as black and gray dots. The circle represents the time between two firings (point at the top of the circle). As time passes, the oscillators move along the circle and the firing of one oscillator reduces the time remaining until the firing of the other oscillator as a function of its current phase value (indicated by arrows). Both oscillators are synchronized after three firings.

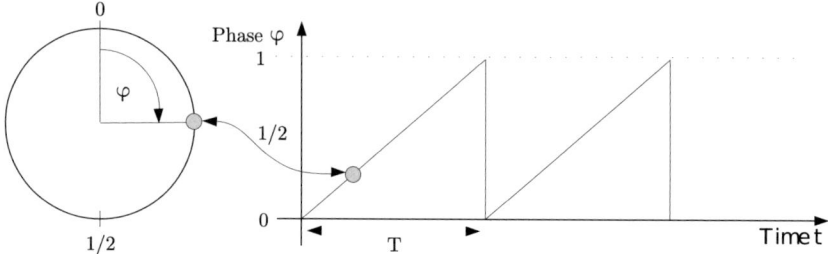

Figure 5.20: Relation between a normalized phase φ of an oscillator and time t.

5.2.1 Pulse-coupled Oscillators

Firefly-algorithms can be used to synchronize clocks and have already been used successfully in MANETs to implement energy-efficient communication mechanisms by Taniguchi et al. [229], Wakamiya et al. [239], and Wakamiya and Murata [238]. The basic algorithmic model for firefly-inspired synchronization was defined by Mirollo and Strogatz [161], in which each oscillator is described by a state variable $x \in [0,1]$. The phase of an oscillator is mapped to the oscillator's state by a function $f : \varphi \to x$, which is required to be increasing and strictly concave. The mapping from phase to state is introduced in order to be able to describe the sensitivity of the phase adjustment as a function of the oscillator's phase at the time of an observed firing. This function is further on referred to as *state-function*. When the state x reaches the value 1, the oscillator fires and x is reset to 0. In the work of Mirollo and Strogatz [161], the state-function is defined as:

$$x(i) = 1 \Rightarrow x(j) \leftarrow \min(1, x(j) + \epsilon), \forall j \neq i \qquad (5.8)$$

When an oscillator i fires, all other oscillators increase their state by the value of ϵ, which is denoted as impulse intensity, until they reach a maximum value of 1 (cf. Equation 5.8). The corresponding phase-shift is determined by the state-function. With this simple rule, any two oscillators can be synchronized and for $n > 2$ oscillators, there are few combinations of initial phase values which do not result in synchrony if the impulse intensity is non-negative and non-zero for all oscillators (cf. Mirollo and Strogatz [161]). In the work of Mathar and Mattfeldt [147], convergence is also shown for a state-function f which is non-differentiable. Further, the concavity of the state-function is abandoned and a linear state-function is shown to be sufficient for nearly all systems to converge if multiple synchronous firings are accounted for by an increased impulse intensity ϵ and $\epsilon \geq 1/n$ holds (cf. Bottani [21]). Lucarelli and Wang [144] demonstrate that neighborhood-coupling, where only firing of neighbors induces a phase shift of the device, is enough for the convergence of a system. For this, they use a linear state-function $f(\varphi) = \varphi$ and a new update model where the state advancement is sensitive to the current state of the affected device by assigning a higher weight to flashes received when the device itself is close to firing:

$$x(i) = 1 \Rightarrow x(j) \leftarrow \min(1, x(j) + \epsilon \cdot x(j)), \forall j \neq i \qquad (5.9)$$

Due to the characteristics of the state-function f, state x and phase φ are the same and Equation 5.9 can also be written as:

$$\varphi(i) = 1 \Rightarrow \varphi(j) \leftarrow \min(1, \varphi(j) + \epsilon \cdot \varphi(j)), \forall j \neq i \qquad (5.10)$$

With this setting, it has been shown experimentally that synchronization can also be achieved in dynamic networks even if connectivity is temporarily lost. In publications of Tyrrell et al. [233] and Werner-Allen et al. [247], delays in firing perception are examined and two algorithms are proposed which can provide synchronization under these circumstances. Although message delays are an issue in MANETs, the following study is based on the algorithm published by Lucarelli and Wang [144] as a simple synchronization algorithm is sufficient to investigate the effect which synchronization has on distance estimates.

5.2.2 Firefly-inspired Hop Counting

In distributed computing systems, message exchange is a time and resource consuming process, which decreases the lifetime of the devices involved (cf. Akyildiz et al. [4], Dietrich and Dressler [52]). Since hop counting is an essential technique for both, routing (cf. Boukerche et al. [22], Chatterjee and Das [38], Chou et al. [42]) and distance estimation (cf. Section 2.4.2), it is desirable to reduce the number and length of messages exchanged. *Firefly-inspired Hop Counting (FIHC)* is an approach to encode hop count information in the timing of a binary signal which has only two states, on and off, instead of exchanging messages with the hop count value as it is done in GA (cf. Section 2.4.2). In addition to the resource saving potential, this approach enables devices which only possess simple communication capabilities to determine hop counts, which could be useful in scenarios where devices are only equipped with rudimentary hardware, such as in *smart dust* applications (cf. Ilyas and Mahgoub [105]).

FIHC requires the network to be synchronous. For FIHC, the devices are assumed to have identical oscillators, i.e., the period of their timers is equal. This assumption is reasonable, since ad hoc networks are often described as containing only identical devices.

As detailed before, the firefly-algorithm described by Lucarelli and Wang [144] can be used for synchronization of such a network. For FIHC, a second signal is used, which is sent by the device with a specific delay to a synchronized signal in order communicate the device's encoded hop count information. When the network is synchronized, the delay of the second signal with respect to the synchronized signal represents the hop count of the device. Hence, all devices with the same hop count emit this signal at the same time, devices with a lower hop count emit the signal beforehand and devices with higher hop counts emit the signal afterwards. Further on, the signal used for synchronization is called *sync-signal* and the delayed signal used to encode hop count information is called *HC-signal*. In order to be able to use the timing of a signal to transport information, a method for encoding and decoding has to be provided.

Encoding

A device i with a hop count value of $h(i)$ sends its *HC-signal*, when the phase of the *sync-signal* has the value

$$\varphi_{sync} = \frac{h(i)}{h(i)+1}. \tag{5.11}$$

For example, a device which is two hops away from the beacon emits its *HC-signal* when the phase of its *sync-signal* has the value of $\frac{2}{2+1} = \frac{2}{3}$. Devices with different hop counts are required to emit their *HC-signal* at different times, which holds for this encoding. Let $h(i) \geq 0, h(j) \geq 0$ be the hop counts of device i and j, and $h(i) \neq h(j)$. It then holds that:

$$h(i) \neq h(j)$$
$$\Rightarrow h(i) + (h(i) \cdot h(j)) \neq h(j) + (h(i) \cdot h(j))$$
$$\Rightarrow h(i) \cdot (1 + h(j)) \neq h(j) \cdot (1 + h(i))$$
$$\Rightarrow \frac{h(i)}{h(i) + 1} \neq \frac{h(j)}{h(j) + 1}$$

Decoding

For decoding, the following equation is used. Let $0 \leq \varphi_{sync} < 1$ be the value of the common *sync-signal's* phase when device j receives the first *HC-signal* from its neighbor i. From this information, device j can compute its own hop count as:

$$h(j) = \frac{\varphi_{sync}}{1 - \varphi_{sync}} + 1 \tag{5.12}$$

Because of $\varphi_{sync} = \frac{h(i)}{h(i)+1}$, it holds that:

$$h(j) \Leftrightarrow \frac{\varphi_{sync}}{1 - \varphi_{sync}} + 1 \Leftrightarrow \frac{\frac{h(i)}{h(i)+1}}{1 - \frac{h(i)}{h(i)+1}} + 1 \Leftrightarrow h(i) + 1$$

Figure 5.21 shows an example of four devices determining their hop counts, assuming that they are already synchronized. The beacon starts by sending an *HC-signal* when the *sync-signal* phase has the value $\varphi_{sync} = 0$. When the next device receives this signal its *sync-signal* phase is also at a value of 0 (since they are synchronous) and the device, therefore, has a hop count value of 1 and emits its *HC-signal* at sync-phase $\varphi_{sync} = \frac{1}{2}$. The next device calculates its own hop count to have a value of 2 and emits its signal at

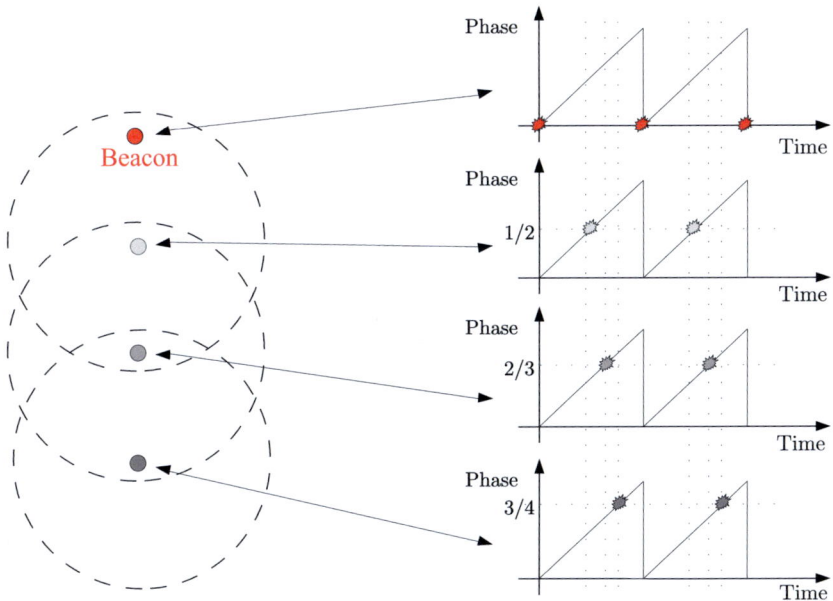

Figure 5.21: Example of the FIHC over three hops via intentional phase shifting of a signal with respect to a synchronized reference signal.

$\varphi_{sync} = \frac{2}{3}$. Analogously, the fourth device will send its *HC-signal* at sync-phase value $\varphi_{sync} = \frac{3}{4}$.

One benefit of using timed signals to encode hop counts is that the order in which the signals are sent corresponds to the ascending order of hop counts. Assuming that there is no delay or message-loss, each device can determine its hop count value within one period. The asynchronous exchange of messages in the GA, on the other hand, can take many periods (depending on the network size) until all devices in the network have determined their hop counts. Additionally, each device knows its hop count immediately after the first reception of an *HC-signal* from its neighbors and can ignore all other signals for the rest of the period. During this time, listening to signals is no longer required and energy can be saved. In contrast, the GA requires all devices to be permanently receptive to new messages sent by neighbors. The FIHC algorithm can be designed in two variants, FIHC or Firefly-inspired Hop Counting with Delay (FIHCd). With FIHC each device emits an *HC-signal* when the phase of its timer corresponds to the device's encoded hop count. The firing is conducted whether or not the device has already received a signal from a neighbor in its current period. In case it receives a signal after its own firing, the hop count is adapted and the device fires again. With FIHCd, a device only fires after having received a signal from another device, except for the beacon, which always fires at phase 0. In the delayed version, the firing frequency is limited to one *HC-signal* per device per period, which reduces the communication overhead even further.

5.2.3 Evaluation

The first set of experiments investigates the synchronization success and duration using the model proposed by Lucarelli and Wang [144] in a neighborhood-coupling setting. In a second set of experiments the distance estimates in a synchronized network using FIHC are compared to results using the asynchronous, message-based GA.

Scenario and Settings

The experiment setting is the same as described in Section 5.2.3, except for the placement of the static beacon, which is now placed in the center of the environment. 1000 devices are randomly placed in the environment and the impulse intensity ϵ is tested for values $\epsilon = 0.05, 0.10$, and 0.15. The communication range r is varied from 5% to 20%. One simulation cycle is equivalent to the period T, which is divided into 100 time slots. Devices listen to signals and messages during the whole period and for the GA they send their hop count messages at the end of their timers' periods. Figure 5.22 shows the simulated scenario. Non-beacons in the network move according to the CM mobility model described in Section 5.1.1, where each device moves with a probability of $p_m = 0.01$ in each time slot. Movements which would lead outside of the plane are not executed.

Synchronization Success

In this section, the effectiveness of the synchronization algorithm is investigated in terms of its ability to successfully synchronize the entire network. For this purpose, an experiment is classified as unsuccessful if complete network synchrony is not achieved within 300 cycles. Each experiment is repeated 40 times and the results are averaged.

Figure 5.23(a) and 5.23(b) show the percentage of successfully synchronized experiments for static and dynamic networks respec-

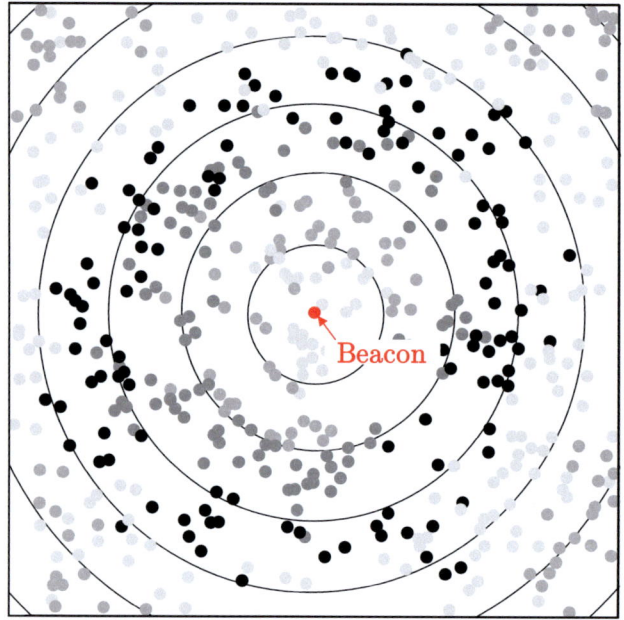

Figure 5.22: Network model for the simulative experimental study. The beacon is placed in the center of the square environment. Devices with the same color have the same hop count value.

tively. Figure 5.24 displays the time elapsed until the networks are in synchrony for both, static and dynamic networks.

It is noticeable that the impulse intensity has a strong impact on the synchronization success in both cases. For a value of $\epsilon = 0.1$, the highest success rates are achieved with up to 100% for communication ranges larger than 9% in static networks and 16% in dynamic networks. The experiments indicate that the performance decrease for $\epsilon = 0.15$ when compared to $\epsilon = 0.1$ could be caused by an increase in synchronization time. This is not the case for $\epsilon = 0.05$, however. In addition, synchronization time has a high dispersion for $\epsilon = 0.15$, which confirms that this impulse intensity is not suitable to synchronize the regarded network. It seems that $\epsilon = 0.1$ is the best choice in both scenarios because it guarantees a high success rate and simultaneously low synchronization time, which is why this setting is used for the experiments investigating FIHC. An increase in the communication range r improves the time until successful synchronization for all impulse intensities considered. Mobility in the network makes the synchronization less likely. Nevertheless, with the right choice for impulse intensity and a sufficiently large communication range the network can be synchronized.

When comparing the results of static and dynamic networks, it becomes apparent that the percentage of successfully synchronized experiments in dynamic networks is lower than in static networks when considering smaller communication ranges. The explanation for this is straight-forward. Synchronization is achieved by mutual influences between neighbors. In dynamic networks, devices sometimes move before this process is finished and then engage in a synchronization process which is possibly at a different state as the previous one. This can have the effect that the signal of the moved device interferes with this new synchronization process and

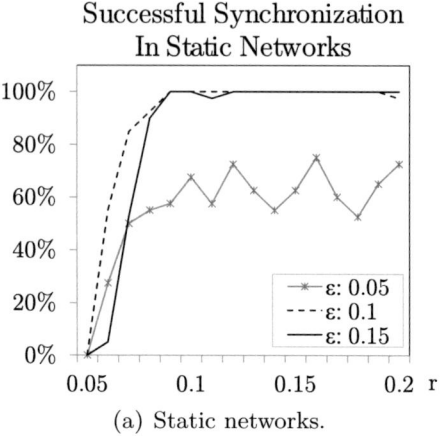

(a) Static networks.

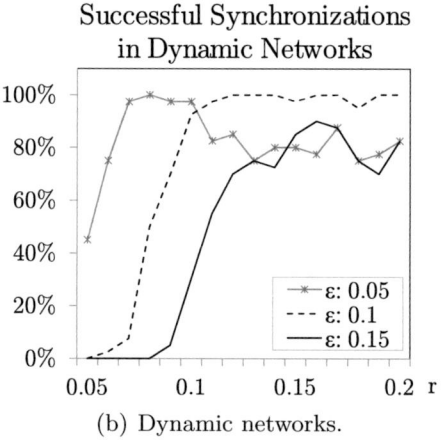

(b) Dynamic networks.

Figure 5.23: Percentage of successful experiments in static (a) and dynamic (b) networks with 1000 devices and a varying communication range r.

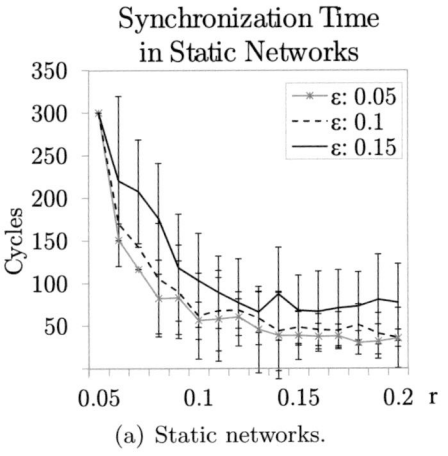

(a) Static networks.

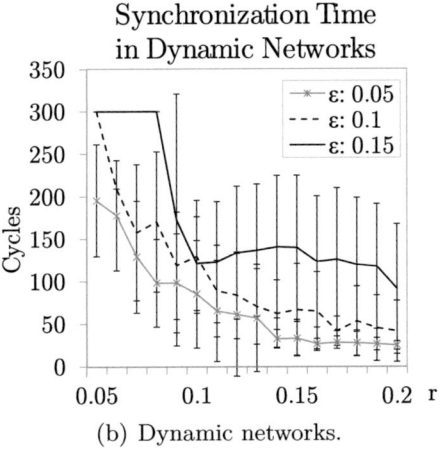

(b) Dynamic networks.

Figure 5.24: Average time until successful synchronization of static (a) and dynamic (b) networks with 1000 devices and a varying communication range r.

causes delays. On the other hand, the absence of the moved device in its old neighborhood can also be the cause for a slowdown in the previous synchronization process. When the communication range increases, a newly added or removed device in a neighborhood has comparatively less impact since more devices are involved in each synchronization process.

Comparison of Firefly-inspired Hop Counting and Asynchronous Gradient Algorithm

The aim of the next experiment is to evaluate the performance of the FIHC and FIHCd algorithms and to compare the resulting distance estimates with the asynchronous GA. For this, the average hop count error is computed over 40 cycles starting after 10 cycles in order to exclude the phase in which hop count values are propagated through the network for the first time. The devices are simulated with a communication range of $r = 7\%$, which corresponds to the settings in the experiments conducted in Section 5.1.3. Results are presented in Figure 5.25. FIHC has the lowest hop count error, followed by GA, and the highest error occurs when using FIHCd. Although this result creates the impression that FIHC should be the algorithm of choice for hop count based distance estimation in MANETs, this is true only to a certain extent.

In order to get a better insight into the deviations in performance, Figure 5.26 shows the average percentage of devices with which a negative or positive hop count error occurs. It becomes apparent that the performance of the algorithms is reflected by the amount of underestimation in the network. The higher the underestimation is, the lower is the overall hop count error. This is due to the fact that underestimation compensates for the natural density induced overestimation in networks. However, as discussed in Section 5.1.2, underestimation is the more aggravating type of error for localization since it cannot be predicted and prevents the application of traditional refinement methods without adjustment, which are proposed to encounter low density issues. As a consequence, FIHCd is the best option in dynamic networks because it results in the lowest amount of negative hop count error. As the experiments in Section 5.1.3 show, movements leading away from the beacon into higher gradient rings create high negative hop count error due to the distortion the moved devices create in their new neighborhoods. FIHCd counteracts this effect because hop count signals are emitted only after a signal was received first. Thus, a device which moves away from the beacon does not affect the new neighborhood since it does not communicate its underestimated hop count before updating. The remaining underestimation can be explained by the fact that a device which has moved to a higher gradient ring underestimates its own distance before updating. Nevertheless, with FIHCd the negative hop count error can be reduced significantly, which has the advantage of being able to treat a dynamic network just like a static one.

5.2.4 Conclusion

In this section, FIHC and FIHCd are proposed, two algorithms for hop counting in MANETs, which are based on synchronized timers and, based on that, timed sending of signals. The basic idea of FIHC is to use an intentional phase shift with respect to a synchronous base signal in order to encode information about the device's hop count with respect to a beacon. To realize this idea, the nature-inspired firefly algorithm by Lucarelli and Wang [144] is used for synchronization. Experiments are performed, which investigate the success rate and duration of synchronization of this method under the constraint of neighborhood-coupling, i.e., only the firing

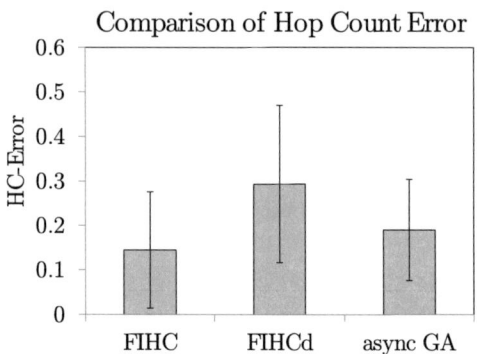

Figure 5.25: Comparison of hop count errors in distance estimation using FIHC, FIHCd, and asynchronous GA (async GA).

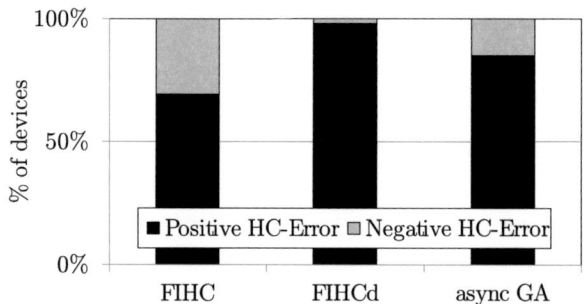

Figure 5.26: Percentage of the devices in the network which overestimate and underestimate their distance to the beacon for FIHC, FIHCd, and asynchronous GA (async GA).

of direct communication partners has an impact on a device's synchronization process. The communication range is varied in order to determine its impact on synchronization performance and three different impulse intensities are testes. Subsequently, both variants of the proposed signal-based hop counting approach, FIHC and FIHCd, are evaluated and compared to results achieved by the standard GA. The difference between FIHC and FIHCd is that in the latter variant devices have to wait before sending an own signal until after having received a signal from any nearby device, whereas with FIHC, the device simply sends its signal at the determined phase shift.

Synchronization success is shown to be 100% on average when impulse intensity is set to $\epsilon = 0.1$ and the communication range is at least 9% in static and 16% in dynamic networks. In general, an increase in the communication range positively influences the synchronization success and the time it takes for the network to be in synchrony. Although mobility in the network slightly hinders synchronization, the produced synchronization delay, can be compensated by an increase of the communication range. Experiments further demonstrate that FIHCd decreases the emergence of negative hop count error in dynamic networks. As discussed in the previous section, this is essential for an improved accuracy of localization based on hop counts in dynamic networks since underestimation cannot be handled as well as the natural occurrence of overestimated distances. FIHCd, thus, provides an alternative for the previously presented MoGA algorithm in order to eliminate underestimation in dynamic networks if synchronization can be achieved.

211

5.3 Geometric Distance Estimation for Mobile Ad Hoc Networks

In the previous two sections, the behavior of distance estimation algorithms based on hop counts in mobile networks is subject to investigation. It is found that mobility has a negative impact on the quality of the derived distance estimates and that the height of this negative impact is hard to predict. In this section, an alternative distance estimation approach is presented which refrains from hop counts as a basis. The approach is called *Geometric Distance Estimation (GeoDE)* and belongs to the second type of range-free distance estimation algorithms addressed in Section 2.4.2, the connectivity-based distance estimation techniques.

5.3.1 Connectivity-based Distance Estimation

In order to understand the concept of connectivity-based distance estimation, the notions of *shared* and *individual* neighbors have to be introduced, which are graphically illustrated in Figure 5.27.

Definition 5.7 (Classification of Neighbors). *Let i, j be two adjacent devices and $N(i)$, $N(j)$ the sets of devices situated in the neighborhood of i and j respectively. The neighbors of i can be categorized with respect to j as:*

$$shared\ neighbors:\ S(i,j) := N(i) \cap N(j)$$

$$individual\ neighbors:\ I_j(i) = N(i) \setminus S(i,j)$$

In connectivity-based distance estimation, the number of shared neighbors between two devices is used to approximate the intersection area A of the two circles which represent the communication

212

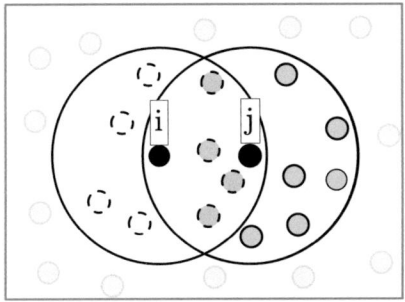

Figure 5.27: An example of the communication range of two adjacent devices i, j. Devices with dotted lines are communication partners of device i and belong to the neighborhood $N(i)$. Gray filled devices are communication partners of device j and, consequently, belong to the neighborhood $N(j)$. Devices in the shaded area are shared neighbors and belong to the set of shared neighbors $S(i,j)$.

ranges of both devices. Figure 5.28 displays the geometric conditions of intersecting circles. In reality, the communication range is not exactly circular, but this assumption is a commonly used simplification in the modeling of ad hoc networks, which is called the *unit-disc-graph model* (cf. Aspnes et al. [11], Breu and Kirkpatrick [24]). The approximation of the intersection area follows the principle of a Monte Carlo integration. Monte Carlo integration approximates the size of a shape's surface by randomly choosing points and determining the proportion of these random points which lie inside the shape relative to the points outside the shape (cf. Evans and Swartz [61]). The standard Circle-Circle Intersection Equation 5.13 establishes a relation between the distance d of the two circles' centers and the intersection area A. Solving Equation 5.13 for d would allow to derive an estimate for the distance d from a given approximation of the intersection surface A and the range r. GeoDE provides a method for deriving such a mapping between an approximation of A and an estimate for the distance d. It should be noted that similar connectivity-based distance estimation approaches have been pursued by Aslam et al. [10], Buschmann et al. [33], Fekete et al. [64], Villafuerte et al. [236], and Huang et al. [99]. However, they differ in the way how the mapping function is derived and do not consider multi-hop distance estimation which is required in the context of beacon-based localization.

$$A = 2r^2 \arccos\left(\frac{d}{2r}\right) - d\sqrt{r^2 - \frac{d^2}{4}} \qquad (5.13)$$

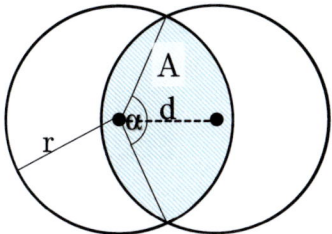

Figure 5.28: Geometric characteristics of two overlapping circles. The intersection area A corresponds to the shaded area, the two black dots represent the circles' centers.

5.3.2 Geometric Distance Estimation

In order to be able to approximate a mapping between the intersection area A and the distance d which is independent of the communication range r, the following considerations are made. The distance d between the centers of two overlapping circles can be described as a ratio θ of the circles' diameters according to Equation 5.14. The intersection area A can be described as a ratio Δ of the circle's surface as shown in Equation 5.15.

$$\theta = 1 - \frac{d}{2r} \qquad (5.14)$$

$$\Delta = \frac{A}{\pi r^2} \qquad (5.15)$$

Standard equations (5.16) and (5.17) are alternative descriptions of A and d which express both values using the communication range r and the segment angle α (cf. Figure 5.28). Substituting A and d in Equations 5.14 and 5.15 by the expressions from Equation 5.17 and 5.16, it becomes apparent that Δ and θ only depend on

215

the segment angle α, which is independent of the communication range r.

$$d = 2r \cos\left(\frac{\alpha}{2}\right) \tag{5.16}$$

$$A = r^2 (\alpha - \sin(\alpha)) \tag{5.17}$$

As a consequence, the relation between θ and Δ is independent of the value r and can be approximated as a third-degree polynomial function using linear regression. Figure 5.29 shows the approximation of the mapping function $f : \Delta \rightarrow \theta$ (dotted line). Putting it all together, the distance d can be calculated from Δ according to Equation 5.18 and Δ is estimated for device i as shown in Equation 5.19. This results in the final Equation 5.20, which device i uses in order to compute an estimate for its distance to device j.

$$d = 2r(1 - f(\Delta)) \tag{5.18}$$

$$\Delta \approx \frac{|S(i,j)|}{|N(i)|} \tag{5.19}$$

$$\bar{d}^{GeoDE}(i,j) = r \cdot \left(a \cdot \bar{\Delta}^3 + b \cdot \bar{\Delta}^2 + c \cdot \bar{\Delta} + e\right) \tag{5.20}$$

With $\bar{\Delta} = \frac{|S(i,j)|}{|N(i)|}$ and corresponding coefficients:

$$a = 3.90 \qquad b = -4.16 \qquad c = 3.04 \qquad e = 0.04.$$

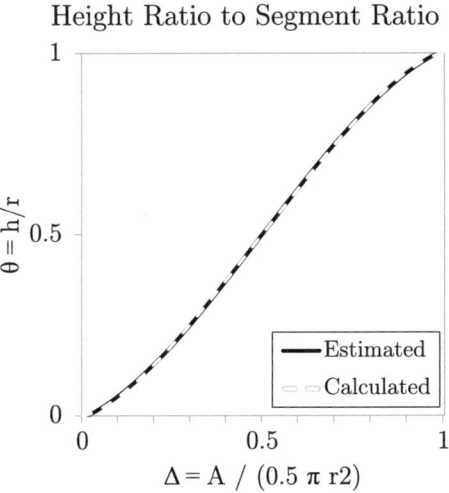

Figure 5.29: Relation of θ to Δ and the approximated third-degree polynomial function f, which maps Δ to θ.

Approximation Error

There are two approximations in GeoDE which influence the accuracy of the computed distance estimates. Firstly, the approximation of Δ as the ratio of shared to total communication partners and, secondly, the approximation of the function f through polynomial regression. Considering the first approximation, there are two sources of error in this approximation. Monte Carlo algorithms base their concept on random numbers that are selected uniformly. Networks, however, do not necessarily have an even distribution of devices. A shift in the positions of the neighbors into a certain direction, shown exemplarily in Figure 5.30, can distort the approximation results. The influence of various device distributions on the estimation accuracy is, therefore, examined in experiments in Section 5.3.3. A second problem is the sampling rate. For $|N(i)|$ neighbors, there are only $|N(i)| + 1$ different values for Δ. As a consequence, the absolute error for the estimation of Δ, assuming the ratio of neighbors indeed reflects the overlap size, lies within the interval of $[0, \frac{1}{|N(i)|})$.

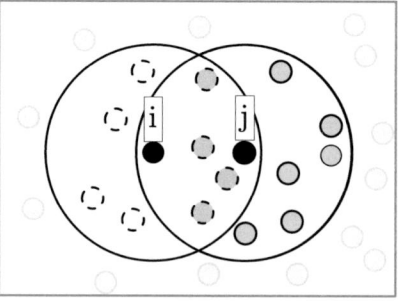

Figure 5.30: Example of an irregular distribution of neighboring devices over the communication range.

The second approximation is that of function f. Figure 5.31 shows the deviation between $f(\Delta)$ and θ. The approximation error with a first order Taylor series expansion, as it is used by Huang et al. [99], is depicted for comparison. For $\theta < 0.9$ the error using polynomial regression is smaller compared to the first order Taylor series approximation. The approximation error is at most 0.04, which leads to a maximum absolute distance estimation error of $0.16r$. The error value depends on the exact value of θ, which in turn depends on r. It follows that GeoDE estimates the same distance with slight variations in accuracy when the communication range r changes.

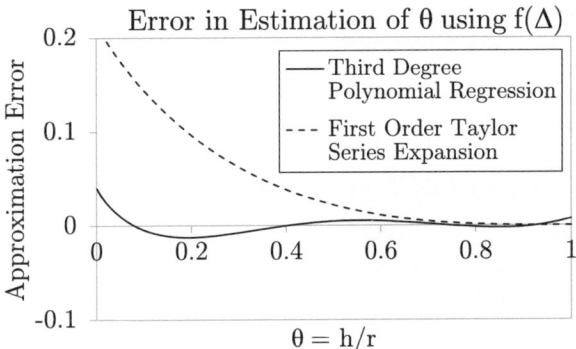

Figure 5.31: The approximation error for function f, which maps Δ to θ, derived by a third-degree polynomial regression compared to the approximation error when f is derived by a first order Taylor series expansion.

Geometric Distance Estimation over Multiple Hops

Although GeoDE could be applied directly to two-hop neighbors, as well as one-hop neighbors, this is not pursued here due to the additional communication overhead. The two devices which need to estimate their distance would exchange all the necessary information via a common communication partner, which burdens that device's resources. Nevertheless, two-hop estimation can be performed analogously and could be useful in situations in which accuracy of distance estimates is prior to resource saving. So far, distance estimates $\bar{d}(i,j)$ can range between 0 and $2r$. The first refinement technique used in GeoDE is to limit calculated estimates to a maximum value of r. The second refinement results from the consideration that the number of neighbors $|N(i)|$ and $|N(j)|$ of the two devices i and j can differ, even in uniform-randomly distributed networks (cf. Figure 5.27 for an example). As a result, device i and device j can compute different estimates of their distance using Equation 5.20. Hence, device i and j exchange their estimates via communication and compute the average value of the estimates $\bar{d}(i,j)$ and $\bar{d}(j,i)$.

Algorithm 5.1 shows how a device i estimates its distance to a neighbor j using the GeoDE approach (note that because of i and j being neighbors it holds that $|N(i)| > 0$).

As stated earlier, the distance between neighboring devices is not enough for the computation of coordinates with beacon-based localization algorithms. Instead, the distance to beacons has to be known, which can be multiple hops away. Algorithm 5.2 shows how GeoDE is expanded to allow for distance estimations between devices in a network and beacons. The algorithm can be executed repeatedly and the necessary iterations for all devices in the network to derive a distance estimate are subject to the neighborhood size and the total number of devices in the network. GeoDE is similar

220

Algorithm 5.1 Geometric Distance Estimation to Neighbors

Require: $N(i)$, neighbors from device i, a neighbor j, and communication range r

Ensure: Estimated distance $\bar{d}(i,j)$

1: Ask list of neighbors $N(j)$ from device j.

2: $S(i,j) \leftarrow N(i) \cap N(j)$

3: $x \leftarrow \frac{|S(i,j)|}{|N(i)|}$

4: $\bar{d}(i,j) \leftarrow r \cdot (3.90 \cdot x^3 - 4.16 \cdot x^2 + 3.04 \cdot x + 0.04)$
   //*Limitation:*

5: **if** $\left(\bar{d}(i,j) > r\right)$ **then**

6:     $\bar{d}(i,j) \leftarrow r$

7: **end if**
   //*Averaging:*

8: Ask j for its non-averaged distance estimate $\bar{d}(j,i)$

9: $\bar{d}(i,j) \leftarrow \frac{1}{2} \cdot \left(\bar{d}(i,j) + \bar{d}(j,i)\right)$

10: **return** $\bar{d}(i,j)$

---

to the distance estimation approach based on hop counts. The difference is that each device computes its own distance estimate to a beacon on the basis of the minimum value any of its neighbors has computed for its distance to the beacon. In contrast to hop count based distance estimation, where the distance estimate is computed on the basis of the minimum hop count value in the neighborhood.

5.3.3 Evaluation

The objective of the following experiments is to evaluate GeoDE in comparison with distance estimation based on hop counts. Firstly, the sensitivity of GeoDE to variations in the communication range r and the network's distribution is examined in static networks. In this first experiment, the results of GeoDE are compared to a simple distance estimation approach based on hop counts proposed by Nagpal et al. [171]. The equation to derive distance estimates with this approach is shown in Equation 5.21, with $h_b(i)$ denoting the hop count of device i with respect to beacon b.

$$\bar{d}^{SGM}(i,b) = r\left(\frac{\sum_{j\in N(i)} h_b(j) + h_b(i)}{|N(i)| + 1} - 0.5\right) \qquad (5.21)$$

In the second set of experiments, the performance of GeoDE is investigated in dynamic networks and compared to a state-of-the-art distance estimation method based on hop counts, which is more complex than the one presented by Nagpal et al. [171]. This method is called *Gradient-based Distance Estimation (GDE)* and is published by Liu et al. [140]. The computations include additional statistical considerations, which are based on the work from Nagpal et al. [171] and Kleinrock and Silvester [122]. The

---

Algorithm 5.2 Geometric Distance Estimation to Beacons

Require: $N(i)$ neighbors of device i, beacon b, communication range r

Ensure: estimated distance $\bar{d}(i, b)$

1: **if** $(b \in N(i))$ **then**
2: $\quad \bar{d}(i, b) \leftarrow$ compute $\bar{d}(i, b)$ using Algorithm 5.1
3: **else**
$\quad$ //*search for neighbor k closest to b:*
4: $\quad \bar{D} \leftarrow \{\ \}$
5: $\quad$ **for** $j \in N(i)$ **do**
6: $\quad\quad$ ask j for $\bar{d}(j, b)$
7: $\quad\quad$ **if** $\bar{d}(j, b) \neq null$ **then**
8: $\quad\quad\quad$ add $\bar{d}(j, b)$ to $\bar{D}$
9: $\quad\quad$ **end if**
10: $\quad$ **end for**
11: $\quad$ **if** $(\bar{D} \leftarrow \{\ \})$ **then**
12: $\quad\quad$ **return** null
13: $\quad$ **else**
14: $\quad\quad$ Select neighbor m: $\bar{d}(m, b) \leftarrow min\left(\bar{D}\right)$ closest to b
15: $\quad\quad \bar{d}(i, m) \leftarrow$ compute $\bar{d}(i, m)$ using Algorithm 5.1
16: $\quad\quad \bar{d}(i, b) \leftarrow \bar{d}(i, m) + \bar{d}(m, b)$
17: $\quad$ **end if**
18: **end if**
19: **return** $\bar{d}(i, b)$

---

necessary calculations to derive a distance estimate $\bar{d}^{GDE}(i, b)$ between beacon b and device i according to Liu et al. [140] are shown in Equation 5.22.

$$\bar{d}^{GDE}(i,b) = r \cdot (G_b^{out}(i) \cdot R^{out}(i) + G_b^{in}(i) \cdot R^{in}(i)$$
$$+(h_b(i) - 1) \cdot d_{hop}(i) \cdot \Delta(R)) \tag{5.22}$$

with:

$$G_b^{out}(i) = \frac{1}{r}\bar{d}^{SMG}(i,b) - (h_b(i) - 1) \cdot (1 - d_{hop}(i)) - 0.5 \cdot (1 - d_{hop}(i))$$

$$R^{out}(i) = 1 - R^{in}(i)$$

$$G_b^{in}(i) = G_b^{out}(i) + 1$$

$$R^{in}(i) = 1 - d_{hop}(i)$$

$$\Delta R(i) = \int_0^1 x \left(\frac{|N(i)| - 2x^2 + 4x - 1}{e^{(x-1)\sqrt{2x-x^2}} + |N(i)|\arccos(1-x)\sqrt{2x - x^2}} \right) dx$$

$$d_{hop}(i) = 1 + e^{|N(i)|} - \int_{-1}^1 e^{-\frac{|N(i)|}{\pi}\left(\arccos t - t\sqrt{1-t^2}\right)} dt$$

In the work of Liu et al. [140], a method is proposed to account for mobility when computing distance estimates. However, for this method the expected mobility pattern has to be known, which is not the case in the scenario of passive mobility considered here. Hence, this method is not applied in the experiments. GDE relies on the computation of numerical integrations. Different methods have been proposed for approximation of numerical integration in the literature (cf. Isaacson and Keller [108]). Here, Riemann integration (cf. Riemann [196]) is used, where the surface area is approximated by the sum of the surfaces of multiple boxes. For the experiments, the numerical integration is approximated using 1000 integration steps (boxes).

Geometric Distance Estimation in Static Networks

For the experiments, the settings described in Section 5.1.3 are used with the difference that a beacon is randomly chosen from the set of devices in each repetition of an experiment. This modification is necessary, in order to increase the chance of creating a connected network, especially for distorted device distributions. Since communication range, neighborhood size, and the distribution of devices are identified to influence the quality of GeoDE, three static network scenarios are considered. In *Scenario 1*, the devices are distributed according to a uniform random distribution. In *Scenario 2*, the devices are distributed using a Gaussian random distribution and in *Scenario 3*, all devices are placed like in a grid (cf. Figure 5.32). In addition, the communication range r is varied to show the influence of the neighborhood size on the estimation error (cf. Section 5.3.2). Mobility is not considered yet. To evaluate the quality of the estimates, *Mean absolute percentage error (MAPE)* is computed as described in Equation 5.23.

$$MAPE\left(\bar{d}\left(i,j\right)\right) = \frac{|d\left(i,j\right) - \bar{d}\left(i,j\right)|}{d\left(i,j\right)} \tag{5.23}$$

where $d\left(i,j\right)$ denotes the Euclidean distance between a device i and its neighbor j and $\bar{d}\left(i,j\right)$ the estimate of that distance. MAPE gives information about the relative deviation of the estimate with respect to the real distance.

Figure 5.33 shows the MAPE for *Scenario 1*, Figure 5.34 shows the results for *Scenario 2*, and Figure 5.35 for *Scenario 3*. It can be observed that GeoDE leads to less error-prone estimates than the estimation based on hop counts for all considered distributions and communication ranges. Furthermore, it can be noted that even the sample standard deviation is less or equal to the MAPE of estimates based on hop counts. This confirms that the GeoDE

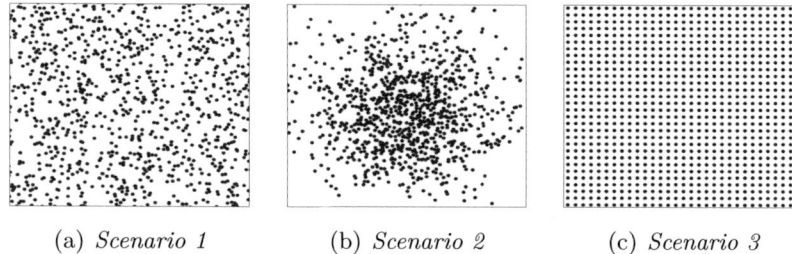

(a) *Scenario 1*   (b) *Scenario 2*   (c) *Scenario 3*

Figure 5.32: Different network structures used for the experimental study. Devices are placed in the environment according to a uniform random distribution (a), a Gaussian random distribution (b), and are evenly distributed in a grid-like fashion (c).

approach is a consistent improvement for distance estimation in static networks compared to distance estimation based on the approach from Nagpal et al. [171].

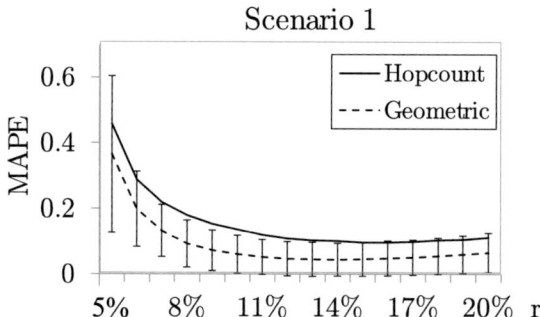

Figure 5.33: MAPE for GeoDE compared to distance estimation based on hop counts on long distance estimation including standard sample deviation in Scenario 1.

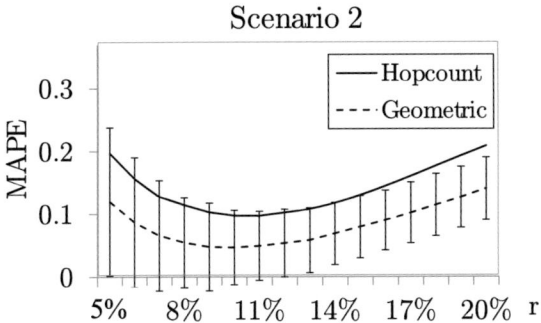

Figure 5.34: MAPE for GeoDE compared to distance estimation based on hop counts on long distance estimation including standard sample deviation in Scenario 2.

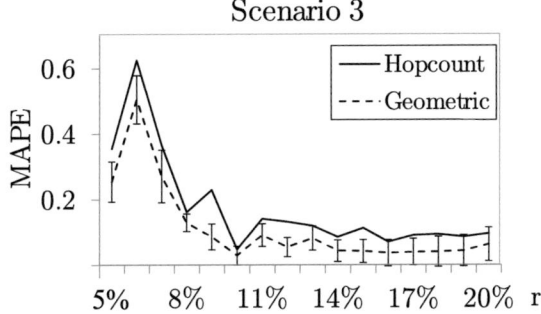

Figure 5.35: MAPE for GeoDE compared to distance estimation based on hop counts on long distance estimation including standard sample deviation in Scenario 3.

Despite the imbalanced distribution of devices, GeoDE performs slightly better in Gaussian networks compared to networks which are distributed according to uniform random distributions. This can be explained by two observations. Firstly, the averaging of estimates from both involved devices could help to overcome the bias introduced by distorted device distributions. An unbalanced distribution of devices leads to an overestimation in one device and an underestimation in the other device, which can provide a good estimate on average. Another factor is the larger average neighborhood size for most devices due to the concentration of devices in the center of the environment. As discussed above, this increases the number of values for Δ and, as a result, improves the estimates. Furthermore, it can be observed that the behavior of the estimation error is different from *Scenario 2* for increasing communication range. After an initial decline, the error starts increasing again. This characteristic can be explained by a higher shift-sensitivity with larger communication range. A small communication range only covers a small area of the network in which the distribution of devices is not as distorted as when looking at a larger area. Nevertheless, the proposed averaging technique seems to be able to keep the overall error to a similar level compared to uniform-randomly distributed networks.

For the grid-like distribution shown in Figure 5.35, one would expect a similar behavior as in *Scenario 1*, because the distribution of devices is even in both networks. The trend of the error behavior with increasing communication range indeed is similar to the error behavior in uniform-randomly distributed networks. The oscillation can be explained by the step-like increase of the neighborhood size. Due to the grid-like distribution, increasing the communication range does not change the neighborhood density until suddenly several new neighbors are included. As a consequence, the error of GeoDE, as well as the hop count based distance estimation, changes erratically.

Geometric Distance Estimation in Mobile Networks

In order to compare localization results on the basis of hop counts with results based on GeoDE, lateration is used to determine locations from the distance estimates to beacons as described in Section 2.4.2. Algorithm 5.3 shows the procedure of lateration. Let i be the device which is to located and $B(i)$ the set of known beacons, $C(i) = \{c(b)\}, \forall b \in B(i)$, with $c(b) = (x(b), y(b))$ denotes the set of all known two-dimensional beacon coordinates, and $\bar{D}(i) = \{\bar{d}(i,b)\}, \forall b \in B(i)$ is the set of all corresponding distance estimates. Algorithm 5.3 shows how the coordinates $c(i)$ for device i are computed.

The iterations are stopped, when the error of the next coordinate-candidate is not a significant reduction to the previous candidate. The significance is determined by a parameter ϵ. α controls the step size of the search for good coordinates, i.e., a smaller α makes coordination more precise but increases the number of necessary iterations. In the experiment, one beacon is placed in each corner of the plane. This corresponds to a beacon placement in a convex hull around the network, which is the optimal beacon placement for localization according to Bachrach and Taylor [12]. The coordinates of the beacons are initialized with (0,0), (0,1), (1,0) and (1,1) and the communication range is set to 15% of the environment's side-length. The devices are assumed to be asynchronous. One cycle is defined as the random execution of 1000 devices. When selected for execution, a device performs the following steps:

1. Ask all neighbors for known beacon coordinates

2. Ask all neighbors for the necessary information to estimate distances (list of neighbors for GeoDE and hop counts for GDE respectively)

Algorithm 5.3 Lateration

Require: beacon coordinates $C(i)$, distance estimates $\bar{D}(i)$
Ensure: coordinates of device i: $c(i) \leftarrow (x(i), y(i))$
    //*Select closest beacon m:* $\bar{d}(i,m) \leftarrow min\left(\bar{D}(i)\right)$
    //*Initialize:*
 1: $\bar{c}(i) \leftarrow c(m) \in C(i)$
 2: $\Delta(E) \leftarrow \infty$
 3: **while** $\Delta(E) > \epsilon$ **do**
 4:     $c(i) \leftarrow \bar{c}(i)$
 5:     $\Delta x(i) \leftarrow 0$
 6:     $\Delta y(i) \leftarrow 0$
 7:     **for** $c(b) \in C(i)$ **do**
 8:         $d(i,b) \leftarrow EuclideanDistance(c(i), c(b))$
 9:         $E \leftarrow E + \left(d(i,b) - \bar{d}(i,b)\right)^2$
10:         $\Delta x(i) \leftarrow \Delta x(i) + (x(i) - x(b))\left(1 - \left(d(i,b)/\bar{d}(i,b)\right)\right)$
11:         $\Delta y(i) \leftarrow \Delta x(i) + (y(i) - y(b))\left(1 - \left(d(i,b)/\bar{d}(i,b)\right)\right)$
12:     **end for**
        //*Calculate new coordinates:*
13:     $\bar{c}(i) \leftarrow (x(i) - \alpha \Delta x(i), y(i) - \alpha \Delta y(i))$
14:     $\bar{E} \leftarrow \sum_{C(i)}\left(EuclideanDistance(\bar{c}(i), c(b)) - \hat{d}(i,b)\right)$
15:     $\Delta(E) \leftarrow \bar{E} - E$
16: **end while**
17: **return** coordinates $c(i)$

3. Calculate distance estimates to all known beacons

4. If at least three beacon locations are known, calculate coordinates with lateration

5. Move according to the applied movement pattern

The examined mobility models are CM, RW, and StrM, which are described in Section 5.1.1. RW is chosen because it is one of the most widely researched mobility models in the literature, e.g., in Zonoozi and Dassanayake [259]. CM is chosen as a contrast to RW, since the trajectories of these two movements differ significantly in range and step size. As a representative for coupled mobility, StrM is selected because it is designed to model stream-like movements, such as caused by natural forces like wind or water. Moreover, movements of evacuees are often modeled as liquid or gas dispersal (cf. Section 2.3.1), which is why the investigation of the StrM model is especially interesting considering the context of this thesis.

For evaluation of the experiments, the average location error E is calculated using Equation 5.24. With N denoting the set of devices in the network, $\bar{c}(i)$ are the estimated coordinates of device i and $c(i)$ are its real coordinates. The function $d(\cdot, \cdot)$ refers to the Euclidean distance.

$$E(\bar{c}(i), c(i)) = \frac{\sum_{i \in N} d(\bar{c}(i), c(i))}{|N|} \qquad (5.24)$$

Figure 5.36 shows the results for localization using GeoDE and GDE in static and dynamic networks. The experiment reveals that GDE delivers better results for static networks but is significantly worse in dynamic environments, which confirms the findings from Section 5.3.3. GDE is also based on hop counts and, as a consequence, suffers from the same weakness of underestimated hop counts under mobility described thoroughly in Section 5.1.

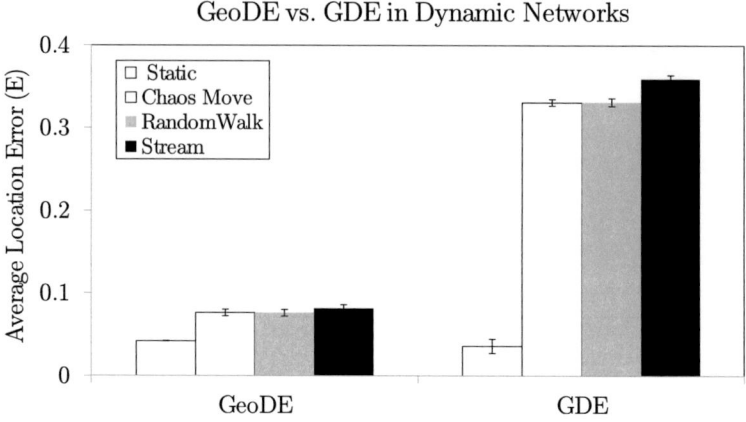

Figure 5.36: Localization error with GeoDE and GDE for static and dynamic networks.

The quality of GDE depends on the approximation of the numerical integration, which influences the computational costs to derive estimates. Since computational resources are limited in MANETs, it is interesting to know how many integration steps (or boxes in case of the Riemann integration method) are necessary to achieve a better performance of GDE compared to GeoDE. Figure 5.37 shows the results for varying approximation steps. Apparently, more than 50 approximation steps are required for GDE to outperform GeoDE.

5.3.4 Conclusion

GeoDE is a range-free distance estimation approach, which does not rely on hop counts but the ratio of shared to total communication partners in order to compute distances. GeoDE offers the possibility to estimate multi-hop distances in a network. It

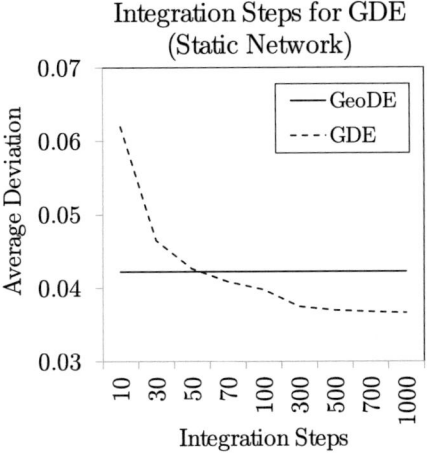

Figure 5.37: Localization error for the GDE for increasingly fine-grained approximation of the necessary integration computations.

is shown that using a third-degree polynomial regression in order to approximate the mapping from neighbors to distances is less error-prone when compared to an approximation via a first-order Taylor series expansion. Furthermore, experiments are performed in order to compare the distance estimation using GeoDE with two hop count based distance estimation methods proposed in the literature. The first method is presented in 2003 by Nagpal et al. [171] and the second choice is a more recently published approach from Liu et al. in 2011 [140], which is called GDE. Three different static network distributions are used for the comparison of GeoDE with the first hop count based method: a uniformly random distribution, a Gaussian random distribution, and a grid-like distribution of devices. The communication range is varied from 5% to 20% and the MAPE of distance estimates is used for evaluation. The more recent hop count based approach is tested in a uniform-randomly distributed static network and in dynamic networks with three different mobility patterns from the study presented in Section 5.1.1. The investigated mobility models are CM and RW, which belong to the group of individual movements, and StrM, which is a coupled mobility model. For evaluation, the derived distance estimates are used to compute locations with an iterative lateration algorithm and the localization error, i.e. the deviation between real and computed coordinates, is calculated for evaluation.

The experiments reveal that GeoDE significantly outperforms the first hop count based distance estimation approach in all considered static networks. Even the standard deviation of the error with GeoDE is mostly lower than the error produced with the hop count based distance estimation approach. Surprisingly, the performance in a Gaussian-randomly distributed network is even better when compared to a uniform-randomly distributed network for certain communication ranges. This indicates that averaging the computed estimates from both involved devices is successful in mitigating the negative effect of distorted neighborhoods. Additionally, the distance estimation approach profits from the higher average number of neighbors in Gaussian-randomly distributed networks, which is another reason why the error is well below that of uniformly random networks. In Gaussian networks, similar to uniform-randomly or evenly distributed networks, the error decreases first with increasing communication range. At a communication range of about 10%, a low point is reached and the error starts increasing again. This can be ascribed to the increased distortion of devices within a neighborhood with higher communication ranges. In evenly distributed networks, GeoDE performs similar to uniform-randomly distributed networks, except for some oscillations in the error behavior for increased communication ranges due to the step-wise increase in the neighborhood size.

Although GeoDE is found to be slightly outperformed by GDE in static networks, it is notably superior in all considered dynamic networks. This is due to the negative effect of mobility identified in Section 5.1, which all hop count based approaches suffer from. The GDE algorithm relies on the computation of numerical integrations which can be computed by different approximation methods. It is shown that with an approximation method for numerical integration from Riemann [196], at least 50 integration steps are required for GDE in order to outperform GeoDE.

A slight change in computing the average estimate of two neighboring devices could be useful in order to prevent an increase in error for higher communication ranges in Gaussian-randomly distributed networks. The higher the distortions of device locations in the neighborhood are, the greater the difference between the total number of neighbors of both involved devices. Since the device with higher number of neighbors has better input data for distance estimation, its resulting estimate is likely to be more precise than the one from its counterpart. This difference could be regarded by weighting both estimates according to the respective number of total neighbors before computing the average distance estimate.

5.4 Optimization of Beacon Placement in Buildings

As discussed before, beacon-based localization algorithms are the only reasonable choice to localize mobile evacuation devices in OBESS because absolute coordinates of devices with respect to a common reference grid, e.g., the building map, are required. Beacons, i.e., devices which know their own locations, for example due to a-priori configuration, are used to derive the locations of all other devices in the network. The placement of beacons is essential to the accuracy of the derived locations (cf. Bachrach and Taylor [12], Nagpal et al. [171]), hence, it is important to think about where optimal locations for beacons are. So far, this problem is considered mainly for SSNs. In static networks, an optimal beacon placement is mostly handled as an optimal coverage problem where beacons are placed in such a way that their communication ranges cover the largest possible area. However, new challenges arise when considering mobile devices because the network's topology is changing constantly and often substantially over time, compared to SSNs where devices only occasionally fail or are newly added. Considering an evacuation scenario makes the problem even more specific. During evacuation, the devices move simultaneously towards certain targets (exits) in the building. As a result, not only the network's topology is changing, but its intrinsic structure changes from a more or less evenly distributed network to a concentrated and fragmented network. Consequently, the ability to communicate with certain static beacons varies strongly over time. Intuitively, a concentration of beacons in higher frequented areas of the building seems advisable. However, in such regions, the density of the MANET is also increased, which makes it more likely to establish connections to beacons over multiple hops, even if there are few of them. This tradeoff has to be taken into account when searching for an optimal solution. In addition, for lateration at least three beacons have to be known to a device in order to compute its position (cf. Nagpal et al. [171]). This further distinguishes the problem from a simple optimal coverage problem. Little is known about the characteristics of a good solution and with operating in a two- or even three-dimensional environment, the search space is large. These are criteria which point to a heuristic optimization approach as a valid strategy for problem solving (cf. Gerdes et al. [74]). In the following, an EA, i.e., a heuristic optimization and search method based on the principles of natural evolution, is introduced to tackle the problem. The EA is used to optimize the placement of static beacons for localization of devices in a MANET during evacuation. A multi-agent evacuation simulation serves as a tool to evaluate the fitness of a specific placement.

5.4.1 Optimization of Network Distributions

As mentioned before, optimal device placement has received attention mainly in the context of SSNs. Also, the research often focuses on achieving an optimal coverage of a specific area with a minimal number of devices (cf. for example Cardei and Wu [35], Heidari and Movaghar [87], Kaplan et al. [115], Katz and Morgenstern [119], So and Ye [219]). In general, this problem is referred to as *minimum disc coverage problem* and can be solved in time $\mathcal{O}(n \log n)$ with n denoting the number of devices in the

237

network (cf. Sun et al. [224]). Research which concerns the optimal placement of beacons for localization in static networks can be found in Akl et al. [3], Savvides et al. [207], and Tatham and Kunz [230]. In the work of Savvides et al. [207], placing beacons at the perimeter of an SSN is recommended. Akl et al. [3] and Tatham and Kunz [230] propose guidelines for beacon placements in the context of specific localization algorithms. Moreover, Bulusu et al. [30] introduce an approach for adaptive beacon placement in order to encounter failure of devices in the network by reorganization. A lower bound for localization accuracy is shown by Salman et al. [203] and the impact of beacon placement on this boundary is examined. Another research area is the improvement of localization results by using mobile beacons, which is, for example, discussed in Liao et al. [137] and Li et al. [134].

Evolutionary Algorithms

Before describing the proposed solution to the problem treated here, some basic information about an EA has to be introduced. EAs describe heuristic optimization algorithms which follow the principles of natural evolution based on Darwin's theory (cf. Darwin [47]). An EA is composed of genetic operators, which are known as reproduction, mutation, and selection. The repeated execution of these operators represents the search process for good solutions to a given problem. Figure 5.38 illustrates the process. At the beginning, a set of so-called individuals, which represent valid solutions to a given problem, is chosen. This set of individuals is called a *population*. The initial population can be selected randomly or by choice if certain prior knowledge about the solution is available. The core of an EA is the fitness evaluation. Here, a given solution, or individual, is evaluated with respect to the optimization objective and a *fitness value* is assigned to it. The

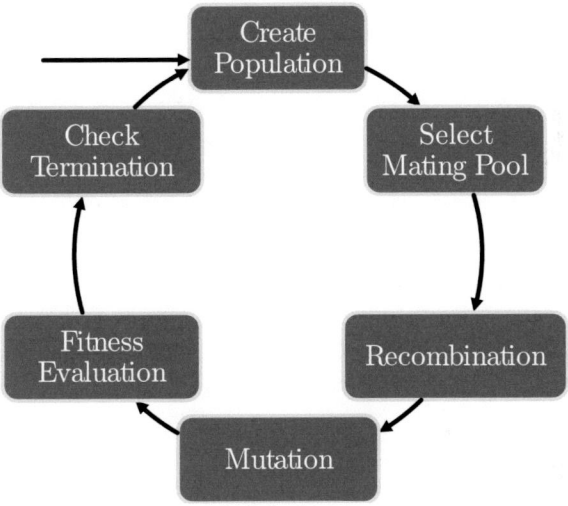

Figure 5.38: Illustration of the general procedure of an EA.

choice of appropriate fitness evaluation criteria is crucial and not always very intuitive. Especially in the research field of Evolutionary Robotics (cf. for example König et al. [124], Merkel et al. [151], Nelson et al. [174]), which is concerned with the evolution of controllers for robots, the performance evaluation of an evolved controller is not straightforward. The scenario of beacon placement optimization faces similar challenges because the criteria which distinct a good beacon placement from a bad one are not obvious. Therefore, some thought has to be put into the design of the fitness evaluation.

After evaluating each individual, some of them are chosen to be recombined. During recombination, their genome is merged to form new individuals, which are called *children*. The children are then slightly altered; this process is commonly described as *mutation*. The iteration is concluded by forming a new population before the procedure starts from the beginning. Various configurations of the genetic operators are conceivable, which have a different impact on the progression of the EA. The termination criteria for an EA can either be a predefined number of repetitions (cycles) or the achievement of a specified fitness level in the population. For more details about EAs, it is referred to Weicker [246] and Gerdes et al. [74].

In the following section, an algorithm proposed by Huang and Tseng [100] is introduced, which can be used to optimize coverage in SSNs. Later, this algorithm is, amongst other methods, used for fitness evaluation in the EA to optimize beacon placements.

Perimeter Coverage Approach

Huang and Tseng [100] propose an approach to compute the so-called *coverage-degree* of an area which is occupied by static devices. Basically, the algorithm decides if and how often the perimeter of a device's communication range is intersected by other devices' communication ranges. If the perimeter of a device is completely contained in the communication range of other devices, it is denoted as covered. Figure 5.39(a) illustrates an example of a first-degree covered beacon perimeter (the middle device).

In order to use this concept for fitness evaluation, some changes are made as follows. An area which is not contained in the communication range of any beacon is denoted as uncovered or zero-degree-covered. An area which is contained in the communication range of a beacon is denoted first-degree covered and an area which is inside the communication range of a beacon, which, in turn, is covered n times by other beacons is denoted as $(n + 1)$-degree covered. For example, the area covered by the middle beacon in Figure 5.39(a) is a two-degree covered area, while the region which is only covered by the surrounding beacons is one-degree covered and the rest is defined as uncovered. If two beacons cover the same slice of the perimeter of a third beacon, the overlapping part is counted for the next coverage degree. Figure 5.39(b) illustrates this procedure.

5.4.2 Evolutionary Algorithm for Optimal Beacon Placement

To find a good placement of beacons for the localization of mobile devices in a MANET, an EA is designed as follows. Firstly, the genome representation of a solution is defined. Here, a solution is represented by a set of two-dimensional coordinates, each denoting the position of a respective beacon. The coordinates of one beacon in a genome is called a *gene*. In Figure 5.40, an example individual and its genetic representation are illustrated.

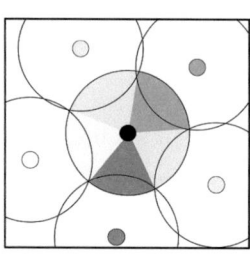

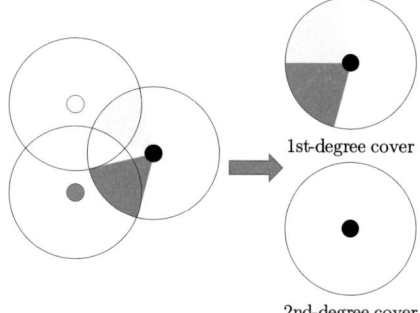

(a) The central beacon 2nd-degree-covers an area.

(b) Treatment of overlapping perimeter covers.

Figure 5.39: Illustration of the process to determine the perimeter coverage-degree of an area.

Selection

The selection process describes the procedure of selecting a certain number $n_{parents}$ of individuals for recombination. Here, the *binary tournament selection* is used, which is a standard method where two individuals are randomly chosen and then compared in terms of their fitness value. The one with the higher fitness value is selected for recombination. Both solutions stay available for further selections. Figure 5.41 describes the tournament-selection graphically.

By changing the size of a tournament, the tournament-selection allows for an easy control of the selection pressure, i.e., the pressure towards keeping good solutions in the population and disposing bad ones. When selection pressure is too high, the algorithm can get stuck in a local optimum because it does not explore

242

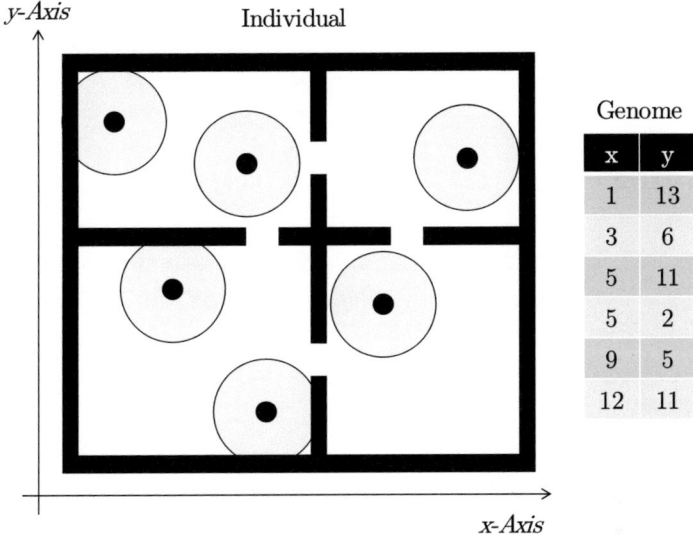

Figure 5.40: An example solution for the placement of beacons inside a building and its corresponding genetic representation.

solutions with low fitness well enough. On the other hand, when the selection pressure is too low, the algorithm could be prevented from converging to an optimal solution. A binary tournament-selection corresponds to a relatively low selection pressure (cf. Weicker [246]).

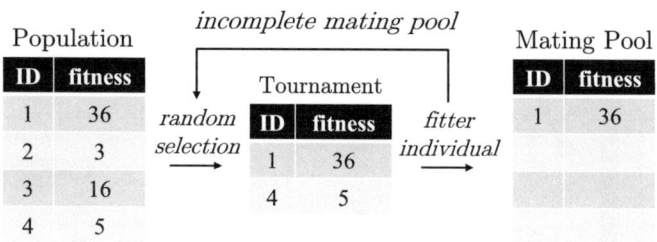

Figure 5.41: Illustration of the tournament selection operator, which is used to select individuals for recombination.

Crossover

All selected individuals belong to a *mating pool*. From this pool, two random individuals are selected and recombined such that they produce two new individuals. For this process two standard methods are implemented and tested in the experiments. Firstly, the *uniform crossover* method is used, in which it is decided randomly for each gene in the genome whether it is part of the first or the second child. The remaining empty genes are taken from the second parent. Figure 5.42(a) illustrates the method.

The second standard method is called *one-point crossover*. Both parents are cut in half at a random position in the genome. The first child is composed by the first half of the first parent and the second half of the second parent. The second child is created analogously. Figure 5.42(b) shows an example of one-point crossover.

244

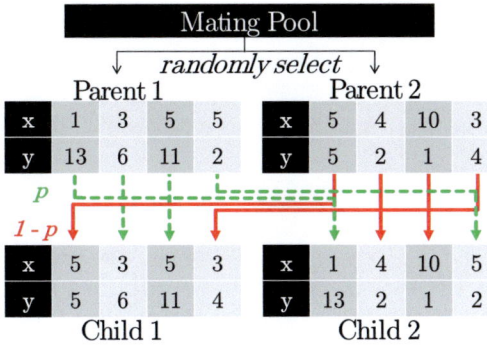

(a) Uniform crossover.

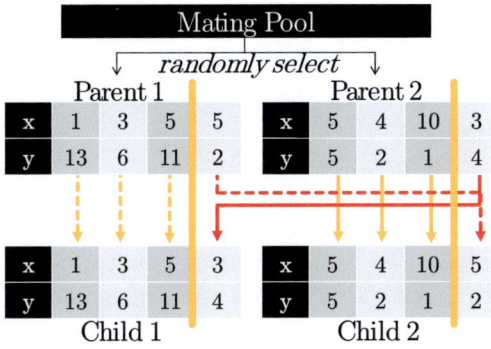

(b) One-point Crossover.

Figure 5.42: Illustration of the two recombination operators used in the experimental study: uniform crossing and one-point crossover.

Mutation

After recombination, n_{mut} random genes from the newly created individuals are slightly altered by mutation. For each gene, it is decided with a probability of p_{mut} whether the mutation is actually performed. The mutated genes, i.e., the altered coordinates of a beacon, are computed according to equation 5.25.

$$c = (\mathcal{N}(x, \sigma), \mathcal{N}(y, \sigma))$$ (5.25)

with c denoting the new coordinates of the mutated beacon, x and y represent the two-dimensional coordinates of the gene before mutation and $\mathcal{N}(m, \sigma)$ is a normally distributed random value with mean m and standard deviation σ. With this mutation method, the new coordinates are selected within a certain range around the old ones. The standard deviation of the normal distribution can be used to adjust the amount of change caused by the mutation.

New Population

The new population is created using the standard $(\mu + \lambda)$-approach, with μ denoting the size of the old population and λ describing the number of children. To build the next generation's population, μ individuals with the highest fitness are selected from the combined set of old population and children (cf. Weicker [246]).

Fitness Evaluation

As mentioned before, selecting a good fitness evaluation method is not trivial but has an important impact on the quality of the derived solutions. Hence, various fitness evaluation criteria are proposed in the following, which are then compared in experiments. To evaluate the fitness of a given solution, a multi agent simulation is used, in which the agents, i.e., evacuees who carry a mobile device, compute their locations while performing an evacuation. For this, lateration is chosen as a localization algorithm (cf. Section 2.4.2) and distance estimation based on hop counts according to Nagpal et al. [171], as well as GeoDE (cf. Algorithm 5.3) are applied. The localization technique based on hop counts is further denoted as HC. The average deviation between real and estimated positions of the mobile devices throughout the simulation period T is computed. For this, the simulation duration T is divided into time steps t, in which localization is performed and the agents move towards the designated exit. The fitness is defined as shown in Equation 5.26. It is the reciprocal term of the average deviation between real and estimated coordinates in one simulation run, with N being the set of all devices, $c_t(n)$ denoting the real position of device n at time step t, and $\bar{c}_t(n)$ its estimated position. In order to navigate people to a safe exit during evacuation, the devices have to know the right room which they are located in rather than their exact locations. This consideration leads to the next suggested fitness criteria shown in Equation 5.27. The percentage of devices which estimate their positions to be in the correct room of the considered building is computed on the basis of hop count based distance estimation and lateration.

$$F_{Pos}(HC/GeoDE) = \frac{|T| \cdot |N|}{\sum_{t \in T} \sum_{n \in N} |c_t(n) - \bar{c}_t(n)|} \tag{5.26}$$

$$F_{Room} = \frac{1}{|T|} \sum_{t \in T} 1 - \frac{|\{n \in N : room(c_t(n)) = room(\bar{c}_t(n))\}|}{|N|} \tag{5.27}$$

Apart from the simulative approach, the perimeter coverage algorithm introduced in Section 5.4.1 is used as fitness criteria. For this, the environment is partitioned into a set of squares S. Then, the coverage-degree of each square $s \in S$ is computed and the fitness value is derived by Equation 5.28, with i-cover $(s) = 1$ if square s is i-th-degree covered. The reason for computing a maximum of third-degree coverage lies in the nature of the localization algorithm. As stated before, lateration requires information from at least three beacons. As a consequence, a third-degree covered area seems to be most valuable and is, therefore, weighted more.

$$F_{PC} = \sum_{i=1}^{3} i \cdot \frac{\sum_{s \in S} i\text{-cover}(s)}{|S|} \qquad (5.28)$$

5.4.3 Evaluation

To test the effectiveness of the presented algorithm and the various fitness criteria, a simulative experiment is performed. For this, the building evacuation described in Section 4.1.2 is repeated with 100 agents, which are distributed randomly across a building (cf. Figure 5.43). The communication range is fixed at 10%. The parameter values for the EA are listed in table 5.3.

To be able to assess how much two individuals differ from each other, the Hausdorff-distance (cf. Rockafellar and Wets [198]) is used as shown in Equation 5.29. The two individuals are denoted as i and j, $B(i)$ refers to the set of beacons from individual i. The Hausdorff-distance reflects the maximum distance there is between any two closest pairs of beacons from both individuals, thus, a Hausdorff-distance of value zero indicates identical individuals. Since $hd(i,j)$ and $hd(j,i)$ are not necessarily the same, the mean value is computed as $\overline{hd}_{ij} = \frac{1}{2}(hd(i,j) + hd(j,i))$, $d(\cdot,\cdot)$ refers to the Euclidean distance.

248

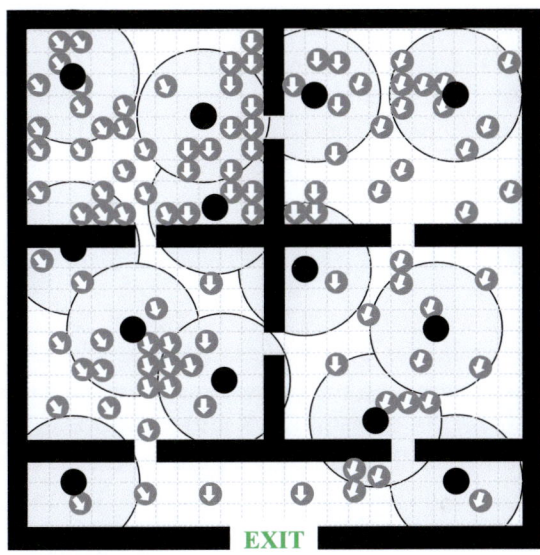

Figure 5.43: Example evacuation scenario used for the experimental study. The mobile devices are depicted as gray circles with arrows pointing to the building's exit. The beacons are depicted as black circles.

Table 5.3: Parameter settings for the simulative experiments to test the EA for beacon placement.

Parameter Name	Value
Population size (μ)	10
Probability for mutation	0.3
Standard deviation for mutation	0.05
Mating pool size ($n_{parents}$)	10
Number of agents	100
Evolutionary iterations	1000

$$hd\,(i,j) = max_{\forall b_i \in B(i)} \left(min_{b_j \in B(j)} d\,(b_i, b_j) \right) \quad (5.29)$$

The first experiment compares the progress of the average fitness value in the population over the course of evolution for all four fitness criteria. Figure 5.44 shows the results for both recombination operators described in Section 5.4.2 and a mutation rate of 1 and 5 genes per iteration. The corresponding standard deviations are depicted in Figure 5.45. It can be observed that the fitness increases steadily over time for all considered evaluation criteria. This indicates that the beacon placements are continuously optimized with respect to the given criteria. The uniform crossover with a mutation rate of 5 genomes yields the best results followed by uniform crossover with a mutation rate of 1 gene per iteration, one-point crossover with a mutation rate of 5 genes per iteration, and one-point crossover with a mutation rate of 1 gene per interation. Except for F_{PC} where one-point crossover with a mutation rate of 5 overtakes the uniform crossover with a mutation rate of 1 after about 200 iterations. Figure 5.45 shows that the standard deviation of fitness values become relatively stable towards the end

250

of the experiments for almost all considered settings, except for $F_{Pos}(GeoDE)$ with uniform crossover and a mutation rate of 5, $F_{Pos}(HC)$ with uniform crossover and a mutation rate of 1, and F_{Room} for all considered settings except uniform crossover and a mutation rate of 1. It should be noted that only the fitness value levels $F_{Pos}(GeoDE)$ and $F_{Pos}(HC)$ are directly comparable.

The most unexpected observation one can make from these results is the exceeding performance of $F_{Pos}(HC)$ when compared to $F_{Pos}(GeoDE)$. As shown in Section 5.3.3, the approach based on hop counts usually delivers localization results with lower quality than GeoDE. Hence, the superior fitness of solutions which are produced by the hop count based fitness criterion is a surprising discovery. One possible reason for this could be that finding an optimal beacon placement is more difficult for GeoDE compared to the approach based on hop counts. This seems reasonable when considering that GeoDE depends much more on the distribution of a device's neighbors compared to the approach based on hop counts. Figure 5.46 displays the individuals from the final population with the highest fitness values $F_{Pos}(HC)$ and $F_{Pos}(GeoDE)$, which are simultaneously the individuals with lowest localization error. It becomes obvious that a good beacon placement for localization based on GeoDE looks differently from a good beacon placement for localization based on hop counts. The corresponding average Hausdorff-distance is $\overline{hd}_{HC,GeoDE} = 0.25$. From these observations, it can be concluded that the applied localization method has a strong impact on the result of the EA. Consequently, it can be assumed that different localization algorithms have different requirements on the beacon placement in a network.

As mentioned before, the results in terms of fitness cannot be compared directly to each other. To overcome this issue, the final beacon placements from all four experiments are evaluated in one

251

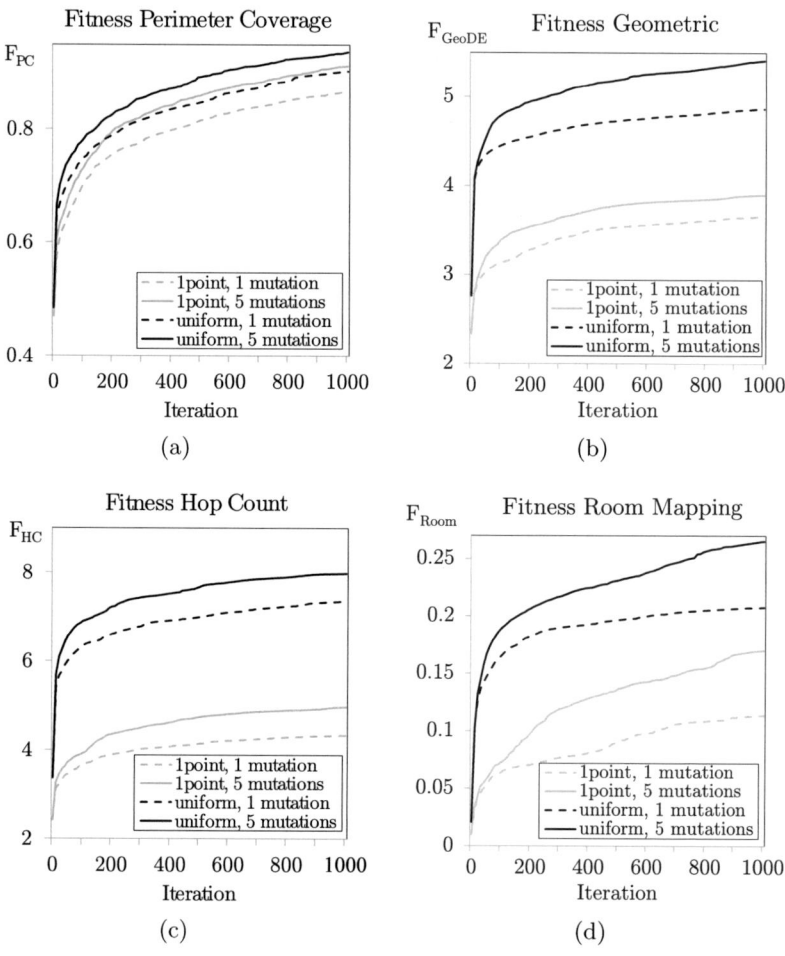

Figure 5.44: Progress of the fitness value during the evolution for perimeter coverage, GeoDE, HC, and the room mapping fitness criteria.

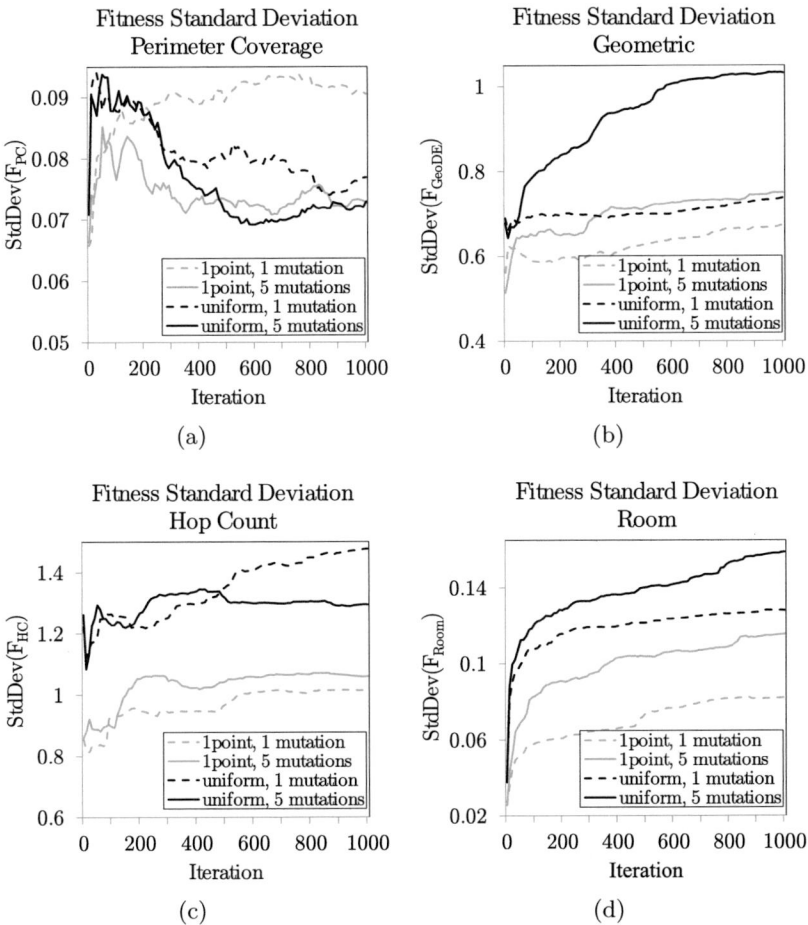

Figure 5.45: Standard deviation of the fitness values during the evolution for perimeter coverage, GeoDE, HC, and the room mapping fitness criteria.

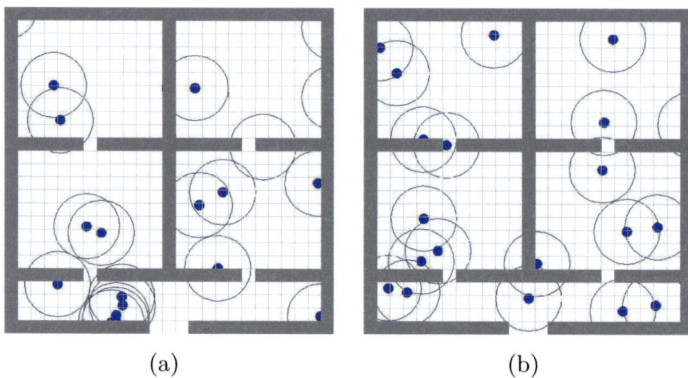

(a)   (b)

Figure 5.46: Solutions with highest fitness value evolved using the simulative GeoDE based localization (a) and localization based on hop counts (b) fitness criteria.

run of the multi-agent evacuation simulation, computing the average localization error as $\frac{1}{F_{Pos}(HC)}$. Figure 5.47 shows these results. The beacon placements evolved with the simulative localization approach based on hop counts are best in terms of localization error followed by the beacon placements evolved with the Perimeter Coverage fitness criteria, and the results produced by GeoDE-based fitness evaluation. The fact that a beacon placement evolved with a hop count based fitness criterion yields the lowest localization error when hop count based localization is applied for evaluation is not surprising. Also, it is understandable that a beacon placement which was optimized for room mapping performs worst in terms of average localization error. However, it is unexpected that the Perimeter Coverage fitness criterion delivers similarly low localization error when compared to hop count based fitness criterion. This does not necessarily mean that an optimal beacon placement

254

for localization is the same as a beacon placement with optimal coverage. The fact that a third-degree perimeter coverage was weighted more heavily than a first-degree coverage could play an important role in the high performance of this approach. This is confirmed by comparing the two best individuals evolved with the perimeter coverage approach in terms of fitness and localization error shown in Figure 5.48. While the fitter individual has a wider area covered by beacons, the individual with lower localization error has a denser beacon placement leaving more squares uncovered. From this it can be concluded that the emphasis on a third-degree covered area in the fitness function is likely to be the reason for the good performance of the perimeter coverage evolution. Nevertheless, it should be noted that the results are in fact similar, while the Perimeter Coverage approach is much less computationally complex since it does not require an evacuation simulation.

Another important discovery is that the room mapping objective obviously delivers different results compared to the criteria which consider localization errors. It becomes apparent that a low localization error is not necessarily the same objective than a good room mapping of coordinates and it has to be thought about which goal priority has before starting the optimization. When looking at the best individual in terms of localization error evolved using $F_{Pos}(HC)$ in Figure 5.46(b), it becomes obvious that placing beacons along a path to the exit seems advisable. When comparing this beacon placement with the best one evolved with perimeter coverage in terms of fitness, which is displayed in Figure 5.48 (b), they look rather different. In fact, their average Hausdorff distance $\overline{hd}_{PC,HC}$ is 0.25. However, the average localization error for both individuals is very similar with 0.11 for perimeter coverage and 0.10 for the hop count based approach. This indicates that an even better placement could be found when beacons are located close to the path leading towards an exit and, at the same time, provide good third-degree coverage.

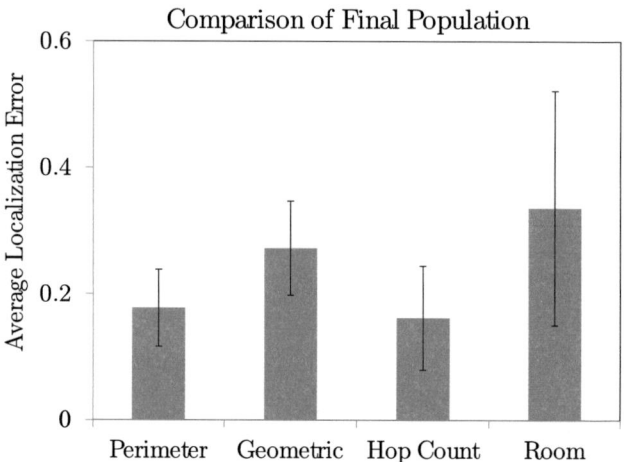

Figure 5.47: Comparison of the last populations evolved with various fitness criteria in terms of localization error.

The importance of a dense beacon placement is reinforced when looking at the best individual in terms of fitness evolved with the room mapping fitness criteria illustrated in Figure 5.49(b). Obviously, the computed coordinates map well to their corresponding room, when beacons are placed densely, even though the localization error is comparatively high in this case (cf. Figure 5.47).

5.4.4 Conclusion

In this section, an EA is introduced with the objective to optimize beacon placements for localization of mobile devices in an ad hoc network during building evacuation. Since mobility of the devices

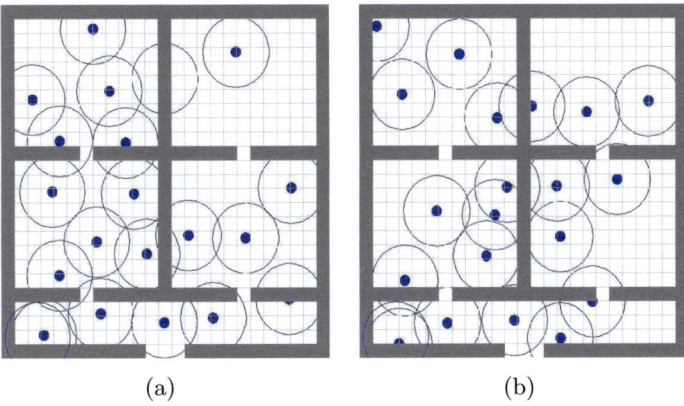

(a)   (b)

Figure 5.48: Solutions with highest fitness value (a) and lowest localization error (b) evolved using the perimeter coverage fitness criteria.

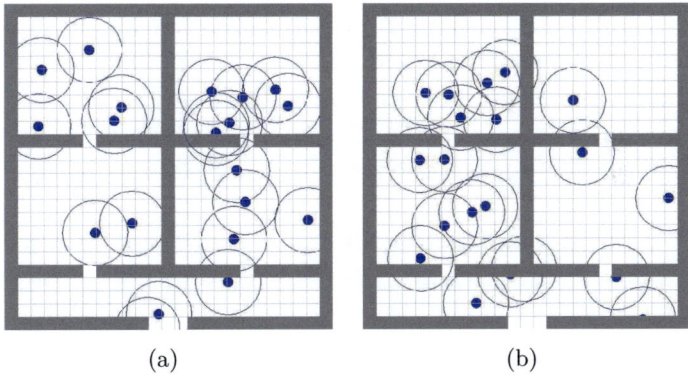

(a)   (b)

Figure 5.49: Solutions with lowest localization error evolved using simulative localization based on hop counts (a) and correct room mapping (b) fitness criteria.

and the evacuation scenario affect the network topology strongly, it is argued that simply increasing the area which is covered by beacons is not the optimal strategy to find good beacon placements. To evaluate the EA, experiments are performed with uniform and one-point crossover as recombination methods and a mutation rate of 1 or 5 genomes per iteration of the algorithm. Four different fitness evaluation criteria are proposed, three of them evaluate a beacon placement by simulating an evacuation scenario in which the devices perform localization. Two of these simulative fitness evaluations measure the average localization error during the simulation by applying lateration to distance estimates produced by a simple hop count based approach and by the GeoDE method proposed in Section 5.3. The third simulative fitness evaluation measures how often locations derived by lateration and hop count based distance estimation lie within the correct room of the building since this is especially important for computing evacuation instructions. In order to make the results comparable, the final populations are evaluated in terms of localization error in one simulation run using lateration and hop count based distance estimation. Additionally, the beacon placements with highest fitness and lowest localization error are compared and their difference is evaluated by applying the Hausdorff distance metric introduced by Rockafellar and Wets [198].

Surprisingly, the distance estimation approach based on hop counts performed best in terms of fitness and localization error closely followed by the Perimeter Coverage method. Subsequently there are GeoDE and room mapping evolution results. Unexpectedly, GeoDE is outperformed in terms of localization error by hop count based localization, even though it is found to be superior in previously investigated network scenarios (cf. Section 5.3.3). A likely reason for this is that it is more difficult to optimize beacon placements for GeoDE based localization compared to hop count based localization. In any case, the selected localization error clearly affects the optimal beacon placement in a network. It is further shown that minimizing the localization error leads to different results when compared to the objective of finding a good room mapping of calculated coordinates. In summary, beacon placements alongside a path which leads towards an exit, as well as a high third-degree coverage, are identified to be essential criteria for low localization error.

It is favorable to have a beacon placement which serves as a basis for a constantly low localization error in contrast to a low average error which is highly volatile. Hence, a further improvement of the presented approach could be to integrate the standard deviation of localization errors in the fitness evaluation.

5.5 Summary

In this chapter, range-free distance estimation, which can be used as a basis to localize devices in ad hoc networks via lateration, is subject to investigation. The focus lies on the influence which mobility of the involved devices has on the accuracy of distance estimation, whether adjustments have to be made in order to account for this impact, and which adjustments could be reasonable. Firstly, a study is presented which examines hop count based distance estimation in MANETs. A so-called hop count error measurement is introduced. It measures the deviation between actual hop counts in a network and an ideal hop count distribution, which would be obtained if the network was perfectly dense and the devices were stationary. This allows deriving general statements about the influence of mobility on any hop count based distance estimation method. Various mobility models from the literature and some novel models, which have been specifically designed for this study, are described and their impact on hop count errors is tested. Experiments reveal that mobility turns naturally positive hop count errors into unpredictably high negative hop count errors, which leads to underestimation of distances. This effect is explained by devices which move and then communicate their hop count values before updating them according to their new locations. This can affect devices at their new locations, which in turn underestimate their distances as well. An increased speed, directions leading away from beacons, and increased heterogeneity in the movements of nearby devices are found to be reinforcing factors for underestimation. MoGA is presented, which is a variant of the standard GA used to determine hop counts, in order to reduce negative hop count errors. Experiments show that this is successfully done; however, a complete elimination is not achieved. As a next step, two indicators are presented called *HC-change* and *ID-change*, which are able to identify and characterize mobility of devices in a network. Additionally, they are computable in a decentralized manner solely based on local information. The aim is to use these indicators in context of learning mechanisms provided by the O/C Architecture in order to reduce hop count errors by adapting the hop count values according to the current network dynamics.

Asynchronous communication and updates of hop counts are identified to be the main reasons for the emergence of negative hop count errors in dynamic networks. Hence, it is subsequently proposed to synchronize the devices in the network by applying a nature-inspired synchronization algorithm. Before investigating the benefit of synchronization for the determination of hop counts in dynamic networks, an assessment of the proposed synchronization algorithm is performed. In order to evaluate its effectiveness in MANETs, it is tested under different parameter constellations. Synchronization duration and synchronization success are measured. It is demonstrated that reliable synchronization success can be achieved for both, static and dynamic networks if the algorithm is initialized with a suitable parameter configuration. Furthermore, increasing the communication ranges of the devices is proven to increase the synchronization success while simultaneously reducing the time duration. An algorithm called FIHC is presented, which can be used to encode hop count information in the time difference between two signals in a synchronized network. Due to the synchrony in the network, now a device can wait until it receives a signal from its neighbors, which confirms its own hop count value, before it reports this value to other nearby devices. Waiting for confirmation before hop count communication aims at reducing negative hop count errors. Experiments confirm that this simple mechanism indeed eliminates negative hop count errors almost entirely.

Apart from hop count based distance estimation, GeoDE is presented in this chapter. This method derives distance estimates between neighboring devices from the ratio of shared to total communication partners. An algorithm is presented which extends this method in order to estimate distances over multiple hops between devices in the network and beacons. The mapping from communication partners to distances is approximated with a third-degree polynomial function, which is shown to be less error-prone when compared to an approximation with a first-order Taylor series expansion. Additionally, a short discussion about potential sources of error in GeoDE is given. The proposed algorithm is evaluated in an experimental study and compared to the results achieved by two different hop count based distance estimation approaches. GeoDE significantly outperforms the more established hop count based distance estimation technique for all considered communication ranges. This result is consistent for all three regarded stationary network distributions, namely a uniformly random network, a Gaussian random network and a network with grid-like distributed devices. Even the standard deviation of the MAPE with GeoDE lies below the error of the hop count based approach. However, when compared with a more sophisticated recently published hop count based approach called GDE, GeoDE produces estimation results of similar, marginally worse, quality in static networks. Nevertheless, in four different dynamic networks, the superiority of GeoDE over GDE is shown to be significant. The main reason for this can be assumed to lie in the previously mentioned sensitivity to negative hop count error under mobile conditions, which hop count based distance estimation methods suffer from. GDE is based on numerical integration and an additional experiment shows that it requires at least 50 steps of the Riemann integration approximation method in order to deliver more accurate distance estimates than GeoDE in static networks.

Because the placement of beacons affects the quality of localization results, an EA is presented to optimize such placements, specifically for localization during an evacuation scenario. Various fitness criteria are proposed in order to evaluate a certain beacon placement. Two fitness criteria are based on the average localization error produced with lateration during a simulated evacuation scenario. One determines locations on the basis of hop counts, the other uses GeoDE. A third fitness evaluation method measures the average percentage of devices which locate themselves in the correct room using lateration and hop count based distance estimation. The last proposed fitness evaluation is based on a method proposed in the literature in order to determine the perimeter coverage-degree of a beacon placement. According to this method, the perimeter of a beacon is denoted as one-degree covered when it's perimeter is completely covered by other beacons' perimeters. The fitness value is computed in a way that third-degree covered beacons are valued the most since at least three beacons are required to compute two-dimensional locations using lateration. An experimental study is conducted to evaluate the proposed EA. It is shown that beacon placements are indeed optimized over time with respect to the individual fitness functions. Two recombination methods, namely uniform and one-point crossing, and a mutation rate of 1 and 5 genes per genome are tested. Uniform crossing with a mutation rate of 5 delivers best results, independently of the underlying fitness evaluation method. While lowest localization errors are produced by beacon placements evolved according to hop count based fitness, perimeter coverage fitness evaluation follows closely behind. Subsequently, there are beacon placements produced by GeoDE based evolution and placements evolved based on the room mapping fitness criterion. Comparison of some evolved beacon placements from final populations reveal that an optimal placement for hop count based distance estimation is rather different from one evolved to be used with GeoDE. Moreover, minimizing localization error yields different beacon placements when compared to optimizing the room mapping of derived locations. Furthermore, the experiments indicated that finding an optimal beacon placement is more challenging for GeoDE than hop count based methods. In general, a beacon placement with a high third-degree coverage and where beacons are located alongside paths towards the building's exit seem to be desirable.

As a summary, it can be concluded from the research presented in this chapter that localization algorithms have huge performance deviations depending on the characteristics of the network, the mobility of the devices in the network, and the placement of beacons. This confirms that learning mechanisms should be applied in order to improve localization in OBESS. Firstly, to the mobile devices such that they learn how to select appropriate localization algorithms at runtime depending on the current environmental state and, secondly, to the CCU in order to optimize beacon placements for localization in that specific building.

CHAPTER 6

CONCLUSION

Increasingly large and complex buildings are the main motivation for a long overdue overhaul of today's building evacuation support. In order to achieve this goal, OBESS has been proposed in this thesis, a system consisting of partly mobile devices used to navigate potential evacuees during an emergency evacuation. This chapter concludes the presented work by summarizing the major contributions in Section 6.1 and describing aspects which remain open for future research in Section 6.2. Section 6.3 gives some final remarks on the work presented.

6.1 Summary

This thesis has made three major contributions to advance the evacuation support equipment in buildings. Firstly, main problems of current emergency equipment have been identified and a concept for an evacuation support system has been presented in order to overcome these limitations. Section 6.1.1 summarizes these findings. Secondly, the concept of decentralized and distributed evacuation route planning with mobile devices has been investigated. The developments regarding this topic are described in Section 6.1.2. Thirdly, localization of mobile devices in ad hoc networks has been addressed. Section 6.1.3 concludes this summary by presenting the research performed in this domain.

6.1.1 Organic Building Evacuation Support System

The preparations of today's buildings for an emergency evacuation mainly consist of stationary, analogous emergency evacuation maps and exit signs installed for the purpose of guiding evacuees towards safe areas or exits. This route guidance system is designed by experts at the time of construction. The objective is to provide for a well-ordered evacuation in case of an emergency situation as it is most likely to occur in that specific building. This includes the estimation of the average number of people located inside that building and their most probable distribution across the rooms. However, this evaluation can be far from reality of an actual evacuation scenario. Furthermore, potential blockages of passages due to collapsed masonry or congestions of evacuees in front of narrow passages or doors can change the optimal route completely. Another problem with today's evacuation support is its stationary nature. Exit signs and evacuation maps are likely to be overlooked, especially when in panic. Consequently, an ideal evacuation support system is desired to react in an adaptive manner to changes in its environment while also being portable. In addition, an ideal evacuation support system should be designed in a way such that the optimal escape route can be personalized according to the specific needs of a particular evacuee. Such individual needs can result, for example from high age or a physical disability of the evacuee, which could make it necessary to avoid narrow passages or stairs. In order to achieve the aforementioned objectives, this thesis has proposed to use mobile devices, such as smart phones or tablet PCs, for evacuation support in buildings. Mobile devices possess computing capacities and digital screens which enable adaptive route guidance. Furthermore, they are usually equipped with means for wireless communication, which allow for the collection of information about the current evacuation situation inside a building. This knowledge can then be incorporated in the escape route planning process. Furthermore, mobile devices are portable and belong to specific users, thereby, fulfilling all previously mentioned desired characteristics for an emergency navigation device.

In this thesis, OBESS has been proposed as an evacuation support system that consists of three main components, a CCU, an SSN, and mobile devices which are capable of establishing ad hoc network connections via local communication. The CCU is used for the configuration of the static sensors which are distributed across the building. The CCU communicates the layout of the building to the sensors, as well as all other information required to support the evacuation route planning and localization process of the mobile devices. This can, for example, be a graph model of the building's layout or information about the sensors' own locations inside the building in order to serve as beacons for the localization of mobile devices. Moreover, the CCU is intended to collect information about the performance of OBESS which can then be used for building-specific optimization. An example of such an optimization is given in Section 5.4 of this thesis, where the placement of sensors in the building is optimized in order to improve localization accuracy. Sensors are able to communicate with each other and with mobile devices whenever they are within reach as well as to provide necessary input for evacuation route planning and localization. Evacuation route planning is performed directly on the mobile devices, which use their ad hoc network connections in order to exchange information about the current evacuation situation and use it to improve evacuation route planning. The computed evacuation paths are then displayed on the devices' screens or provided as voice instructions to the user.

Although there is a CCU in this system architecture, OBESS is designed as a decentralized system in order to avoid having a single point of failure. Therefore, in case the CCU fails to work, the evacuation system still continues to function. In addition, occasional sensors can be defective without rendering the entire evacuation support system useless. It is even conceivable to install some navigation devices inside the building in order to provide guidance for evacuees without or with broken mobile devices. Consequently, due to this design, OBESS is quite robust against failures. This is of special importance as building evacuation is usually a life-threatening situation where a support system is expected to work robustly.

Another crucial virtue of OBESS is the concept of self-organization between the mobile devices in order to employ adaptive evacuation route planning and localization, such that the ability to react to unforeseen changes in the environment is provided for. Self-organization, however, can lead to undesired emergent system behavior, which can be avoided by using the generic O/C Architecture from Organic Computing. This architecture provides means for controlled self-organization and, hence, allows a system to be flexible as well as robust and trustworthy at the same time. This thesis has shown how the generic O/C Architecture can be applied to mobile evacuation devices in order to allow for controllable self-organization in evacuation route planning, as well as in the localization procedure. For evacuation planning, the online learning mechanism can be used to decide if an evacuation instruction has to be updated due to changes in the environment. Additionally, offline-learning allows for validating an evacuation instruction in a simulative environment before it is made available to the evacuee. This quality management is meant to improve evacuation instructions and, thus, the resulting evacuation process. Moreover, it has been described how the two-level learning mechanism of the O/C Architecture can be used for the selection of an appropriate localization algorithm from a set of different algorithms available to the device. The choice is made by taking into account the current topology of the MANET or other criteria, such as the state-of-charge of the mobile device's battery. The intrinsic control mechanism of the O/C Architecture uses feedback mechanisms such as consistency checks and dead-reckoning methods for evaluating the performance of the selected algorithm and decides about an appropriate control action, which can be a change of the applied localization algorithm. Furthermore, a simulation of the current network topology can be set-up and algorithms can be tested in this simulative environment before they are applied during runtime. In addition to these intrinsic control mechanisms, possibilities for direct user control have been presented, such as correcting computed locations by tapping on the device's screen or triggering an update of the evacuation instruction by simply walking in another direction than the one suggested by the current navigation instruction.

6.1.2 Swarm Evacuation Planning

After having introduced the architecture for a self-organizing and robust evacuation support system, this thesis has addressed the task of decentralized evacuation route planning with mobile devices. In contrast to standard path planning approaches, which use global knowledge of the evacuation situation in order to optimize escape routes, the main challenge for OBESS is the uncertainty of the information basis available to each mobile device for finding an optimal evacuation route for its user. Due to the decentralized system architecture, the mobile devices can only rely on local communication with devices within their proximity and information dissemination over ad hoc network connections for generating and updating their knowledge base. SEP refers to such decentralized evacuation planning methods which use only local information as a basis. Two SEP algorithms have been developed and evaluated in this thesis. Both algorithms are adaptive to changes in this knowledge base and are shown to accelerate the evacuation process when compared to a situation in which evacuees' choose the shortest path towards an exit of the building.

The first method is called CC-SEP. It uses a macroscopic graph model of the building and a flow optimization approach to find optimal evacuation routes for each evacuee. This is done by scheduling all evacuees such that the overall evacuation time is minimized and by subsequently selecting an appropriate path for the device's specific user. This approach has been subject to thorough investigation. Varying numbers of evacuees, distributions inside the building, communication ranges of the mobile devices, and several configuration parameters of CC-SEP have been investigated. Moreover, different building layouts have been used for evaluation in order to confirm the generality of the results. Additionally, a robustness test has been performed, in which the number of evacuees who follow the provided navigation instructions have been varied. In summary, it has been shown that CC-SEP leads to a lower overall evacuation time in almost all considered scenarios when compared to a situation in which all evacuees follow the shortest path. Furthermore, the approach has been proven to be robust in scenarios with up to 30% of evacuees which deviate from suggested evacuation routes. Although the evacuation time has been shown to increase slightly when the evacuation planning is performed repeatedly in order to adapt to changes in the knowledge base, it is still faster than in the scenario where evacuees simply follow the shortest paths.

DMO-SEP is the second SEP algorithm, which has been proposed in this thesis. This algorithm uses a discretized version of the building layout instead of a macroscopic graph model as a basis for route planning, a complex cost function to evaluate different routes, and a dynamic path finding algorithm. This dynamic algorithm adapts evacuation paths to newly available information, which reduces the necessary computations when compared to methods which compute the optimal path from scratch. Moreover, DMO-SEP is suited to take into account user specific objectives in the evacuation route optimization process, such as an individual level of risk aversion or others. For the evaluation of different evacuation paths with regard to their potential for congestions, two congestion indicators have been proposed. The first one is called *load* and it is based on the number of evacuees with respect to the size of the room in which they are located in. The second indicator focuses on the *entropy* of evacuees' locations in rooms, i.e., their concentration. An experimental study has been performed in which DMO-SEP is compared to CC-SEP and the different optimization objectives are investigated. It has been shown that DMO-SEP can further improve the overall evacuation time when compared to CC-SEP.

Additionally, DMO-SEP is demonstrated to be able to consider different objectives when optimizing the evacuation path, such as risk aversion or congestion avoidance. Moreover, both congestion indicators have been compared and it is revealed that *load* is an indicator better suited to improve the overall evacuation time than *entropy*, although both indicators lead to an overall faster evacuation when compared to minimizing travel distance only.

6.1.3 Range-free Distance Estimation in Mobile Ad hoc Networks

Distance-based localization has been identified to be the first choice for localization of mobile devices in OBESS since such algorithms are decentralized, deliver absolute localization results, do not necessarily require bulky hardware, and are more accurate than proximity-based localization approaches. In order to apply distance-based localization, distance estimates between the devices to be located and beacons, i.e., devices which know their own locations, have to be determined. For this purpose, many distance estimation techniques have been proposed in the literature and described in this thesis. Range-free distance estimation is especially suited for an application in OBESS because it exploits ad hoc network connections instead of relying on the analysis of a physical communication signal. This way, the hardware requirements of the mobile devices, as well as the number of required beacons in the system are reduced, hence, reducing the total installation costs of such an evacuation support system. However, most range-free distance estimation concepts have not yet been subject to research when applied to mobile devices instead of static ones. Since the devices in OBESS are mobile, the application of such algorithms to MANETs has been addressed in this thesis.

In the first instance, an extensive study has been performed to investigate the effect various mobility models have on distance estimation based on hop counts, i.e., the minimum number of relay devices between the device to be located and the beacon. This study has revealed that mobility has a negative impact on the accuracy of hop count based distance estimation due to asynchronous computation and communication of hop counts. While hop count based distance overestimation is a common problem in static networks, to which many solutions have already been proposed in the literature, mobility of devices can turn this overestimation into an unpredictably high underestimation. It has been argued thoroughly in this thesis that it is crucial to avoid such an underestimation in order to improve the accuracy of localization in mobile networks. In this study, speed and direction of a device's movement with respect to beacons have been shown to have a significant impact on the underestimation. Additionally, similarity in the movements of devices which are close together has been identified to have an impact on this kind of underestimation. MoGA, a modified version of a standard algorithm for determining hop counts has been proposed in this thesis and has been shown to reduce mobility induced underestimation. Furthermore, two indicators have been introduced, which can be computed based on local information from the hop counting algorithm. These indicators have been shown to be suited for identifying whether a device moves and which characteristics its movement has. In the context of O/C Architecture, these indicators could be used for letting the devices learn how to adjust hop count based distance estimation results in order to compensate for mobility induced underestimation.

Since asynchronous hop count computation and communication have been identified to be the main reasons for the negative impact of mobility, this thesis has examined whether a MANET can be synchronized in order to reduce mobility induced underestimation. A nature-inspired, decentralized synchronization algorithm has been investigated in static and dynamic network scenarios with varying communication ranges and configuration parameters. It has been shown that synchronization can be achieved reliably in both, static and dynamic networks, when initialized with suitable parameter values. Based on synchronized networks, FIHC, an algorithm for scheduling the communication of hop count values, has been introduced. Two variants of this hop counting algorithm have been investigated and compared to the standard hop count algorithm. Experiments have revealed that this scheduling of hop count messages in a network can significantly reduce mobility induced underestimation, up to an almost complete elimination of underestimation in the scenario considered.

Apart from hop count based distance estimation, a connectivity-based distance estimation approach called GeoDE has been developed in this thesis. This approach utilizes the ratio of shared to total communication partners between two devices for estimating the distance between them. It has been shown how this algorithm can be used for the purpose of estimating distances between beacons and devices in the network. As for the mapping of ratios to distance estimates, two approximation approaches have been compared, and it has been shown that the linear regression yields a lower approximation error when compared to a first order Taylor series expansion. GeoDE has been evaluated for varying communication ranges of the mobile devices and for different static network topologies. Additionally, dynamic networks using different mobility models have been investigated. It has been demonstrated that GeoDE outperforms two different state-of-the-art hop count based distance estimation techniques in static and dynamic networks for almost all cases considered. Only when compared to GDE from Liu et al. [140] in a uniformly random distributed static network, GeoDE does not significantly outperform the hop count based estimation method, but rather delivers quite similar localization errors. However, an additional experiment has shown that this is only the case when numerical integration in GDE is approximated with a sufficiently high accuracy. In any other case, GeoDE is superior to this estimation method as well.

The final contribution of this thesis to the research areas of evacuation management and localization alike is an EA which optimizes the placement of beacons for the application of mobile device localization during building evacuation. Building evacuation leads to a change in the distribution of mobile devices in the building over time, with devices temporarily concentrating at bottleneck-areas, such as doors or narrow passages, and tending to cluster around the exits of the building after a certain time. This dynamically changing topology poses a special challenge for finding an optimal beacon placement to support localization during the whole evacuation process. Since only little is known about the characteristics of a potentially good beacon placement for this specific application scenario and the search space is quite large, a heuristic optimization approach has been chosen to tackle the problem. Four different evaluation criteria for the fitness evaluation process have been proposed in this thesis. Three of these evaluation criteria are based on a simulative building evacuation, during which the mobile devices determine their locations via distance-based localization. The first variant uses hop count based distance estimation for localization, the second variant is based on GeoDE. The average localization error of all devices during the evacuation has been taken as an evaluation criterion for determining the fitness, i.e., quality, of a specific beacon distribution. The third simulative evaluation method also uses hop count based distance estimation for the localization of the devices, but a room mapping criterion, instead of the average localization error, forms the basis for fitness evaluation. This criterion measures how often the determined locations match the correct room in which the devices are actually located in. As a fourth fitness evaluation criterion a so-called perimeter coverage approach has been examined. A beacon distribution has high perimeter coverage when a large area is covered by the communication ranges of the beacons and the perimeters of their communication ranges have many overlaps. The experimental evaluation has delivered some valuable insights into an optimal beacon placement for localization during a building evacuation scenario. Beacon placements with a high perimeter coverage placed alongside a path towards the exit of the building have been found suitable to support localization in the considered scenario. Furthermore, it has been shown that a beacon placement which results in a low average localization error is not necessarily optimal when it comes to determining the correct room in which devices are located in and vice versa. Hence, it is important to determine the appropriate optimization objective before choosing a beacon placement. In addition, the study has revealed that GeoDE, although previously proven to be superior to hop count based distance estimation in mobile networks, can under certain conditions result in a higher average localization error when applied to an evacuation scenario. This finding indicates that alternating between localization algorithms during runtime in response to changing conditions of the environment can improve localization results. This finding confirms the strategy for an adaptive evacuation and localization approach proposed in this thesis.

6.2 Outlook

With the introduction of the concept of OBESS and the proposal for decentralized path planning and localization, this thesis has laid the foundation for a long overdue changeover in building evacuation support. By applying the O/C Architecture from Organic Computing to the mobile devices used in OBESS, the devices are capable of autonomously computing their locations in the building and of finding optimal evacuation instructions while at the same time maintaining their controllability by the user. With the introduction of this concept, the development of decentralized evacuation planning methods, and the new insights about range-free localization in dynamic networks, the research objectives of this thesis have been fulfilled. However, the main ambition of this thesis is to initiate a process, in which researchers improve and reconsider the presented ideas in order to further develop the vision of building evacuation support via mobile devices. In the following, some initial thoughts on potential improvements are presented.

6.2.1 Organic Building Evacuation Support System

While the focus of this thesis has been laid on the mobile evacuation devices used in OBESS, the design of the CCU is another important factor. As already mentioned, the CCU could also be implemented according to the generic O/C Architecture, allowing for the learning of building-specific characteristics in order to improve the performance of OBESS over time. Information about the number of people inside the building at specific days or about the most frequented rooms, et cetera, can be collected from the mobile devices using the SSN connections, transferred to the CCU and incorporated in the building-specific optimization process. Using this data, potential bottleneck-passages in the building could be

277

identified and removed. In Section 2.3.2, several publications are presented which address the optimization of buildings to enable faster or less dangerous evacuation. Such optimization includes the deliberate placement of barriers inside the building or additional doors in order to prevent congestions. This optimization could be performed on the CCU in OBESS, with the great benefit of being able to use building-specific characteristics as a basis for evaluating measures before they are applied to the building. Since adaptation of buildings via constructional measures can be cost intensive, this is a major advantage of OBESS. Additionally, the CCU can use collected data in order to improve the localization of mobile devices in OBESS. One example of such an optimization approach has been presented in Section 5.4 of this thesis, where an EA is used to find appropriate placements of beacons in a building with the aim of supporting localization during an evacuation scenario. This idea could be expanded even further by collecting data from multiple CCUs in OBESS-ready buildings on external servers in order to provide an even broader learning basis.

Apart from developing building-specific optimization concepts, the general design of OBESS needs to be considered. For example, the user interfaces provided by the CCU or the mobile devices have to be defined. Questions have to be addressed, such as which data should be displayed to the user and in which form should the layout of the building be provided to OBESS, et cetera. When talking about the building layout, it is essential to consider certain standards for layouts, as well as a way to make them automatically readable by OBESS. Moreover, further research is required which focuses on the automatic transformation of building layouts to macroscopic evacuation graphs, which can be used as a basis for CC-SEP. Additionally, it would be useful to enhance the layout by providing information about the location of first-aid kits, fire extinguishers, or others. It is also conceivable to add information about other points-of-interest inside the building. Such information could be anything, from the locations of paintings in a museum accompanied by additional background information, over the locations of printers or conference rooms in an office building, up to the location of restrooms, check-in desks, or gates at an airport. Similar to computing evacuation instructions, the mobile devices in OBESS could be used for navigating users to such points-of-interest in non-hazardous situations. Furthermore, OBESS could be used to help users to find each other by sending a search request via the SSN and waiting for a response from the user that is searched for.

Another important feature of the CCU in OBESS is the configuration of all sensors in the SSN as to their respective locations inside the building. The question arises how this can be done in a way that the manual configuration to be carried out by the user is kept to a minimum. One approach to reduce this overhead could be to configure only a small amount of sensors manually and derive the locations of all other sensors by applying any of the proposed localization algorithms in Section 2.4.1. In order to do so, it has to be investigated which sensors in the network require manual configuration and which localization algorithm has to be applied to determine the locations of the remaining sensors.

So far, it has been argued in this thesis that a central approach to evacuation support is undesirable due to the high risk of failure. However, it could be reasonable to rely on centralized evacuation planning, as long as the CCU is unimpaired, and to use decentralized mechanisms either supplementary or as a fallback. This could reduce the amount of communication and computation which mobile devices have to perform and, hence, increase the lifetime of their batteries. When it comes to the development of software running on mobile evacuation devices in OBESS, a challenge which has to be faced are well-known technical issues which arise with wireless communication between a multitude of devices, e.g., signal collisions, interferences, et cetera (cf. Rappaport [190]). However, there are already several proposals to remedy such problems, for example published by Priyantha et al. [183].

6.2.2 Swarm Evacuation Planning

In the proposed SEP approaches, the age-value of a message is solely used to resolve conflicts, although it provides additional knowledge about how much time has passed since the location has been computed. Evacuation planning is likely to deliver even better results, when reported locations of other evacuees in the building are extrapolated using the age-values of the respective messages and knowledge about the evacuees' traveling speeds and directions, which can be computed using historic location information. Another field of application is to utilize the age-value for evaluating the reliability of a certain piece of information. When two paths are only slightly different with respect to their congestion potential, it could be reasonable to select the path for which the obtained information is more recent and, hence, more reliable. For DMO-SEP, additional work is to be done in order to answer the question how to determine the right weights of different objectives. Ideally, the weights are derived automatically from user preferences. However, since a user cannot be expected to define the degree of its own risk aversion, learning a user's preferences and characteristics from its behavior could be one direction of future research in the area of evacuation management. Smart phones are often connected to social media platforms, where personal information about the user can be stored. This could be of help when approaching the task of identifying a user's preferences. Nevertheless, this remains an open challenge and, surely, the protection of the user's privacy has to be considered when pursuing such an approach.

6.2.3 Range-free Distance Estimation in Mobile Ad Hoc Networks

In the study about the performance of hop count based distance estimation under mobile conditions, which has been presented in this thesis, two indicators have been proposed in order to assess the mobility in a network. In a next step, these indicators have to be mapped to a specific adaptation of the hop count values such that underestimation is compensated and the accuracy of the hop count values is improved. Such a mapping could, for example, be derived using a supervised machine learning approach. The multitude of mobility models described in this thesis forms a rich basis for generating suitable training data. If it were possible to derive a fixed mapping, this mapping could then be used to improve the results of any hop count based distance estimation technique when applied to dynamic networks.

Apart from refining the standard GA by using hop count adaptation, a synchronization based hop counting method called FIHCd has been presented in this thesis. One limitation of this method is that it assumes devices to be able to send signals at arbitrarily short time intervals. There are cases, however, in which this assumption does not hold. Especially in large networks, the difference between two successive hop count signals becomes very small with the proposed method. In order to overcome this drawback and preserve the benefit of negative hop count error reduction, FIHCd can be modified as follows. The network is still assumed to be synchronous but mobile devices send their hop count information in the form of a message instead of simple signals at the end of their timers' periods, similar to standard GA. However, the devices now alternate between a listening and a sending period and they are only allowed to send messages during the sending period after having received a message during the listening period which confirms their hop count value or leads to an update respectively. In any other case, the sending period turns into a listening period until a message is received. This method can avoid having devices send messages before they managed to update their hop counts after having moved away from their current gradient ring similar to FIHCd.

As for GeoDE, a potential improvement could be to use a weighted average of the computed distance estimates between two neighbors. A device which has a higher number of neighbors in its communication range can be expected to deliver a more accurate estimate; hence, its initial estimate should be assigned a higher weight when computing the average value.

Finally, there are several potential improvements of the EA for optimizing beacon placements, which has been presented in the last section of Chapter 5. Firstly, the evolutions could be initialized with regular beacon placements, such as grid-like distributions, in order to examine whether such simple structures leave room for improvements. Another improvement could be to refine the fitness function of the EA. So far, only the average localization error was taken as a basis for evaluating a particular beacon placement. Another objective, however, could be to obtain localization errors which are constant for the time of the entire evacuation and similar for all evacuees in the building. Furthermore, it could be interesting to look at a combination of the fitness evaluation criteria proposed. In general, EAs have many more configuration parameters, which have not yet been examined, such as the population size, the number of parents or children during recombination, the mutation operator employed, and many more. Before an EA is used productively in an OBESS system, finding an optimal configuration should be subject to thorough investigation.

6.3 Final Remarks

While certainly not aiming at providing final solutions to the challenges of modern and adaptive evacuation management for buildings, this thesis has demonstrated the huge potential that lies within the usage of mobile devices for navigation support, especially during an emergency. The ability of the devices to communicate with each other offers the opportunity to collect relevant and up-to-date information about the evacuation situation, which can be used for dynamic and adaptive evacuation route planning. Two approaches are provided in this thesis for accomplishing this goal. Moreover, it has been shown how an evacuation system can be designed in a decentralized and self-organizing manner by applying concepts from Organic Computing. This provides for a system which exhibits an almost life-like adaptability and flexibility towards unforeseen changes in its environment and, at the same time, stays robust, trustworthy, and controllable. Especially, in an unpredictable and dynamic situation such as a life-threatening emergency evacuation, these traits are crucial system properties. Apart from suggesting a concept for future evacuation management, the challenge of localizing mobile device inside a building, where GPS-signals are not available, has been addressed. Problems which arise due to the mobility of the devices have been identified and various solution approaches have been suggested and successfully evaluated in experiments. It is, therefore, believed that the insights gained in this thesis have the potential to significantly improve indoor navigation systems. In conclusion, this thesis has laid the foundation for a changeover in the evacuation support of modern buildings, meeting the standards of the technological progress which has already found its way into most other areas of human life.

LIST OF TABLES

LIST OF FIGURES

LIST OF DEFINITIONS

LIST OF ALGORITHMS

LIST OF ABBREVIATIONS

ACO Ant Colony Optimization

AoA Angle of Arrival

APIT Approximated Point-in-Triangle Test

BMBF German Federal Ministry for Education and Research

BR Bounded Random Walk

CM Chaos Move

ColM Column Mobility

CCRP Capacity Constrained Routing Planner

CC-SEP Capacity Constrained Swarm Evacuation Planner

CCU Central Control Unit

DFG German Research Foundation

DMO-SEP Dynamic Multi-objective Swarm Evacuation Planner

EA Evolutionary Algorithm

FIHC Firefly-inspired Hop Counting

FIHCd Firefly-inspired Hop Counting with Delay

GA Gradient Algorithm

GDE Gradient-based Distance Estimation

GeoDE Geometric Distance Estimation

GI German Informatics Society

GM Gauss Markov Move

GPS Global Positioning System

IETF Internet Engineering Task Force

ITG Information Technology Society

LCS Learning Classifier System

MANET Mobile Ad Hoc Network

MAPE Mean absolute percentage error

MDF Maximum Dynamic Flow

MDS-Map Multidimensional Scaling Map

MoGA Maximum-oriented Gradient Algorithm

NomM Nomadic Move

OBESS Organic Building Evacuation Support System

O/C Architecture Observer/Controller Architecture

PR Probabilistic Random Walk

QF Quickest Flow

RD Random Direction Walk

RefM Reference Point Mobility

RSSI Radio Signal Strength Indication

RW Random Walk

SDP Semi-definite Programming

SEP Swarm Evacuation Planning

SSN Static Sensor Network

StrM Stream Mobility

SuOC System under Observation and Control

TDoA Time Difference of Arrival

ToA Time of Arrival

ToF Time of Flight

UMF Universal Maximum Flow

WLAN Wireless Local Area Network

BIBLIOGRAPHY

[1] N. Abramson. The ALOHA system: Another alternative for computer communications. In *Proceedings of the 1970 Fall Joint Computer Conference*, pages 281–285. ACM Press, 1970.

[2] AG Optimierung - TU Kaiserslautern. REPKA - Regionale Evakuierung: Planung, Kontrolle und Anpassung, January 2013. http://www.repka-evakuierung.de.

[3] R. Akl, K. Pasupathy, and M. Haidar. Anchor nodes placement for effective passive localization. In *Proceedings of the 2011 International Conference on Selected Topics in Mobile and Wireless Networking*, pages 127–132. IEEE, 2011.

[4] I. F. Akyildiz, W. Su, Y. Sankarasubramaniam, and E. Cayirci. Wireless sensor networks: A survey. *Computer Networks*, 38:393–422, 2002.

[5] R. Alizadeh. A dynamic cellular automaton model for evacuation process with obstacles. *Safety Science*, 49(2):315–323, 2011.

[6] F. Allerding, B. Becker, and H. Schmeck. Decentralised energy management for smart homes. In C. Müller-Schloer, H. Schmeck, and T. Ungerer, editors, *Organic Computing - A Paradigm Shift for Complex Systems*, Autonomic Systems, pages 605–607. Springer, 2011.

[7] K. K. Almuzaini and T. A. Gulliver. A new distributed range-free localization algorithm for wireless networks. In *Proceedings of the 70th IEEE Vehicular Technology Conference*, pages 174–178. IEEE, 2009.

[8] T. Amemiya, J. Yamashita, K. Hirota, and M. Hirose. Virtual leading blocks for the deaf-blind: a real-time way-finder by verbal-nonverbal hybrid interface and high-density RFID tag space. In *Proceedings of the 2004 IEEE Virtual Reality Conference*, pages 165–287. IEEE, 2004.

[9] M. Arikawa, S. Konomi, and K. Ohnishi. Navitime: Supporting pedestrian navigation in the real world. *IEEE Pervasive Computing*, 6(3):21–29, 2007.

[10] F. Aslam, C. Schindelhauer, and A. Vater. Improving geometric distance estimation for sensor networks and unit disk graphs. In *Proceedings of the 2009 International Conference on Ultra Modern Telecommunications Workshops*, pages 1–5, 2009.

[11] J. Aspnes, D. Goldenberg, and Y. R. Yang. On the computational complexity of sensor network localization. In

Proceedings of 1st International Workshop on Algorithmic Aspects of Wireless Sensor Networks, pages 32–44. Springer, 2004.

[12] J. Bachrach and C. Taylor. Localization in sensor networks. In *Handbook of Sensor Networks*, pages 277–310. John Wiley & Sons, 2005.

[13] P. Bahl and V. N. Padmanabhan. RADAR: an in-building RF-based user location and tracking system. In *Proceedings of the 19th Annual Joint Conference of the IEEE Computer and Communications Societies*, pages 775–784. IEEE Computer Society, 2000.

[14] S. M. Ballew. *Managing IP networks with Cisco Routers.* O'Reilly, 1997.

[15] D. Bartlett. *Essentials of Positioning and Location Technology.* Cambridge University Press, 2013.

[16] J. Baus, A. Krüger, and W. Wahlster. A resource-adaptive mobile navigation system. In *Proceedings of the 7th International Conference on Intelligent User Interfaces*, pages 15–22. ACM Press, 2002.

[17] P. Bergamo and G. Mazzini. Localization in sensor networks with fading and mobility. In *Proceedings of the 13th IEEE International Symposium on Personal, Indoor and Mobile Radio Communications*, pages 750–754. IEEE, 2002.

[18] M. Bessho, S. Kobayashi, N. Koshizuka, and K. Sakamura. A space-identifying ubiquitous infrastructure and its application for tour-guiding service. In *Proceedings of the 2008 ACM*

symposium on Applied computing, pages 1616–1621. ACM Press, 2008.

[19] K. Bing, L. Fu, Y. Zhuo, and L. Yanlei. Design of an internet of things-based smart home system. In *Proceedings of the 2nd International Conference on Intelligent Control and Information Processing*, pages 921–924. Curran Associates, 2011.

[20] Bluetooth SIG, Inc. Bluetooth technology, July 2013. http://www.bluetooth.com.

[21] S. Bottani. Pulse-coupled relaxation oscillators: From biological synchronization to self-organized criticality. *Physical Review Letters*, 74(21):4189–4192, 1995.

[22] A. Boukerche, B. Turgut, N. Aydin, M. Z. Ahmad, L. Bölöni, and D. Turgut. Routing protocols in ad hoc networks: A survey. *Computer Networks*, 55(13):3032–3080, 2011.

[23] J. Branke, M. Mnif, C. Müller-Schloer, H. Prothmann, U. Richter, F. Rochner, and H. Schmeck. Organic Computing - addressing complexity by controlled self-organization. In *Proceedings of the 2nd International Symposium on Leveraging Applications of Formal Methods, Verification and Validation*, pages 185–191. IEEE, 2006.

[24] H. Breu and D. G. Kirkpatrick. Unit disk graph recognition is NP-hard. *Computational Geometry*, 9(1-2):3–24, 1998.

[25] W. Brockmann, E. Maehle, K.-E. Grosspietsch, N. Rosemann, and B. Jakimovski. ORCA: An organic robot control architecture. In C. Müller-Schloer, H. Schmeck, and T. Ungerer,

editors, *Organic Computing - A Paradigm Shift for Complex Systems*, Autonomic Systems, pages 385–398. Springer, 2011.

[26] R. Brown. *Social Psychology, 2nd Ed.* Free Press, 2003.

[27] R. Bucher and D. Misra. A synthesizable VHDL model of the exact solution for three-dimensional hyperbolic positioning system. *VLSI Design*, 15(2):507–520, 2002.

[28] J. B. Buck. Synchronous rhythmic flashing of fireflies. *The Quarterly Review of Biology*, 13(3):301–314, 1938.

[29] N. Bulusu, J. Heidemann, and D. Estrin. GPS-less low-cost outdoor localization for very small devices. *IEEE Personal Communications*, 7(5):28–34, 2000.

[30] N. Bulusu, V. Bychkovskiy, D. Estrin, and J. Heidemann. Scalable, ad hoc deployable RF-based localization. *Proceedings of the Grace Hopper Conference on Celebration of Women in Computing*, 2002.

[31] R. Burkard, K. Dlaska, and B. Klinz. The quickest flow problem. *Mathematical Methods of Operations Research*, 37 (1):31–58, 1993.

[32] C Burstedde, K. Klauck, A. Schadschneider, and J. Zittartz. Simulation of pedestrian dynamics using a two-dimensional cellular automaton. *Physica A: Statistical Mechanics and its Applications*, 295(3-4):507–525, 2001.

[33] C. Buschmann, H. Hellbrück, S. Fischer, A. Kröller, and S. P. Fekete. Radio propagation-aware distance estimation based on neighborhood comparison. In *Proceedings of the 4th European Conference on Wireless Sensor Networks*, pages 325–340. Springer, 2007.

[34] T. Camp, J. Boleng, and V. Davies. A survey of mobility models for ad hoc network research. *Wireless Communications and Mobile Computing, Special Issue On Mobile Ad Hoc Networking: Research, Trends and Applications*, 2:483–502, 2002.

[35] M. Cardei and J. Wu. Energy-efficient coverage problems in wireless ad-hoc sensor networks. *Computer Communications*, 29(4):413–420, 2006.

[36] L. G. Chalmet, R. L. Francis, and P. B. Saunders. Network models for building evacuation. *Fire Technology*, 18(1):90–113, 1982.

[37] Y.-J. Chang, S.-K. Tsai, and T.-Y. Wang. A context aware handheld wayfinding system for individuals with cognitive impairments. In *Proceedings of the 10th International ACM SIGACCESS Conference on Computers and Accessibility*, pages 27–34. ACM Press, 2008.

[38] P. Chatterjee and N. Das. A distributed algorithm for load-balanced routing in multihop wireless sensor networks. In *Proceedings of the 9th International Conference on Distributed Computing and Networking*, pages 332–338. Springer, 2008.

[39] N. Cheng. An optimization method for dynamic evacuation route programming based on improved ant colony algorithm. In *Proceedings of the 2010 International Conference on Intelligent System Design and Engineering Application*, pages 265–267. IEEE, 2010.

[40] K. K. Chintalapudi, A. Dhariwal, R. Govindan, and G. Sukhatme. Ad-hoc localization using ranging and sectoring. In *Proceedings of the 23rd Annual Joint Conference of*

the IEEE Computer and Communications Societies, pages 2662–2672. IEEE, 2004.

[41] H. M. Choset. *Principles of Robot Motion: Theory, Algorithms, and Implementation.* MIT Press, 2005.

[42] C.-H. A. Chou, K.-F. Ssu, H. C. Jiau, W.-T. Wang, and C. Wang. A dead-end free topology maintenance protocol for geographic forwarding in wireless sensor networks. *IEEE Transactions on Computers*, 60(11):1610–1621, 2011.

[43] B. N. Clark, C. J. Colbourn, and D. S. Johnson. Unit disk graphs. *Discrete Mathematics*, 86(1–3):165–177, 1990.

[44] D. Coore. Establishing a coordinate system on an amorphous computer. Techreport MIT/LCS/TR-737, MIT Laboratory for Computer Science, 1998.

[45] D. Corona and B. De Schutter. Adaptive cruise control for a smart car: A comparison benchmark for MPC-PWA control methods. *IEEE Transactions on Control Systems Technology*, 16(2):365–372, 2008.

[46] G. Daniels, K. Wallasch, and B. Stock. BS 9999 - Neue Vorgehensweise bei der risikobasierten Auslegung des Brandschutzes. *vfdb-Zeitschrift Forschung, Technik und Management im Brandschutz*, 58:93–101, 2009.

[47] C. Darwin. *On the Origin of the Species by Means of Natural Selection: Or, The Preservation of Favoured Races in the Struggle for Life.* John Murray, 1859.

[48] E. D'Atri, C. M. Medaglia, A. Serbanati, and U. B. Ceipidor. A system to aid blind people in the mobility: A usability

test and its results. In *Proceedings of the 2nd International Conference on Systems*, pages 35–35. IEEE, 2007.

[49] P. Davidsson and M. Boman. Distributed monitoring and control of office buildings by embedded agents. *Information Sciences*, 171(4):293–307, 2005.

[50] L. Dawei, G. Lihua, and W. Li. Emergency evacuation based on the nested game analysis. In *Proceedings of the 29th Chinese Control Conference*, pages 1733–1737. IEEE, 2010.

[51] B. de Ruyter and E. Pelgrim. Ambient assisted-living research in carlab. *Interactions*, 14(4):30–33, 2007.

[52] I. Dietrich and F. Dressler. On the lifetime of wireless sensor networks. *ACM Transactions on Sensor Networking*, 5(1): 1–39, 2009.

[53] E. W. Dijkstra. A note on two problems in connexion with graphs. *Numerische Mathematik*, 1(1):269–271, 1959.

[54] B. Ding, H. Yuan, X. Zang, and L. Jiang. The research on blind navigation system based on RFID. In *Proceedings of the 2007 International Conference on Wireless Communications, Networking and Mobile Computing*, pages 2058–2061. IEEE, 2007.

[55] L. Doherty, K. S. J. Pister, and L. El Ghaoui. Convex position estimation in wireless sensor networks. In *Proceedings of the 20th Annual Joint Conference of the IEEE Computer and Communications Societies*, pages 1655–1663. IEEE, 2001.

[56] M. Dorigo. *Optimization, learning and natural algorithms.* Ph.D. dissertation, Politecnico di Milano, Milano, Italy, 1992.

[57] M. Dorigo, V. Maniezzo, and A. Colorni. Ant system: Optimization by a colony of cooperating agents. *IEEE Transactions on Systems, Man, and Cybernetics, Part B: Cybernetics*, 26(1):29–41, 1996.

[58] R. C. Eberhart, Y. Shi, and J. Kennedy. *Swarm Intelligence*. Morgan Kaufmann, 2001.

[59] J. M. Epstein, R. Pankajakshan, and R. A. Hammond. Combining computational fluid dynamics and agent-based modeling: A new approach to evacuation planning. *PLOS ONE*, 6 (5):e20139, 2011.

[60] T. Eren. Cooperative localization in wireless ad hoc and sensor networks using hybrid distance and learing (angle of arrival) measurements. *EURASIP Journal on Wireless Communications and Networking*, 2011(73):1–18, 2011.

[61] M. Evans and T. Swartz. *Approximating Integrals via Monte Carlo and Deterministic Methods*. Oxford University Press, 2000.

[62] R. F. Fahy and G. Proulx. Analysis of published accounts of the world trade center evacuation. federal building and fire safety investigation of the world trade center disaster. Federal Building and Fire Safety Investigation Report (NIST NCSTAR 1-7A), US Department of Commerce, NIST, 2010.

[63] N. Fallah, I. Apostolopoulos, K. Bekris, and E. Folmer. Indoor human navigation systems: A survey. *Interacting with Computers*, 25(1):21–33, 2013.

[64] S. P. Fekete, A. Kröller, C. Buschmann, and S. Fischer. Geometric distance estimation for sensor networks and unit

disk graphs. In *Proceedings of the 16th International Fall Workshop on Computational Geometry*, 2006.

[65] S. P. Fekete, B. Hendriks, C. Tessars, A. Wegener, H. Hellbrück, S. Fischer, and S. Ebers. Methods for improving the flow of traffic. In C. Müller-Schloer, H. Schmeck, and T. Ungerer, editors, *Organic Computing - A Paradigm Shift for Complex Systems*, Autonomic Systems, pages 447–460. Springer, 2011.

[66] A. Filippoupolitis, G. Gorbil, and E. Gelenbe. Spatial computers for emergency management. In *Proceedings of the 5th IEEE Conference on Self-Adaptive and Self-Organizing Systems Workshops*, pages 61–66. IEEE, 2011.

[67] C. Fischer, K. Muthukrishnan, M. Hazas, and H. Gellersen. Ultrasound-aided pedestrian dead reckoning for indoor navigation. In *Proceedings of the 1st ACM International Workshop on Mobile Entity Localization and Tracking in GPS-less Environments*, pages 31–36. ACM Press, 2008.

[68] L. R. Ford and D. R. Fulkerson. *Flows in Networks*. Princeton University Press, 1962.

[69] G. A. Frank and C. O. Dorso. Room evacuation in the presence of an obstacle. *Physica A: Statistical Mechanics and its Applications*, 390(11):2135–2145, 2011.

[70] N. Fredivianus, U. Richter, and H. Schmeck. Collaborating and learning predators on a pursuit scenario. In M. Hinchey, B. Kleinjohann, L. Kleinjohann, P. A. Lindsay, F. J. Rammig, J. Timmis, and M. Wolf, editors, *Distributed, Parallel and Biologically Inspired Systems*, volume 329 of *IFIP Advances*

in Information and Communication Technology, pages 290–301. Springer, 2010.

[71] D. Gale. Transient flows in networks. *The Michigan Mathematical Journal*, 6(1):59–63, 1959.

[72] A. Garrett, B. Carnahan, R. Muhdi, J. Davis, G. Dozier, M. P. SanSoucie, P. V. Hull, and M. L. Tinker. Evacuation planning via evolutionary computation. In *Proceedings of the 2006 IEEE Congress on Evolutionary Computation*, pages 157–164. IEEE, 2006.

[73] J. Gehrke and S. Madden. Query processing in sensor networks. *IEEE Pervasive Computing*, 3(1):46–55, 2004.

[74] I. Gerdes, F. Klawonn, and R. Kruse. *Evolutionäre Algorithmen: Genetische Algorithmen, Strategien und Optimierungsverfahren, Beispielanwendungen.* Vieweg und Teubner, 1st edition, 2004.

[75] P. Ghosekar, G. Katkar, and P. Ghorpade. Mobile ad hoc networking: Imperatives and challenges. *International Journal of Computer Applications, Special Issue on MANETs*, 3: 153–158, 2010.

[76] P. G. Gipps and B. Marksjö. A micro-simulation model for pedestrian flows. *Mathematics and Computers in Simulation*, 27(2-3):95–105, 1985.

[77] L. Girod and D. Estrin. Robust range estimation using acoustic and multimodal sensing. In *Proceedings of the 2001 IEEE/RSJ International Conference on Intelligent Robots and Systems*, pages 1312–1320. IEEE, 2001.

[78] A. R. Golding and N. Lesh. Indoor navigation using a diverse set of cheap, wearable sensors. In *The Third International Symposium on Wearable Computers*, pages 29–36. IEEE, 1999.

[79] R. Y. Guo and H. J. Huang. A mobile lattice gas model for simulating pedestrian evacuation. *Physica A: Statistical Mechanics and its Applications*, 387(2-3):580–586, 2008.

[80] F. Gustafsson and F. Gunnarsson. Positioning using time-difference of arrival measurements. In *Proceedings of the 2003 IEEE International Conference on Acoustics, Speech, and Signal Processing*, pages 553–556. IEEE, 2003.

[81] Z. J. Haas, J. Y. Halpern, and L. Li. Gossip-based ad hoc routing. *IEEE/ACM Transactions on Networking*, 14(3): 479–491, 2006.

[82] H. W. Hamacher and S. A. Tjandra. Mathematical modelling of evacuation problems : A state of art. *Pedestrian and Evacuation Dynamics*, 24:227–266, 2001.

[83] P. E. Hart, N. J. Nilsson, and B. Raphael. A formal basis for the heuristic determination of minimum cost paths. *IEEE Transactions on Systems Science and Cybernetics*, 4(2):100–107, 1968.

[84] P. E. Hart, N. J. Nilsson, and B. Raphael. Correction to "A formal basis for the heuristic determination of minimum cost paths". *SIGART Bulletin*, 37:28–29, 1972.

[85] A. Harter, A. Hopper, P. Steggles, A. Ward, and P. Webster. The anatomy of a context-aware application. In *Proceedings of the 5th Annual ACM/IEEE International Conference on*

Mobile Computing and Networking, pages 59–68. ACM Press, 1999.

[86] T. He, C. Huang, B. M. Blum, J. A. Stankovic, and T. Abdelzaher. Range-free localization schemes for large scale sensor networks. In *Proceedings of the 9th Annual International Conference on Mobile Computing and Networking*, pages 81–95. ACM Press, 2003.

[87] E. Heidari and A. Movaghar. An efficient method based on genetic algorithms to solve sensor network optimization problem. *International Journal on Applications of Graph Theory in Wireless Ad Hoc Networks and Sensor Networks*, 3(1):18–33, 2011.

[88] D. Helbing. A fluid dynamic model for the movement of pedestrians. *Complex Systems*, 6:391–415, 1998.

[89] D. Helbing and P. Molnar. Social force model for pedestrian dynamics. *Physical Review E*, 51(5):4282–4286, 1995.

[90] D. Helbing, I. Farkas, and T. Vicsek. Simulating dynamical features of escape panic. *Nature*, 407(6803):487–490, 2000.

[91] L. F. Henderson. The statistics of crowd fluids. *Nature*, 229 (5284):381–383, 1971.

[92] L. F. Henderson. On the fluid mechanics of human crowd motion. *Transportation Research*, 8(6):509–515, 1974.

[93] T. Hestermeyer, O. Oberschelp, and H. Giese. Structured information processing for self-optimizing mechatronic systems. In H. Araújo, A. Vieira, J. Braz, B. Encarnação,

and M. Carvalho, editors, *Proceedings of the 2004 International Conference on Informatics in Control, Automation and Robotics*, pages 230–237. IEEE, 2004.

[94] J. Hightower and G. Borriello. Location systems for ubiquitous computing. *Computer*, 34(8):57–66, 2001.

[95] J. Hightower, G. Borriello, and R. Want. SpotON: An indoor 3D location sensing technology based on RF signal strength. Techreport 2000-02-02, University of Washington, 2000.

[96] T. Höllerer, D. Hallaway, N. Tinna, and S. Feiner. Steps toward accommodating variable position tracking accuracy in a mobile augmented reality system. In *In Proceedings of the 2nd International Workshop on Artificial Intelligence in Mobile Systems*, pages 31–37. AAAI Press, 2001.

[97] L. Hu and D. Evans. Localization for mobile sensor networks. In *Proceedings of the 10th Annual International Conference on Mobile Computing and Networking*, pages 45–57. ACM Press, 2004.

[98] Y.-C. Hu, A. Perrig, and D. B. Johnson. Packet leashes: A defense against wormhole attacks in wireless networks. In *Proceedings of the 22nd Annual Joint Conference of the IEEE Computer and Communications*, volume 3, pages 1976–1986. IEEE, 2003.

[99] B. Huang, C. Yu, B. D. O. Anderson, and G. Mao. Connectivity-based distance estimation in wireless sensor networks. In *Proceedings of the 2010 Global Telecommunications Conference*, pages 4565–4569. IEEE, 2010.

[100] C.-F. Huang and Y.-C. Tseng. The coverage problem in a wireless sensor network. In *Proceedings of the 2nd ACM International Conference on Wireless Sensor Networks and Applications*, pages 115–121. ACM Press, 2003.

[101] H. Huang, G. Gartner, M. Schmidt, and Y. Li. Smart environment for ubiquitous indoor navigation. In *Proceedings of the 2009 International Conference on New Trends in Information and Service Science*, pages 176–180. IEEE, 2009.

[102] Q. Huang and S. Selvakennedy. A range-free localization algorithm for wireless sensor networks. In *Proceedings of the 63rd IEEE Conference on Vehicular Technology*, pages 349–353. IEEE, 2006.

[103] A. Hub, J. Diepstraten, and T. Ertl. Design and development of an indoor navigation and object identification system for the blind. In *Proceedings of the 6th international ACM SIGACCESS conference on Computers and accessibility*, pages 147–152. ACM Press, 2003.

[104] IEEE Standards Association. IEEE 802.11 Standards, October 2013. http://standards.ieee.org/about/get/802/802.11.html.

[105] M. Ilyas and I. Mahgoub. *Smart Dust: Sensor Network Applications, Architecture And Design*. CRC Taylor & Francis, 2006.

[106] Y. Inoue, A. Sashima, T. Ikeda, and K. Kurumatani. Indoor emergency evacuation service on autonomous navigation system using mobile phone. In *Proceedings of the 2nd International Symposium on Universal Communication*, pages 79–85. IEEE, 2008.

[107] Internet Engineering Task Force (IETF). Mobile ad-hoc networks (MANET) - charter, November 2011. http://datatracker.ietf.org/wg/manet/charter.

[108] E. Isaacson and H. B. Keller. *Analysis of Numerical Methods.* Dover Publications, reprint edition, 1994. ISBN 0486680290.

[109] J. Izquierdo, I. Montalvo, R. Pérez, and V.S. Fuertes. Forecasting pedestrian evacuation times by using swarm intelligence. *Physica A: Statistical Mechanics and its Applications*, 388(7):1213–1220, 2009.

[110] H.-C. Jang, Y.-N. Lien, and T.-C. Tsai. Rescue information system for earthquake disasters based on MANET emergency communication platform. In *Proceedings of the 2009 International Conference on Wireless Communications and Mobile Computing: Connecting the World Wirelessly*, pages 623–627. ACM Press, 2009.

[111] J. J. Jarvis and H. D. Ratliff. Some equivalent objectives for dynamic network flow problems. *Management Science*, 28 (1):106–109, 1982.

[112] X. Ji and H. Zha. Sensor positioning in wireless ad-hoc sensor networks using multidimensional scaling. In *Proceedings of the 23rd Annual Joint Conference of the IEEE Computer and Communications Societies*, pages 2652–2661. IEEE, 2004.

[113] A. Johansson and D. Helbing. Pedestrian flow optimization with a genetic algorithm based on boolean grids. In N. Waldau, P. Gattermann, H. Knoflacher, and M. Schreckenberg, editors, *Pedestrian and Evacuation Dynamics 2005*, pages 267–272. Springer, 2007.

[114] W. Kai and C. Chun. Using RSS with difference method in localization algorithm for sensor networks. In *Proceedings of the 2nd International Conference of Information Science and Engineering*, pages 2500–2502. IEEE, 2010.

[115] H. Kaplan, M. J. Katz, G. Morgenstern, and M. Sharir. Optimal cover of points by disks in a simple polygon. In M. Berg and U. Meyer, editors, *European Symposium on Algorithms*, volume 6346 of *LNCS*, pages 475–486. Springer, 2010.

[116] D. Karaboga and B. Akay. A survey: Algorithms simulating bee swarm intelligence. *Artificial Intelligence Review*, 31(1-4): 61–85, 2009.

[117] C. Karlof and D. Wagner. Secure routing in wireless sensor networks: attacks and countermeasures. In *Proceedings of the 1st IEEE International Workshop on Sensor Network Protocols and Applications*, pages 113–127. IEEE, 2003.

[118] V. Kaseva, T. D. Hamalainen, and M. Hannikainen. Range-free algorithm for energy-efficient indoor localization in wireless sensor networks. In *Proceedings of the 2011 Conference on Design Architectures for Signal Image Processing*, pages 1–8. IEEE, 2011.

[119] M. J. Katz and G. Morgenstern. A scheme for computing minimum covers within simple regions. In *Proceedings of the 11th International Symposium on Algorithms and Data Structures*, pages 447–458. Springer, 2009.

[120] L. Kellenberger and R. Müller. A genetic algorithm module for spatial optimization in pedestrian simulation. In W.W.F.

Klingsch, C. Rogsch, A. Schadschneider, and M. Schrecken-berg, editors, *Pedestrian and Evacuation Dynamics 2008*, pages 359–370. Springer, 2010. ISBN 978-3-642-04503-5, 978-3-642-04504-2.

[121] J. O. Kephart and D. M. Chess. The vision of autonomic computing. *Computer*, 36(1):41–50, 2003.

[122] L. Kleinrock and J. Silvester. Optimum transmission radii for packet radio networks or why six is a magic number. In *Proceedings of the 1978 National Telecommunications Conference*, pages 431–435, 1978.

[123] S. Koide and M. Kato. 3-d human navigation system considering various transition preferences. In *Proceedings of the 2005 IEEE International Conference on Systems, Man and Cybernetics*, pages 859–864. IEEE, 2005.

[124] L. König, S. Mostaghim, and S. Schmeck. A markov-chain-based model for success prediction of evolution in complex environments. In *Proceedings of the 3rd International Joint Conference on Computational Intelligence*, pages 90–102. IEEE Computer Society, 2011.

[125] S. König and M. Likhachev. Improved fast replanning for robot navigation in unknown terrain. In *Proceedings of the 2002 IEEE International Conference on Robotics and Automation*, volume 1, pages 968–975, 2002.

[126] T. Kretz. Pedestrian traffic: On the quickest path. *Journal of Statistical Mechanics: Theory and Experiment*, 2009(3): P03012, 2009.

[127] A. Kröller, S. P. Fekete, C. Buschmann, S. Fischer, and D. Pfisterer. Koordinatenfreies Lokationsbewusstsein (localization without coordinates). *it Information Technology*, 47 (2):15, 2005.

[128] J. Krumm, S. Harris, B. Meyers, B. Brumitt, M. Hale, and S. Shafer. Multi-camera multi-person tracking for EasyLiving. In *Proceedings of the 3rd IEEE International Workshop on Visual Surveillance*, pages 3–10. IEEE, 2000.

[129] V. Kulyukin, C. Gharpure, J. Nicholson, and G. Osborne. Robot-assisted wayfinding for the visually impaired in structured indoor environments. *Autonomous Robots*, 21(1):29–41, 2006.

[130] V. Kumar and S. R. Das. Performance of dead reckoning-based location service for mobile ad hoc networks: Research articles. *Wireless Communications and Mobile Computing*, 4 (2):189–202, 2004.

[131] Y. Kwon, K. Mechitov, S. Sundresh, W. Kim, and G. Agha. Resilient localization for sensor networks in outdoor environments. In *Proceedings of the 25th IEEE International Conference on Distributed Computing Systems*, pages 643–652. IEEE, 2005.

[132] S. M. LaValle. *Planning Algorithms*. Cambridge University Press, 2006.

[133] H. Li, J. Wang, X. Li, and H. Ma. Real-time path planning of mobile anchor node in localization for wireless sensor networks. In *Proceedings of the 2008 IEEE International Conference on Information and Automation*, pages 384–389. IEEE, 2008.

[134] X. Li, H. Shi, and Y. Shang. Selective anchor placement algorithm for ad-hoc wireless sensor networks. In *Proceedings of the 2008 International Conference on Communications*, pages 2359–2363. IEEE, 2008.

[135] S. Y. Liana, R. L. Hecker, and R. G. Landers. Machining process monitoring and control: The state-of-the-art. *Journal of manufacturing science and engineering*, 126(2):297–310, 2004.

[136] W.-H. Liao, Y.-C. Tseng, and J.-P. Sheu. GRID: a fully location-aware routing protocol for mobile ad hoc networks. *Telecommunication Systems*, 18(1-3):37–60, 2001.

[137] W.-H. Liao, Y.-C. Lee, and S. P. Kedia. Mobile anchor positioning for wireless sensor networks. *IET Communications*, 5(7):914–921, 2011.

[138] Y.-N. Lien, H.-C. Jang, and T.-C. Tsai. A MANET based emergency communication and information system for catastrophic natural disasters. In *Proceedings of the 29th IEEE International Conference on Distributed Computing Systems Workshops*, pages 412–417. IEEE, 2009.

[139] J. G. Lim and S. V. Rao. Mobility-enhanced positioning in ad hoc networks. In *Proceedings of the 2003 IEEE Conference on Wireless Communications and Networking*, volume 3, pages 1832–1837, 2003.

[140] Q. Liu, A. Pruteanu, and S. Dulman. GDE: a distributed gradient-based algorithm for distance estimation in large-scale networks. In *Proceedings of the 14th ACM International Conference on Modeling, Analysis and Simulation of Wireless and Mobile Systems*, pages 151–158. ACM Press, 2011.

[141] S. M. Lo, H. C. Huang, P. Wang, and K. K. Yuen. A game theory based exit selection model for evacuation. *Fire Safety Journal*, 41(5):364–369, 2006.

[142] Q. Lu, Y. Huang, and S. Shekhar. Evacuation planning: A capacity constrained routing approach. In H. Chen, R. Miranda, D. D. Zeng, C. Demchak, J. Schroeder, and T. Madhusudan, editors, *Intelligence and Security Informatics*, volume 2665 of *LNCS*, pages 111–125. Springer, 2003.

[143] Q. Lu, B. George, and S. Shekhar. Capacity constrained routing algorithms for evacuation planning: A summary of results. In C. B. Medeiros, M. J. Egenhofer, and E. Bertino, editors, *Advances in Spatial and Temporal Databases*, volume 3633 of *LNCS*, pages 291–307. Springer, 2005.

[144] D. Lucarelli and I.-J. Wang. Decentralized synchronization protocols with nearest neighbor communication. In *Proceedings of the 2nd International Conference on Embedded Networked Sensor Systems*, pages 62–68. ACM Press, 2004.

[145] C. Maihofer. A survey of geocast routing protocols. *IEEE Communications Surveys Tutorials*, 6(2):32–42, 2004.

[146] G. Mao, B. Fidan, and B. D. O. Anderson. Wireless sensor network localization techniques. *Computer Networks*, 51(10): 252–2553, 2007.

[147] R. Mathar and J. Mattfeldt. Pulse-coupled decentral synchronization. *SIAM Journal on Applied Mathematics*, 56(4): 1094–1106, 1996.

[148] M. K. McClintock. Menstrual synchrony and suppression. *Nature*, 229(5282):244–245, 1971.

[149] L. Meertens and S. Fitzpatrick. The distributed construction of a global coordinate system in a network of static computational nodes from inter-node distances. Techreport KES.U.04.04, Kestrel Institute, 2004.

[150] S. K. Meghani, M. Asif, and S. Amir. Localization of WSN node based on time of arrival using ultra wide band spectrum. In *Proceedings of the 13th Annual Wireless and Microwave Technology Conference*, pages 1–4. IEEE, 2012.

[151] S. Merkel, L. König, and H. Schmeck. Age based controller stabilization in evolutionary robotics. In *Proceedings of the 2nd World Congress on Nature and Biologically Inspired Computing*, pages 84–91. IEEE, 2010.

[152] S. Merkel, C. W. Becker, and H. Schmeck. Firefly-inspired synchronization for energy-efficient distance estimation in mobile ad-hoc networks. In *Proceedings of the 31st International Performance Computing and Communications Conference*, pages 205–214. IEEE, 2012.

[153] S. Merkel, S. Mostaghim, and H. Schmeck. Distributed geometric distance estimation in ad hoc networks. In D. Hutchison, T. Kanade, J. Kittler, J. M. Kleinberg, F. Mattern, J. C. Mitchell, M. Naor, O. Nierstrasz, C. Pandu Rangan, B. Steffen, M. Sudan, D. Terzopoulos, D. Tygar, M. Y. Vardi, G. Weikum, X.-Y. Li, S. Papavassiliou, and S. Ruehrup, editors, *Ad-hoc, Mobile, and Wireless Networks*, volume 7363 of *LNCS*, pages 28–41. Springer, 2012.

[154] S. Merkel, S. Mostaghim, and H. Schmeck. A study of mobility in ad hoc networks and its effects on a hop count

based distance estimation. In *Proceedings of the 5th International Conference on New Technologies, Mobility and Security*, pages 39–43. IEEE, 2012.

[155] S. Merkel, S. Mostaghim, D. Blum, and H. Schmeck. Distributed swarm evacuation planning. In *Proceedings of the 2013 IEEE Symposium on Swarm Intelligence*, pages 276–283. IEEE, 2013.

[156] S. Merkel, S. Mostaghim, and H. Schmeck. Hop count based distance estimation in mobile ad hoc networks - challenges and consequences. *Ad Hoc Networks*, 11(8), 2013. (to appear).

[157] S. Merkel, P. Unger, and H. Schmeck. Evolutionary algorithm for optimal anchor node placement to localize devices in a mobile ad hoc network during building evacuation. In *Proceeding of the 15th Annual Conference Companion on Genetic and Evolutionary Computation Conference Companion*, pages 1407–1414. ACM Press, 2013.

[158] S. Merkel, A. Kesseler, and H. Schmeck. Dynamic multi-objective evacuation path planning in mobile ad hoc networks. Techreport 3044, Karlsruhe Institute of Technology (KIT), 2014.

[159] S. Merkel, S. Mostaghim, and H. Schmeck. Self-organized swarm display. *International Journal of Swarm Intelligence*, 2014. revision submitted on 10th of December 2013.

[160] Yoshihiro Ishibashi Minoru Fukui. Jamming transition in cellular automaton models for pedestrians on passageway. *Journal of The Physical Society of Japan*, 68(11):3738–3739, 1999.

[161] R. E. Mirollo and S. H. Strogatz. Synchronization of pulse-coupled biological oscillators. *SIAM Journal on Applied Mathematics*, 50:1645–1662, 1990.

[162] M. Mnif and C. Müller-Schloer. Quantitative emergence. In C. Müller-Schloer, H. Schmeck, and T. Ungerer, editors, *Organic Computing - A Paradigm Shift for Complex Systems*, Autonomic Systems, pages 39–52. Springer, 2011.

[163] M. Mnif, U. Richter, J. Branke, H. Schmeck, and C. Müller-Schloer. Measurement and control of self-organised behaviour in robot swarms. In P. Lukowicz, L. Thiele, and G. Tröster, editors, *Architecture of Computing Systems*, volume 4415 of *LNCS*, pages 209–223. Springer, 2007.

[164] Evacuation modelling community. Evacuation modelling portal, January 2013. http://evacmod.net.

[165] S. Morishita and T. Shiraishi. Evaluation of billboards based on pedestrian flow in the concourse of the station. In S. E. Yacoubi, B. Chopard, and S. Bandini, editors, *Cellular Automata*, volume 4173 of *LNCS*, pages 716–719. Springer, 2006.

[166] G. Muehl, M. Werner, M. A. Jaeger, K. Herrmann, and H. Parzyjegla. On the definitions of self-managing and self-organizing systems. In *Proceedings of the 2007 ITG-GI Conference on Communication in Distributed Systems*, pages 1–11. IEEE, 2007.

[167] R. Muhdi, A. Garrett, R. Agarwal, J. Davis, G. Dozier, and D. Umphress. The application of evolutionary computation in evacuation planning. In *Proceedings of the 2006 IEEE Intelligent Transportation Systems Conference*, pages 600–605. IEEE, 2006.

[168] C. Müller-Schloer. Organic computing - on the feasibility of controlled emergence. In *Proceedings of the 2004 International Conference on Hardware/Software Codesign and System Synthesis*, pages 2–5, 2004.

[169] C. Müller-Schloer and H. Schmeck. Organic Computing: A grand challenge for mastering complex systems. *it - Information Technology*, 52(3):135–141, 2010.

[170] C. Müller-Schloer, H. Schmeck, and T. Ungerer. *Organic Computing - A Paradigm Shift for Complex Systems*. Springer, 2011.

[171] R. Nagpal, H. Shrobe, and J. Bachrach. Organizing a global coordinate system from local information on an ad hoc sensor network. In F. Zhao and L. Guibas, editors, *Information Processing in Sensor Networks*, volume 2634, pages 333–348. Springer, 2003.

[172] G. Nan and M. Li. Evolutionary based approaches in wireless sensor networks: A survey. In *Proceedings of the 4th International Conference on Natural Computation*, volume 5, pages 217–222, 2008.

[173] A. Nasipuri and K. Li. A directionality based location discovery scheme for wireless sensor networks. In *Proceedings of the 1st ACM International Workshop on Wireless Sensor Networks and Applications*, pages 105–111. ACM Press, 2002.

[174] A. L. Nelson, G. J. Barlow, and L. Doitsidis. Fitness functions in evolutionary robotics: A survey and analysis. *Robotics and Autonomous Systems*, 57(4):345–370, 2009.

[175] M. Neshat, G. Sepidnam, M. Sargolzaei, and A. N. Toosi. Artificial fish swarm algorithm: A survey of the state-of-the-art, hybridization, combinatorial and indicative applications. *Artificial Intelligence Review*, pages 1–33, 2012.

[176] D. Niculescu and B. Nath. Ad hoc positioning system (APS). In *Proceedings of the 2001 IEEE Global Telecommunications Conference*, pages 2926–2931. IEEE, 2001.

[177] D. Niculescu and B. Nath. DV based positioning in ad hoc networks. *Telecommunication Systems*, 22(1):267–280, 2003.

[178] D. Niculescu and Badri Nath. Ad hoc positioning system (APS) using AOA. In *Proceedings of the 22nd Annual Joint Conference of the IEEE Computer and Communications*, volume 3, pages 1734–1743. IEEE, 2003.

[179] R. J. Orr and G. D. Abowd. The smart floor: A mechanism for natural user identification and tracking. In *Extended Abstracts on Human Factors in Computing Systems*, pages 275–276. ACM Press, 2000.

[180] N. Patwari and A. O. Hero. Using proximity and quantized RSS for sensor localization in wireless networks. In *Proceedings of the 2nd ACM International Conference on Wireless Sensor Networks and Applications*, pages 20–29. ACM Press, 2003.

[181] C. S. Peskin. Mathematical aspects of heart physiology. *New York University Press*, 1975.

[182] N. B. Priyantha. *The Cricket Indoor Location System*. Ph.D. dissertation, Massachusetts Institute of Technology, Massachusetts, USA, 2005.

[183] N. B. Priyantha, A. K. L. Miu, H. Balakrishnan, and S. Teller. The cricket compass for context-aware mobile applications. In *Proceedings of the 7th Annual International Conference on Mobile Computing and Networking*, pages 1–14. ACM Press, 2001.

[184] N. B. Priyantha, H. Balakrishnan, E. Demaine, and S. Teller. Anchor-free distributed localization in sensor networks. Techreport 892, MIT Laboratory for Computer Science, 2003.

[185] H. Prothmann, S. Tomforde, J. Branke, J. Hähner, C. Müller-Schloer, and H. Schmeck. Organic traffic control. In C. Müller-Schloer, H. Schmeck, and T. Ungerer, editors, *Organic Computing - A Paradigm Shift for Complex Systems*, Autonomic Systems, pages 431–446. Springer, 2011.

[186] H. Prothmann, S. Tomforde, H. Lyda, H. Branke, H. Hähner, C. Müller-Schloer, and H. Schmeck. Self-organised routing for road networks. In Fernando A. Kuipers and Poul E. Heegaard, editors, *Self-Organizing Systems*, volume 7166 of *LNCS*, pages 48–59. Springer, 2012.

[187] F. H. Raab, E. B. Blood, T. O. Steiner, and H. R. Jones. Magnetic position and orientation tracking system. *IEEE Transactions on Aerospace and Electronic Systems*, AES-15 (5):709–718, 1979.

[188] J. Rajamäki, P. Viinikainen, J. Tuomisto, T. Sederholm, and M. Säämänen. LaureaPOP indoor navigation service for the visually impaired in a WLAN environment. In *Proceedings of the 6th WSEAS International Conference on Electronics, Hardware, Wireless and Optical Communications*, pages 96–101. World Scientific and Engineering Academy and Society (WSEAS), 2007.

[189] L. Ran, S. Helal, and S. Moore. Drishti: an integrated indoor/outdoor blind navigation system and service. In *Proceedings of the 2nd Annual Conference on Pervasive Computing and Communications*, pages 23–30. IEEE, 2004.

[190] T. Rappaport. *Wireless Communications: Principles and Practice*. Prentice Hall, 2 edition, 2002.

[191] G. Retscher. Pedestrian navigation systems and location-based services. In *Proceedings of the 5th IEEE International Conference on 3G Mobile Communication Technologies*, pages 359–363. IEEE, 2004.

[192] O. Ribock, U. Richter, and H. Schmeck. Using Organic Computing to control bunching effects. In U. Brinkschulte, T. Ungerer, C. Hochberger, and R. G. Spallek, editors, *Architecture of Computing Systems*, volume 4934 of *LNCS*, pages 232–244. Springer, 2008.

[193] U. Richter. *Controlled self-organisation using learning classifier systems*. Ph.D. dissertation, Karlsruhe Institute of Technology, Karlsruhe, Germany, 2009.

[194] U. Richter and M. Mnif. Learning to control the emergent behaviour of a multi-agent system. In F. Klügl, K. Tuyls, and S. Sen, editors, *Proceedings of the 2008 Workshop on Adaptive Learning Agents and Multi-Agent Systems*, pages 33–40, 2008.

[195] U. Richter, M. Mnif, J. Branke, C. Müller-Schloer, and H. Schmeck. Towards a generic Observer/Controller architecture for Organic Computing. In C. Hochberger and R. Liskowsky, editors, *GI Jahrestagung*, volume 93 of *LNI*, pages 112–119. Gesselschaft für Informatik, 2006.

[196] B. Riemann. Über die Darstellbarkeit einer Funktion durch eine trigonometrische Reihe. In *Abhandlungen der Königlichen Gesellschaft der Wissenschaften in Göttingen.* Weidmann, 1868.

[197] B. Ristic, S. Arulampalam, and N. Gordon. *Beyond the Kalman Filter: Particle Filters for Tracking Applications.* Artech House, 2004.

[198] R. T. Rockafellar and R. J.-B. Wets. *Variational Analysis.* Springer, 2011.

[199] D. Rodriguez, S. Heuer, C. Kunze, and B. Weber. Management of mass casualty of incidents using an autonomous sensor network. In *Proceedings of the 14th International Symposium on Wireless Personal Multimedia Communications,* pages 1–5. IEEE, 2011.

[200] M. J. Russell, G. M. Switz, and K. Thompson. Olfactory influences on the human menstrual cycle. *Pharmacology, Biochemistry, and Behavior,* 13(5):737–738, 1980.

[201] S. Helal S. Willis. RFID information grid for blind navigation and wayfinding. In *Proceeding of the 9th IEEE International Symposium on Wearable Computers,* pages 34–37. IEEE, 2005.

[202] M. Saadatseresht, A. Mansourian, and M. Taleai. Evacuation planning using multiobjective evolutionary optimization approach. *European Journal of Operational Research,* 198 (1):305–314, 2009.

[203] N. Salman, H. K. Maheshwari, A. H. Kemp, and M. Ghogho. Effects of anchor placement on mean-CRB for localization.

In *Proceedings of the 10th IFIP Annual Mediterranean Ad Hoc Networking Workshop*, pages 115–118. IEEE, 2011.

[204] K. Sangho, S. Shekhar, and M. Min. Contraflow transportation network reconfiguration for evacuation route planning. *IEEE Transactions on Knowledge and Data Engineering*, 20 (8):1115–1129, 2008.

[205] C. Savarese, J. M. Rabaey, and K. Langendoen. Robust positioning algorithms for distributed ad-hoc wireless sensor networks. In *Proceedings of the 2002 USENIX Annual Technical Conference*, pages 317–327. USENIX Association, 2002.

[206] A. Savvides, C.-C. Han, and M. B. Strivastava. Dynamic fine-grained localization in ad-hoc networks of sensors. In *Proceedings of the 7th Annual International Conference on Mobile Computing and Networking*, pages 166–179. ACM Press, 2001.

[207] A. Savvides, H. Park, and M. B. Srivastava. The bits and flops of the n-hop multilateration primitive for node localization problems. In *Proceedings of the 1st ACM International Workshop on Wireless Sensor Networks and Applications*, pages 112–121. ACM Press, 2002.

[208] A. Savvides, H. Park, and M. B. Srivastava. The n-hop multilateration primitive for node localization problems. *Mobile Network Applications*, 8(4):443–451, 2003.

[209] A. Schadschneider. Cellular automaton approach to pedestrian dynamics - theory. In M. Schreckenberg and S. D. Sharm, editors, *Pedestrian and Evacuation Dynamics*, pages 75–86. Springer, 2001.

[210] A. Schadschneider, W. Klingsch, H. Klüpfel, T. Kretz, C. Rogsch, and A. Seyfried. Evacuation dynamics: Empirical results, modeling and applications. In R. A. Meyers, editor, *Encyclopedia of Complexity and Systems Science*, pages 3142–3176. Springer, 2009.

[211] V. Schau, C. Erfurth, G. Eichler, S. Späthe, and W. Rossak. Geolocated communication support in rescue management. In *Proceedings of the 8th International Conference on Information Systems for Crisis Response and Management*, 2011.

[212] H. Schmeck. Organic Computing. *Künstliche Intelligenz*, 5 (3):68–69, 2005.

[213] H. Schmeck. Organic Computing - a new vision for distributed embedded systems. In *Proceedings of the 8th IEEE International Symposium on Object-Oriented Real-Time Distributed Computing*, pages 201–203. IEEE, 2005.

[214] H. Schmeck. DFG priority program 1183 Organic Computing, January 2013. http://www.organic-computing.de/spp.

[215] Y. Shang, W. Ruml, Y. Zhang, and M. P. J. Fromherz. Localization from mere connectivity. In *Proceedings of the 4th ACM International Symposium on Mobile Ad Hoc Networking and Computing*, pages 201–212. ACM Press, 2003.

[216] A. Sherman, J. Rinzel, and J. Keizer. Emergence of organized bursting in clusters of pancreatic beta-cells by channel sharing. *Biophysical Journal*, 54(3):411–425, 1988.

[217] F. Sivrikaya and B. Yener. Time synchronization in sensor networks: A survey. *IEEE Network*, 18(4):45–50, 2004.

[218] A. Smailagic and R. Martin. Metronaut: a wearable computer with sensing and global communication capabilities. In *Proceedings of the 1st International Symposium on Wearable Computers*, pages 116–122. IEEE, 1997.

[219] A. M.-C. So and Y. Ye. On solving coverage problems in a wireless sensor network using voronoi diagrams. In *Proceedings of the 1st International Conference on Internet and Network Economics*, pages 584–593. Springer, 2005.

[220] J. Soar, A. Livingstone, and S.-Y. Wang. A case study of an ambient living and wellness management health care model in australia. In M. Mokhtari, I. Khalil, J. Bauchet, D. Zhang, and C. Nugent, editors, *Ambient Assistive Health and Wellness Management in the Heart of the City*, volume 5597 of *LNCS*, pages 48–56. Springer, 2009.

[221] W. Song, X. Xu, B.-H. Wang, and S. Ni. Simulation of evacuation processes using a multi-grid model for pedestrian dynamics. *Physica A: Statistical Mechanics and its Applications*, 363(2):492–500, 2006.

[222] V. Srovnal, Z. Machacek, R. Hercik, R. Slaby, and V. Srovnal. Intelligent car control and recognition embedded system. In *Proceedings of the 2010 International Multiconference on Computer Science and Information Technology*, pages 831–836. Polskie Towarzystwo Informatyczne, 2010.

[223] H. Sun, Z. Fang, T. Wang, Y. Ma, and N. Ren. CDHL: a hybrid range-free localization algorithm in wireless sensor networks. In *Proceedings of the 5th International Conference on Frontier of Computer Science and Technology*, pages 180–183. IEEE, 2010.

[224] M.-T. Sun, C.-W. Yi, C.-K. Yang, and T.-H. Lai. An optimal algorithm for the minimum disc cover problem. *Algorithmica*, 50(1):58–71, 2007.

[225] M. Swenne and T. Bäck. Optimizing pedestrian environments with evolutionary strategies. In U. Weidmann, U. Kirsch, and M. Schreckenberg, editors, *Pedestrian and Evacuation Dynamics*. Springer, 2012. to appear.

[226] R. Szewczyk, E. Osterweil, J. Polastre, M. Hamilton, A. Mainwaring, and D. Estrin. Habitat monitoring with sensor networks. *Communications of the ACM - Wireless sensor networks*, 47(6):34–40, 2004.

[227] J. Szwedko, C. Shaw, A. G. Connor, A. Labrinidis, and P. K. Chrysan. Demonstrating an evacuation algorithm with mobile devices using an e-scavenger hunt game. In *Proceedings of the 8th ACM International Workshop on Data Engineering for Wireless and Mobile Access*, pages 49–52, 2009.

[228] A. S. Tanenbaum. *Computer networks*. Prentice Hall, 2002.

[229] Y. Taniguchi, N. Wakamiya, and M. Murata. A communication mechanism using traveling wave phenomena for wireless sensor networks. In *Proceedings of the 2007 IEEE International Symposium on a World of Wireless, Mobile and Multimedia Networks*, pages 1–6. IEEE, 2007.

[230] B. Tatham and T. Kunz. Anchor node placement for localization in wireless sensor networks. In *Proceedings of the 7th International Conference on Wireless and Mobile Computing, Networking and Communications*, pages 180–187. IEEE, 2011.

[231] V. Torre. A theory of synchronization of heart pace-maker cells. *Journal of Theoretical Biology*, 61(1):55–71, 1976.

[232] V. Tsetsos, C. Anagnostopoulos, P. Kikiras, and S. Hadjiefthymiades. Semantically enriched navigation for indoor environments. *International Journal of Web Grid Services*, 2 (4):453–478, 2006.

[233] A. Tyrrell, G. Auer, and C. Bettstetter. Fireflies as role models for synchronization in ad hoc networks. In *Proceedings of the 1st International Conference on Bio-inspired Models of Network, Information and Computing Systems*. ACM Press, 2006.

[234] A. Varas, M. D. Cornejo, D. Mainemer, B. Toledo, J. Rogan, V. Muñoz, and J. A. Valdivia. Cellular automaton model for evacuation process with obstacles. *Physica A: Statistical Mechanics and its Applications*, 382(2):631–642, 2007.

[235] VDE/ITG/GI. Organic Computing. Positionspapier, VDE/ITG/GI, 2003.

[236] F. L. Villafuerte, K. Terfloth, and J. Schiller. Using network density as a new parameter to estimate distance. In *Proceedings of the 7th International Conference on Networking*, pages 30–35. IEEE, 2008.

[237] A. U. Kemloh Wagoum, A. Seyfried, and S. Holl. Modelling dynamic route choice of pedestrians to assess the criticality of building evacuation. Techreport arXiv e-print 1103.4080, Forschungszentrum Jülich GmbH and Bergische Universität Wuppertal, 2011.

[238] N. Wakamiya and M. Murata. Synchronization-based data gathering scheme for sensor networks. *IEICE Transactions on Communications*, 88(3):873–881, 2005.

[239] N. Wakamiya, S. Kashihara, and M. Murata. A synchronization-based data gathering scheme in unstable radio environments. In *Proceedings of the 4th International Conference on Networked Sensing Systems*, pages 10–18. IEEE, 2007.

[240] T. J. Walker. Acoustic synchrony: Two mechanisms in the snowy tree cricket. *Science*, 166(3907):891–894, 1969.

[241] T. Walther and R. P. Würtz. Learning to look at humans. In C. Müller-Schloer, H. Schmeck, and T. Ungerer, editors, *Organic Computing - A Paradigm Shift for Complex Systems*, Autonomic Systems, pages 309–322. Springer, 2011.

[242] C.-L. Wang, Y.-W. Hong, and Y.-S. Dai. A decentralized positioning method for wireless sensor networks based on weighted interpolation. In *Proceedings of 2007 IEEE International Conference on Communications*, pages 3167–3172. IEEE, 2007.

[243] Y.-H. Wang, C.-P. Hsu, C.-M. Lee, K.-F. Huang, and T.-W. Chang. A location mechanism with mobile reference nodes in wireless sensor networks. In *Proceedings of the 21st International Conference on Advanced Information Networking and Applications Workshops*, pages 48–55. IEEE, 2007.

[244] R. Want, A. Hopper, V. Falcão, and J. Gibbons. The active badge location system. *Transactions on Information Systems*, 10(1):91–102, 1992.

[245] D. J. Watts and S. H. Strogatz. Collective dynamics of small-world networks. *Nature*, 393(6684):440–442, 1998.

[246] K. Weicker. *Evolutionäre Algorithmen*. Vieweg und Teubner, 2nd edition, 2007.

[247] G. Werner-Allen, G. Tewari, A. Patel, M. Welsh, and R. Nagpal. Firefly-inspired sensor network synchronicity with realistic radio effects. In *Proceedings of the 3rd International Conference on Embedded Networked Sensor Systems*, pages 142–153. ACM Press, 2005.

[248] G. Werner-Allen, K. Lorincz, J. Johnson, J. Lees, and M. Welsh. Fidelity and yield in a volcano monitoring sensor network. In *Proceedings of the 7th Symposium on Operating Systems Design and Implementation*, pages 381–396. USENIX Association, 2006.

[249] S. Y. Wong, J. G. Lim, S. V. Rao, and W. K. G. Seah. Density-aware hop-count localization (DHL) in wireless sensor networks with variable density. In *Proceedings of 2005 IEEE Wireless Communications and Networking Conference*, pages 1848–1853. IEEE, 2005.

[250] H. Wu, A. Marshall, and W. Yu. Path planning and following algorithms in an indoor navigation model for visually impaired. In *Proceedings of the 2nd International Conference on Internet Monitoring and Protection*, pages 38–45. IEEE, 2007.

[251] M. Xiong, Y. Chen, H. Wang, and M. Hu. An agent-based model for simulating human-like crowd in dense places. In

Z. Li, X. Li, Y. Liu, and Z. Cai, editors, *Computational Intelligence and Intelligent Systems*, Communications in Computer and Information Science, pages 8–19. Springer, 2012.

[252] L. Z. Yang, D. L. Zhao, J. Li, and T. Y. Fang. Simulation of the kin behavior in building occupant evacuation based on cellular automaton. *Building and Environment*, 40(3): 411–415, 2005.

[253] Z. You, M. Q.-H. Meng, H. Liang, S. Li, Y. Li, W. Chen, Y. Zhou, S. Miao, K. Jiang, and Q. Guo. A localization algorithm nin wireless sensor networks using a mobile beacon node. In *Proceedings of 2007 International Conference on Information Acquisition*, pages 420–426, 2007.

[254] B. Zhang and F. Yu. An energy efficient localization algorithm for wireless sensor networks using a mobile anchor node. In *Proceedings of the 2008 International Conference on Information and Automation*, pages 215–219. IEEE, 2008.

[255] B. Zhang, F. Yu, and Z. Zhang. A high energy efficient localization algorithm for wireless sensor networks using directional antenna. In *Proceedings of the 11th IEEE International Conference on High Performance Computing and Communications*, pages 230–236. IEEE, 2009.

[256] X. Zheng, T. Zhong, and M. Liu. Modeling crowd evacuation of a building based on seven methodological approaches. *Building and Environment*, 44(3):437–445, 2009.

[257] ZigBee Alliance. ZigBee technology, July 2013. http://www.zigbee.org.

[258] X. Zong, S. Xiong, Z. Fang, and Q. Li. Multi-objective optimization for massive pedestrian evacuation using ant colony algorithm. In Y. Tan, Y. Shi, and K. C. Tan, editors, *Advances in Swarm Intelligence*, volume 6145 of *LNCS*, pages 636–642. Springer, 2010.

[259] M. M. Zonoozi and P. Dassanayake. User mobility modeling and characterization of mobility patterns. *IEEE Journal on Selected Areas in Communications*, 15(7):1239–1251, 1997.